# THE LIFE AND LETTERS

OF

# HARRISON GRAY OTIS

## 1765–1848

IN TWO VOLUMES

VOLUME I

# THE LIFE AND LETTERS OF
# HARRISON GRAY OTIS
## FEDERALIST
### 1765–1848

BY

SAMUEL ELIOT MORISON, Ph.D. (Harv.)

**WITH PORTRAITS AND OTHER
ILLUSTRATIONS**

### VOL. I

BOSTON AND NEW YORK
HOUGHTON MIFFLIN COMPANY
The Riverside Press Cambridge
1913

TO MY MOTHER

Tell me, ye learned, shall we for ever be adding so much to the *bulk* — so little to the *stock*?

Shall we for ever make new books, as apothecaries make new mixtures, by pouring only out of one vessel into another?

Are we for ever to be twisting, and untwisting the same rope? for ever in the same track — for ever at the same pace?

Shall we be destined to the days of eternity, . . . to be shewing the *relicks of learning*, as monks do the relicks of their saints — without working one — one single miracle with them?

— *Life and Opinions of Tristram Shandy, Gentleman*
Vol. V, Chap. I.

# PREFACE

In the following pages I have attempted to describe the life of a man of vigorous and fascinating personality, who was born in Boston ten years before the Revolution commenced, who entered national politics during Washington's second administration, who was a leader in the interesting movement that culminated in the Hartford Convention of 1814, and who lived to take a part in the presidential campaign of 1848. Harrison Gray Otis was not a great statesman, but rather a typical representative of that political and social organization which has passed into history under the name of the Federal or Federalist party. This fact alone has made his biography worth writing from a historical point of view. I have endeavored therefore, not only to relate the events of his life, but critically to describe his ideas, his feelings, and his prejudices, and to discover the motives guiding his action in the political crises of his day. I have not confined myself, however, to political biography, for, in addition to being a politician, Otis was an orator and a lawyer of the very first rank, a leader in social life, and a man whose personality did much to influence the community in which he lived.

I may as well confess to my readers at the start that I am a descendant of Harrison Gray Otis, four generations removed. Contrary to general opinion, I believe that a statesman's biography can best be written by a descendant, if he can preserve the natural sympathy that comes from kinship and family tradition, without sacrificing historical judgment and criticism. My readers can best judge how far I have succeeded in keeping the balance.

The materials for this work have been drawn primarily from the papers that Otis left behind him. They are now used for literary purposes for the first time. Confident, as I am, that the well-springs of political action can be traced mainly through the personal correspondence of the actors, I have quoted freely from the Otis manuscripts, and printed such documents of historical value as are too long to be incorporated in the text, after the chapters that they illustrate. Other contemporary political correspondence now available, as well as newspapers and official sources, has been utilized, and an earnest search has been made for manuscript material outside the usual repositories. For secondary material, the few sketches of Otis's life printed heretofore have proved of little value, beyond giving details of his early life; but the general works and monographs covering the period have afforded me much assistance.

All quotations from manuscript sources are given without change of wording, capitalization, spelling, or punctuation, with the exception that canceled passages have been suppressed, raised letters have been reduced to the line of the text (Gov$^r$ rendered as Govr., y$^e$ as ye, etc.), and in punctuation, the dash, where obviously ending a sentence, has been replaced by a period. In a very few instances punctuation has been supplied where the lack of it obscured the meaning. It will be understood that all matter printed in the smaller type is quoted.

This undertaking would have been impossible without the assistance and advice rendered by many individuals and institutions. I am indebted most of all to Professor Albert Bushnell Hart, at whose suggestion this work was begun, and under whose direction and encouragement it has been carried out; to Professors Edward Channing and Frederick J. Turner for their helpful criticism; to Mr. Charles K. Bolton, for granting me every facility at the Boston Athenæum; and to Mr. Worthington C. Ford, for opening to me the manuscript collections of the Massachusetts Historical Society, and for giving me his constant personal interest and coöperation. Finally, whatever merit my book may possess is due primarily to the historical training that I have received at Harvard University.

BOSTON,
*December*, 1912.

# CONTENTS

# ILLUSTRATIONS

# ABBREVIATIONS USED IN FOOTNOTES

*Amer. Hist. Rev.*       *American Historical Review.* Vols. I–XVII (1895–1912).

Gibbs       George Gibbs (ed.), *Memoirs of the Administrations of Washington and Adams, edited from the papers of Oliver Wolcott.* 2 vols., New York, 1846.

King       Charles R. King, *The Life and Correspondence of Rufus King.* 6 vols., New York, 1894–1900.

Loring       James S. Loring, *The Hundred Boston Orators.* Boston, 1852.

*New Eng. Hist. Gen. Reg.*       *New England Historical and Genealogical Register.* Vols. I–LXVI (1847–1912).

*N. E. Federalism*       Henry Adams (ed.), *Documents relating to New England Federalism, 1800–1815.* Boston, 1877.

Niles       Hezekiah Niles (ed.), *The Weekly Register.* Baltimore, 1810–1848.

*Otis' Letters*       H. G. Otis, *Otis' Letters in Defence of the Hartford Convention.* Boston, 1824.

*Proc. Mass. Hist. Soc.*       *Proceedings of the Massachusetts Historical Society.* Vols. I–XX (first series, 1791–1886); 2d ser., vols. I–XX (second series, 1887–1906); vols. XLI–XLV (third series, 1907–1912).

References to the *Works* of Hamilton, Jefferson, and Madison, are to the "Congress," editions (1851, 1856, and 1865, respectively).

All letters, documents, and quotations are from the original papers in the Otis MSS., unless reference to another source is given in a footnote.

# THE LIFE AND LETTERS OF HARRISON GRAY OTIS

## CHAPTER I

### FAMILY AND CHILDHOOD

#### 1765–1775, ÆT. 1–10

HARRISON GRAY OTIS was born in Boston, on the 8th day of October, 1765. At that time every one of his three names stood for respectability and long-established position in the Province of Massachusetts Bay. The name of Otis, in particular, was already famous throughout the British Empire.

With his birth, the Otis family reached its sixth generation in America.[1] The pioneers of the family, John Otis, father and son, were yeomen of Glastonbury, Somersetshire, whence they emigrated during the third decade of the seventeenth century, and settled at Hingham in the colony of Massachusetts Bay. The younger John later removed to the township of Barnstable, in the lower part of Cape Cod, and there, near the "Great Marshes," built the substantial homestead that sheltered future generations of Otises. Nothing further seems to be known

---

[1] The facts regarding the earlier Otises are taken from H. N. Otis, "Genealogical and Historical Memoir of Otis Family " (*New Eng. Hist. Gen. Reg.*, II, 281; IV, 143; also published separately, Boston, 1850); Eliot's *Biographical Dictionary*; A. Otis & C. F. Swift, *Genealogical Notes of Barnstable Families*; W. H. Whitmore, *The Mass. Civil List* (Albany, 1870); Alice Brown, *Mercy Warren*, and Wm. Tudor, *James Otis*. The family name, during the seventeenth century, was spelled indifferently Otis, Ottis, Oates, Otey.

about him, except that he was fined forty shillings for selling cider in 1675, and died in 1683.

John Otis the third, born at Hingham in 1657, eldest son of the cider-selling John, attained membership in the colonial aristocracy by the familiar route of law and public service. Judge Otis, as he was generally called, held various military and judicial appointments in Barnstable County, and represented the town of Barnstable for twenty successive years in the Great and General Court. In 1708 he was chosen a member of His Majesty's Council for Massachusetts, the highest position that the colony could offer a native son, and until his death in 1727 he was annually reëlected to that honourable board. His character was easy-going and genial, with the same humor and charm of manner for which his great-grandson, Harrison Gray Otis, became famous. His sixth child James, the grandfather of Harrison Gray Otis, was born in 1702.

James Otis, like his father, was largely self-educated, and followed a similar career; but he possessed an entirely different temperament. His portrait by Copley shows a man forcible in his opinions, conscious of his dignity, and lacking any trace of humor. "Colonel" James (as he was called, in order to distinguish him from his famous son of the same name), studied law, became, according to John Adams, the "undisputed head of the bar in Barnstable, Plymouth, and Bristol Counties," and in 1748 received the appointment of Attorney-General of the Province. Three years before Harrison Gray Otis was born, in 1762, this distinguished lawyer was elected for the first time to the Council.

Colonel Otis's gradual rise in the estimation of his contemporaries is indicated by the fact that his eldest son's name was placed eleventh in a class of thirty-one on the records of Harvard College, and his youngest son's, second in a class of thirty-five.[1] He never permanently joined the court circles at Boston, however, but resided in his grandfather's homestead at Barnstable, where thirteen children were born to him and his wife Mary Allyne. Infant mortality was high in colonial days, even under the best conditions, and no less than six of the thirteen died within six months of their births. But the record of the survivors shows that quality was not sacrificed to quantity in the family of James and Mary Otis. Of the six who reached maturity, Joseph and Samuel were fairly prominent in the American Revolution, and James and Mercy became leaders in the same cause.

Samuel Allyne Otis, the father of Harrison Gray Otis, was the tenth child of this large family, and the youngest of those who reached maturity. He was born in 1740, graduated from Harvard College in 1759, and then returned to the parental roof with the intention of taking up the study of law. At that time his eldest brother and senior by fifteen years, James Otis "the Patriot," had resided nearly a decade in Boston, and was already the leading lawyer of the province. James, who took a great interest in the education of young Sam, wrote their father in 1760:

Very sure I am, if he should stay a year or two from the time of his degree, before he begins with the law, he will be able to make better progress in one week, than he could now, without a miracle, in six. . . . I hold it to be of vast importance that a young man should be able to make some eclat at his opening, which it is vain to expect from one under twenty five: missing of this is very apt to discourage and dispirit him, and what is of worse consequence, may prevent the application of clients ever after. It has been observed before I was born, if a man don't obtain a character in any profession soon after his first appearance, he hardly will ever obtain one.[2]

[1] Until 1774, class lists at Harvard College were arranged according to the social position of the students' parents.

[2] Tudor, *James Otis*, 11.

Sam followed his brother's advice, but, finding the study of law distasteful, asked his father to set him up as a merchant in Boston. Although the earlier Otises were self-made men, the Colonel could not but humor his youngest and favorite son. Before long we find advertisements in the Boston *Evening Post*, to the effect that "Samuel Allyne Otis will sell very cheap, at his store No. 5 South Side of the Town Dock, New Flour, cordage & boltrope, Lead & Shott, New England Rum made under his own inspection etc." As one would expect of a petted younger son, Samuel never developed the high ability of his father and grandfather; but he inherited from the latter, and transmitted to his son, a gift of personal charm and popularity that stood him in good stead in reverses.

Soon after he settled in Boston, Samuel contracted an alliance with Elizabeth, the only daughter of Harrison Gray, and they were married on the last day of 1764. It was the second time that the families were connected by marriage. The Grays were wealthy townspeople, although a newer family than the Otises. Elizabeth's grandfather, Edward Gray, who had emigrated to Boston from Lincolnshire as an apprentice in 1686, became in course of time the owner of large rope-walks, the profit from which allowed him to bring up a family of nine children in considerable luxury. At the time of his death, in 1757, his son Harrison was serving his fourth term as Treasurer and Receiver-General of the Province, a well-remunerated position of great dignity. Harrison Gray married Elizabeth Lewis, the daughter of Ezekiel Lewis, another prominent Boston merchant. Elizabeth Gray, their only daughter and youngest child, was said to have been a beautiful woman; and her character, as we shall have occasion to observe, was one of singular beauty.

After their marriage, Mr. and Mrs. Samuel Allyne Otis

purchased a house in Boston near the present Bowdoin Square, adjoining the site of the Revere House. There, on October 8, 1765, their first child was born, and named Harrison Gray Otis after his maternal grandfather. No one, however, thought of calling him Harrison. "Harry" he was nicknamed from the first, and Harry Otis he always remained to his family and friends.

Enough has been said of Harry's forbears to show with what advantages he was endowed from his birth. Of pure English stock, strengthened by five generations on New England soil, and refined by three generations of public service and social position, he could have asked nothing more of heredity. His environment was equally advantageous. Boston, with its surroundings of water, open spaces, and hilly pastures, was then an ideal place in which to bring up a boy. Harry made full use of his opportunities for play and mischief, and developed a rugged constitution that carried him past his eighty-third birthday. He was a sturdy, healthy little fellow, with ruddy cheeks, dark hair, and inquisitive blue eyes. Every year, on Guy Fawkes' day, a new pair of leather breeches was given him, and reserved for "best" so long as the breeches of the previous vintage held out. Thomas Handasyd Perkins, one of his lifelong friends, afterwards said, "Harry Otis was always the handsomest, brightest, and most charming boy of all our companions. Everything he did was better done than any of the rest of us could do it."

Harry was given the best education that the time and place afforded. Luckily for him, the old Puritan ideas of education were much mitigated among such broadminded persons of the upper class as his parents were. His childhood was not clouded by a severe repression of his natural boyish impulses, or by a constant reminder

that the mark of Adam was upon him. But he was given
a good religious training at home, and sent at an early age
to schools where female teachers were unheard of, and
where a liberal use was made of the rod. The first school
that he attended was on Hanover Street, kept by one
Master Griffiths, a queer old fellow who used to reward
the good scholars every Saturday by letting them scramble
for shellbarks which he threw from his window into the
courtyard. At the age of seven, Harry was promoted to
the Latin School, where Master John Lovell and his son
James were the reigning tyrants. We shall let Mr. Otis
recall his school life in his own words: [4]

*Latin School at 7*

I perfectly remember the day I entered the School, July,
1773, being then seven years and nine months old. Immediately after the end of Commencement week, I repaired, according to the rule prescribed for candidates for admission to the
lowest form, to old Master Lovell's house, situate in School
Street, nearly opposite the site of the old School house. I was
early on the ground, anticipated only by Mr. John Hubbard,
who lived near — it being understood that the boys were to
take their places on the form in the same routine that they presented themselves at the house. The probationary exercise
was reading a few verses in the Bible. Having passed muster in
this, I was admitted as second boy on the lowest form.

I attended school from that time until April, 1775, (the day
of Lexington battle), being then on the second form. The School
was divided into seven classes. A separate bench or form was
allotted to each, besides a *skipping* form, appropriated for a
few boys who were intended to be pushed forward one year
in advance. The books studied the first year were Cheever's
Accidence, a small Nomenclature, and Corderius' Colloquies.
The second year, Aesop's Fables, and towards the close of it,
Eutropius and Ward's Lilly's Grammar. The third year Eutropius and Grammar continued, and a book commenced

[4] From a letter of December 17, 1844, printed in H. F. Jenks, *Historical
Sketch of the Boston Latin School* (preface to the School Catalogue, Boston,
1886), 35–37.

called Clarke's Introduction. In the fourth year, the fourth form, as well as the fifth and sixth, being furnished with desks, commenced "making Latin," as the phrase was, and to the books used by the third form Caesar's Commentaries were added. After this were read in succession by the three upper classes, Tully's Orations, the first books of the Aeneid, and the highest classes dipped into Xenophon and Homer. School opened at 7 in summer and 8 in winter, A.M., and at 1 P.M. throughout the year. It was ended at 11 A.M. and 5 P.M., at which hours the greater part went to writing school for an hour at a time — but a portion remained and took lessons in writing of "Master James," son of the Preceptor, and some young girls then came into school.

The discipline of the School was strict but not severe. The Master's — Old Gaffer, as we called him — desk was near the south-west corner of the room; Master James's desk was in the north-east corner. I remember to have seen no other instrument of punishment but the ferule in Master Lovell's day. Gaffer's ferule was a short, stubbed, greasy-looking article, which, when not in use, served him as a stick of sugar candy. The lightest punishment was one clap, the severest four — the most usual, two, one on each hand. The inflictions of the old gentleman were not much dreaded; his ferule seemed to be a mere continuation of his arm, of which the center of motion was the shoulder. It descended altogether with a whack, and there was the end of it, after blowing the fingers. But Master James's fashion of wielding his weapon was another affair. He had a gymnastic style of flourishing altogether unique — a mode of administering our experimentum ferules that was absolutely terrific. He never punished in Gaffer's presence, but whenever the old gentleman withdrew, all began to contemplate the "day's disaster," and to tremble, not when he "frown'd," for he did not frown, nor was he an ill-tempered person, but rather smiled sardonically, as if preparing for a pugilistic effort, and the execution as nearly resembled the motion of a flail in the hands of an expert thrasher as could be acquired by long practice. School broke up at 10 A.M. on Thursday, — a relic of an old custom to give opportunity to attend the "Thursday lecture" — which was I believe never improved in my day. School opened with "attendamus" to a short prayer. It ended with "deponite libros." The boys had a recess of a few minutes to go out in the yard — eight at a time. No leave was asked in words; but there was a short club of a yard in length which was caught up by some boy, round whom those who wished to go out clustered, and were drilled down to eight. The club was then held up near Master's nose, who nodded assent, when the eight vanished club in hand. Upon their return there was a rush to seize the club which was placed by the door, and a new conscription of eight formed, and so *toties quoties*.

To live in Boston was an education in itself during Harry's childhood and youth. The first ten years of his life were a period of economic prosperity, when Boston Harbor was thronged with vessels from Europe, Africa, the West Indies, and the southern colonies. It was, moreover, a period decisive in the history of the country. Between 1765 and 1775 the struggle between Parliament and the colonies passed through all the preliminary stages of resistance, compromise, unorganized rebellion, and attempted punishment, that finally ended in civil war. It was a struggle in which Harry's family played an important part from the first. Every argument was threshed out in the home circle. The Boston of his boyhood was an admirable nursery for statesmen.

In the year of Harry's birth, both sides of his family were in the Whig or opposition party. His grandfather Otis was a prominent opposition member of the Council, and his uncle James, whose famous speech against the writs of assistance had been delivered in 1761, was at the very height of his reputation and power as a patriot leader in the lower house of the General Court. James Otis, Jr., represented Massachusetts at the Stamp Act Congress, which met at Albany on October 7, 1765, the day before Harry was born; and the following years were the most active, if not the most fruitful of his career. Politics gradually absorbed his time, to the entire exclusion of his lucrative law practice. He was at the head of every measure taken up in legislature or town meeting to oppose the obnoxious acts of Parliament, and in constant correspondence with patriot leaders in other colonies. But his genius seemed to burn itself out under this stress of work, and his nature, ordinarily pleasure-loving, easygoing, and genial, became morose, resentful, and irascible. As early as 1763, entries in John Adams's diary testify to an extravagance of behavior and a violence of temper on the part of Otis which can be accounted for only by the charitable explanation of mental unsoundness. Towards the close of the sixties, these manifestations became more frequent. In the autumn of 1769 occurred his fatal altercation with a government official, in which he received a severe cut on the head. This blow permanently unbalanced his reason. With the exception of a few lucid intervals, the brilliant orator, lawyer, and patriot was never again himself. He retired to the country, and in December, 1771, on representation to the Probate Court that James Otis, Jr., was *non compos mentis*, Harry's father was appointed his guardian.

The insanity of James Otis was a grave loss to the patriot cause, and a heavy blow to Harry's family circle. The example of the elder man was a constant inspiration in after years to the youth, who unfortunately did not come into contact with his uncle while he was in possession of his faculties.

Another cause of uneasiness in Harry's family was the growing Toryism of his grandfather Gray. At the time Harry was born, Treasurer Gray was a somewhat shaky member of the popular party, but soon afterwards he began to gravitate toward the other side.[5] John Adams subse-

[5] Cf. S. E. Morison, "The Property of Harrison Gray, Loyalist," *Publications of Colonial Society of Mass.*, XIV.

quently ascribed his apostasy to Whiggery to the death, in 1766, of his political and religious mentor, the Reverend Jonathan Mayhew. "Had Mayhew lived, it is believed that Gray would never have been a refugee; but the seducers prevailed, though he had connected his blood with an Otis." The worthy Treasurer was, indeed, fond of religious exercise and susceptible to ecclesiastical influence, but no particular circumstance is necessary to explain his march toward Toryism. Men of means and established position, although liberal in their ideas, generally take the conservative side when the issue is fairly joined between rebellion and loyalty. Self-interest would have led Harrison Gray to remain a Whig, for his tenure of office was dependent on the popularly elected General Court. But the natural feelings of the wealthy merchant asserted themselves. He believed that Parliament had conceded enough in repealing the Stamp Act; and, abhorring the boycotts, riots, and other illegal methods employed by the patriots, he had no wish to make an issue out of the tax on tea.

Until the time came when there was no middle ground, Harrison Gray was a moderate Tory, and managed to retain his position of Treasurer by advancing to impecunious patriots in the General Court their salaries out of his own pocket, when the treasury was empty. But in 1774 came an event that forced him to choose irrevocably between patriotism and loyalism. Among the five coercive measures of that year by which Parliament intended to punish rebellious Boston for its mobs and tea parties, was the Massachusetts Government Act, suspending the Province Charter, and providing that the Council should henceforth be appointed by the Governor on a legal writ of *mandamus*.[6] Harrison Gray's name appeared sixth on

[6] By the Province Charter, the Council was annually chosen by the whole legislature, and subject to the veto only of the Governor.

the list of Governor Gage's *mandamus* Councillors. Against the advice and persuasion of most of his friends, he accepted the call, and thus recognized the right of King and Parliament to suspend at will the rights and liberties of Massachusetts Bay. The immediate consequences of his action were estrangement from most of his friends, loss of his position, and unwelcome attentions from the mob; the final consequences were confiscation of his property and a permanent separation from friends and country.

The fact that Grandfather Gray became a loyalist had an important effect on the mind of young Harry. He heard both sides of the great questions of the day discussed in the family circle. In after years he could testify from personal conviction that it was possible to be at the same time a loyalist and an honest man, and that the relentless persecution of the loyalists both during and after the Revolution, was unjust. The full import of the Treasurer's acceptance of the King's *mandamus*, of course was not realized at the time either by Harry or by his parents. For the present he knew only that Grandfather Gray had become the object of popular opprobrium, and was no longer on speaking terms with Grandfather Otis.

The Otis family, who had quite as much at stake as Treasurer Gray, remained true to the patriot cause while the latter was treading the road that led to exile. Colonel Otis in 1770 renewed his active opposition in the Council, his election to which had been vetoed by Governor Bernard since 1766. In 1774, though seventy-two years of age, he was chosen President of the Council in the revolutionary Provincial Congress, at Watertown, one of the first of whose acts was to order the people of Massachusetts to cease paying taxes to Treasurer Gray. Harry's father was in close business and personal relations with the Adamses, Warrens, and Gerrys, but he did not take

an active part in politics until after the Revolution broke
out.

Meanwhile another member of the Otis family, Harry's
"Aunt Warren,"[7] was rising into fame as the poetess
laureate of the patriot party.  Mercy Otis, married in
1754 to James Warren, a wealthy farmer of Plymouth,
led the humdrum life of a New England housewife down
to the exciting period of the Tea Party.  Her husband then
became a prominent member of the General Court and
the Caucus Club, and Mercy blossomed forth as a *femme
politique*.  With heart and soul in the patriot cause, she
applied her pen in its aid — a proceeding that other and
less gifted patriots' wives believed highly unbecoming to
her sex.  In 1774 she published a satirical poem on the
Tea Party, entitled "The Squabble of the Sea-nymphs,"
and a more serious poem, "A Political Reverie," in which
she looks

". . . with rapture at the distant dawn

. . . . . . . . . . .

When Patriot States in laurel crowns may rise,
And ancient kingdoms greet them as allies."

In May, 1775, began the issue, in parts, of her "Group,"
a dramatic satire on the Tory Party that gave keen delight to the patriots.  Though not deficient in her duties
as wife and mother, Mercy took an Amazonian delight
in the political arena, and all through the war advised her
husband on political matters, corresponded with statesmen, and shot barbed shafts of satire into the enemy's
flank.

This year 1775 brought Harry to his tenth year, when he
could observe and understand much concerning the great

[7] Down to a period within the memory of persons now living, American
children never addressed their aunts and uncles by their Christian names.  Otis
always referred to Mercy Warren as "Aunt Warren."

events that were taking place in his native town. He always retained a vivid remembrance of the historic 19th of April, 1775. A part of the British soldiery was quartered in the Lechmere distillery, at the corner of Hancock and Cambridge Streets, not far from his parents' residence. The evening of the 18th was unusually hot for that season of the year. A general uneasiness was apparent in the streets; citizens conversed in low tones in groups of two or three; and a careful watch was kept on the movements of the troops. In the middle of the night Harry was taken from his bed and brought to the window, where, through the mist hanging over the pasture before his door, he saw the British regulars marching silently along on their way to Lexington and Concord. The following day, to quote his own words,[8] "I went to school for the last time. In the morning, about seven, Percy's brigade was drawn up, extending from Scollay's building thro' Tremont Street nearly to the bottom of the Mall, preparing to take up their march for Lexington. A corporal came up to me as I was going to school, and turned me off to pass down Court St. which I did, and came up School St. to the School-house. It may well be imagined that great agitation prevailed, the British line being drawn up only a few yards from the School-house door. As I entered the school, I heard the announcement of *deponite libros*, and ran home for fear of the regulars."

News of the Concord fight brought thousands of armed country people swarming around Boston, until it became apparent that the town would be besieged, in order to force out General Gage and his troops. Harry's father decided to follow the example of many patriot families, and remove his family before it became too late. The Otis homestead at Barnstable offered a convenient refuge. In

[8] Letter cited above, in *Catalogue of the Boston Latin School*, 37.

the second week of May, 1775, Harry and his mother, bidding good-bye to Grandfather Gray and the Gray uncles and aunts, set out in the family chaise for the Great Marshes. Samuel A. Otis followed by sea with part of the household goods. It was the final parting of the ways for the Otis and Gray families: a separation that lasted the rest of their lives. Luckily for Harry, his father remained true to the cause which his uncle James had done so much to create. That cause must have seemed desperate enough in May, 1775, to an intelligent man who could compare the resources of Great Britain with those of the thirteen colonies. But the father's choice meant for Harry an opportunity for distinguished public service in a republican state, while the Gray uncles and cousins, who doubtless expected to reap the rewards of loyalty on this side of the water, were doomed to a monotonous life of pensioned exile at the court in which they had placed their trust.

# CHAPTER II

## BOYHOOD AND YOUTH

### 1775–1783, ÆT. 10–18

SHORTLY after the Otis family arrived at Barnstable, Harry's mother wrote her father as follows:

Barnstable, May 1775.

Hond Sir

I have only time to inform you, I arrived here this day at twelve, and have been treated with the greatest kindness upon the Road, every one rejoicing that we have left *Boston*. The Sloop did not arrive here till yesterday; I have not seen Mr. Otis yet, he thinks it best not to come on shore, untill he can get his goods all out of the vessel, which will be to morrow, the children are all well with me, except the Baby, who I have left for the present, with her Nurse. I wish you with the rest of my dear Friends were out of Town, not that I am apprehensive of any danger, except that of *starving*. I have many things to say, but I forbear as I know not whose hands this may fall into, so with wishing you all the support of Heaven which is necessary at this day of Trial and distress, I conclude

Your dutiful Daughter E OTIS [1]

---

[1] This and the subsequent letters from Elizabeth Gray Otis to Harrison Gray are taken from copies made by the recipient, and sent by his grand-daughter Sophia to her cousin, Harrison Gray Otis, in 1833. He writes in reply, on February 17, 1833: "You did me a greater favor than you were aware of in sending me the little rubrics of my Grandfather. They have reference to scenes impressed on my bosom in childhood, with indelible interest. I was with my mother when she wrote those letters, which showed that her heart was beginning to break as break it did at her separation from her father tho' united to a worthy and affectionate husband, whom she loved. Think of her being at a place distant only 70 miles from her father, which the mail now reaches in 10 or 12 hours; with which the intercourse was so interrupted by a civil war, that letters were weeks & months in the transit from one place to the other."

¹ Harry looked on the removal to Barnstable as a huge lark, not that he was allowed to waste time, for on their arrival he was sent to school with Mr. Hilliard, pastor of the East Parish. There he passed every week from Mondays to Saturdays, returning to the patriarchal mansion for the Sabbath. His progress was satisfactory, at least to his mother, for she wrote to his grandfather on January 8, 1776, "I shall inclose you a letter from Harry of his own handwriting as well as of inditing, which will enable you to form a Judgment of his Genius which his Tutor tells me is very uncommon to say the least." Another pupil at the same school was Thomas Handasyd Perkins, Harry's young friend, whose family, also, had taken refuge at Barnstable. Colonel Perkins afterwards told of the famous times they used to have together:

In vacation and on Saturday during fishing season we used, with my brother James, to go trout fishing in Mashapee and Santuit Rivers with great success. We never kept trout much under a pound, putting the smaller ones back into the stream. Although we were so young, we were allowed to use guns; my mother saying that she did not know but that we might be called upon some day or other to fight for our country and she wished us to understand the use of a gun. Sometimes we joined the deer-hunts on the hills, or during the autumn shot flight-birds on Barnstable Great Marshes.²

For the boys' elders, however, it was a time of much anxiety. They had not been in Barnstable long before news came of the battle of Bunker Hill, and the burning of Charlestown. "This came to us," Otis remembered, "not in the shape which it has since assumed, as a real victory, though nominal defeat; but with the unmitigated horrors of conflagration and massacre, and as a specimen of the mode in which our peaceful villages were intended to

² A. T. Perkins, *Memoir of H. G. Otis*, 147.

THE PARENTS

ELIZABETH GRAY OTIS
From a portrait by John Singleton Copley

GRAY OTIS

SAMUEL ALLYNE OTIS

From a portrait by Gilbert Stuart

be swept with fire and sword." [2] Barnstable was in a state of perpetual alarm, its militia constantly on the alert, since the coast frequently was threatened by British tenders and privateers. Harry's mother was full of grief at the parting from her father and brothers, and of apprehension for their welfare in the beleaguered town. So difficult were communications between Boston and the outside world, that for three whole months in the autumn of 1775 there came no word from Grandfather Gray. Later in the year, however, communication became fairly easy, to judge from a letter of Christmas day, 1775, from Mrs. Otis to her father:

If it would not be giving my Papa and Brother too much trouble, I should be exceeding glad [if] they would send me out a trunk of Apparel I left in the little Chamber, with my beding counterpin Curtains and Carpets which may be put in a Trunk. I should not have asked this had I not been credibly informed Mr Bowdoin has lately got out several large Trunks over the Neck and the things I mention are absolutely necessary. I need not add I most ardently long to see you, but whether ever I shall is known only to him, who orders all things with unerring Wisdom.

We have already felt heavy trials — and are daily expecting greater. May Heaven take pity on us, and remove those heavy Judgments that are now hanging over us —'prays your obedient Daughr. E O

The family at the Otis mansion consisted of Harry's father and mother, his younger brother Sam, two babies, Grandfather Otis, and Harry's uncle Joseph. The last two were absent a large part of the time, — the old gentleman being President of the Council at Watertown, and Joseph a member of the lower house of the Provincial Congress. Early in 1776 they received an unexpected ac-

[2] Letter of H. G. Otis of August 31, 1839, in *The Cape Cod Centennial Celebration at Barnstable* (Barnstable, 1840), 74–76.

quisition in the person of Mrs. Otis' younger brother, John
Gray. "Jack," as he was generally called, was a spirited
young loyalist of twenty, with a faculty for getting into
trouble. At the beginning of the siege of Boston he sailed
for England, but not long after, thinking that the rebellion would soon be over, he reëmbarked for Boston. His
vessel was captured by an American privateer, and brought
to Newburyport, where the boy was thought sufficiently
dangerous to be put under close confinement. By the in-
tercession of his Otis relatives, however, the Provincial
Congress passed an order releasing him into their custody,
on giving a bond for £1000 not to leave Barnstable or to
have any dealings with the enemy. Under these conditions Jack was allowed to join the family at the Great
Marshes. Since his sister writes "he is in very good spirits,
and treated like a gentleman," the young loyalist, highly
pleased with himself and his adventure, was doubtless a
great source of entertainment to his relatives.

After the evacuation on March 17, 1776, the Otis
family returned to Boston, and reopened the house that
Grandfather Gray had abandoned. It was a different town
from the Boston they had left ten months before. The
change was not so much in the outward aspect of the place,
although, it is true, shot and shells were still scattered
about, and many houses had been pillaged by the British
soldiery during the confusion of evacuation. The real
change that the siege had brought about in Boston was a
total subversion of the social structure, caused by the
wholesale emigration of loyalists. When Lord Howe came
to his sudden decision to retire from the town, the Boston
Tories saw that they, also, must leave. In the words of
one loyalist, "neither Hell, Hull nor Halifax" would be
worse than remaining to face the enraged and victorious
patriots. For three days confusion reigned, while panic-

stricken British sympathizers rushed to and fro, trying
to find corners for themselves and their household goods
on one of the transports. When they were all finally embarked, Abigail Adams could look down from Penn's Hill,
upon the largest fleet ever seen in America, upwards of a
hundred and seventy sail, ready to set forth for Halifax.

It was an emigration comparable only to that which
took place from France sixteen years later. The exodus
drained the community of some of its most prosperous
and valuable elements, and left great gaps in the social
structure that time alone could fill.[4] Among the exiles
were Harrison Gray and his sons Lewis and Harrison.
Their absence alone made it a sad home-coming for
Harry's mother, as her pathetic letters indicate.

My dear, dear Pappa, [she writes on June 29, 1776], — Although I see no great probability this will ever reach you, yet
I cannot let the opportunity pass without a few lines. It's not
in the power of words to express how much I have suffered for
you and the rest of my dear friends since you left Boston, having never received any Intelligence from Halifax, till yesterday. A few lines from Mrs Hughes informs me you with my
Brother and Sister embarked for London May 12th. Hard is
my fate to be thus separated from the tenderest, the best of
Parents. . . . You may well suppose the Town wears a gloomy
appearance to me who has lost so many dear connections. . . .
I had no other Inducement to return to it, but on account of
the little folks, who were destitute of Schools when in the
Country.

And again, on August 15:

My dear papa I must entreat, if there is any possible way
of conveying a line, you would improve it, and tell me
whether you think there is the least probability of our ever
meeting again on Earth. I own I sometimes indulge the

---

[4] The list given in Justin Winsor, *Memorial Hist. of Boston*, III, 175, of refugee Boston loyalists contains 536 names, mostly heads of families, and including men of all classes and occupations.

pleasing hope, however slender the foundation. As I ever make it a rule not to say anything upon political matters, you will not expect anything in that way now. I have many things to say in the domestic way, but as I know not whose hands this may fall into I forbear. . . .

Your dutiful Daughtr E. O.

My good partner with the little folks joins me in duty and Love. I wish you would not mention anything in the political way, as it may be a means of my not seeing it.

Harry and his father, on the contrary, adjusted themselves easily to the new conditions. Harry was sent back to the Latin School, to prepare for college. With his friend Tom Perkins, who also had returned from Barnstable, he often shot snipe at the foot of the Common, on the site of the present playground, and went gunning for teal in a creek near the present site of Dover Street. On one memorable occasion they took a trip to Barnstable, where, Colonel Perkins relates, "Otis and I went out on the marshes to shoot against one another, he going to the north toward Sandwich and I keeping to the south. At the end of the day I brought in some seventy large birds, half of them killed by single shots with a gun having but one barrel and a flint lock, and was delighted to find I had beaten Harry, who had, however, killed but a very few birds less than I had."

Samuel A. Otis, at this time, resumed his mercantile business, in partnership with a Mr. Andrews, and began likewise a political career. In May, 1776, he was chosen one of the Boston Representatives to the General Court. Shortly after, he was appointed to the Massachusetts Board of War, together with his brother-in-law James Warren, the husband of the redoubtable Mercy. This was a responsible position of great importance, for the Board of War acted not only as a state executive for military affairs, but as an intermediary between the state and Congress. Meanwhile the business of Mr. Otis was thriving. It is a mistake to suppose that the majority of Americans suffered hardship and privation during the Revolution. In that contest, as in all wars, large fortunes were made out of privateering, speculating, supplying government, and contraband trade. The early enthusiasm for homespuns and raspberry tea soon passed away; and from 1778 on, the demand for luxuries and British goods was so great as to make a person of Roman virtues like Mercy Warren think that corruption and decay had already entered the body politic. There is no reason to suppose that Mr. Otis shut his eyes to any of these modes of making money.

In November, 1777, Messrs. Otis & Andrews received the appointment of Collectors of Clothing for the Continental Army. Although, as Mr. Otis acknowledged,[5] "the emoluments were considerable," it was an exacting and difficult position. The Continental army was in constant need of clothing. A sudden order would come for ten thousand uniforms to equip Pulaski's Legion, and Messrs. Otis & Andrews would first have to procure the materials as best they could, then see that the garments were made up, and finally forward them to the Clothier-General. They wrote Timothy Pickering, the Quartermaster-General, on July 2, 1778: "We have sent on from the beginning of Dec. from 16 to 18000 suits of cloathes, besides shirts, shoes, Hatts, blankets, &c; . . . for about six months we were near £200,000 Lmy in debt on account of the United States, during which time, we were perpetually embarassed by people calling for their money, & much of our time was taken up, in apologizing."

The varied character of Mr. Otis's business during the

[5] Otis to Timothy Pickering. Pickering MSS.

war is revealed in his letters [6] to his brother Joseph, who was at once brigadier-general of the militia of Barnstable County, country merchant, and member of the local committee on clothing. On June 8, 1778, he wrote:

Dear Brother

Will procure the 160 hard dollars if I can and write you. Am sorry for Weeks's Misfortune. am indifferent about the Cloth but wont refuse it at 10/.

Have no thots of reducing the price of anything past, future reductions is all I have an Idea of.—The melasses cost Andrews 26/ he refused 40/ declined letting you have it at less 24/ and as is riseing you must not think hard of it. You may as well keep yourself calm because if you sware as you threaten at this distance nobody will mind it. Salt Works Freeman insists on managing and we cant honorably decline it tho his political fagaries hurt all he is connected with. Have so many Irons in the fire dont incline to Speculate at Sea but will sell you the Salt. Yours Affectionately, SAM A OTIS.

And on September 10 of the same year:

Am afraid you will be in too much in a hurry about your winter goods, but you may as well make 100 prc as 5 they grow exceedingly scarce and will be at 20 for one in a short time yours were put at 12 . . .

As you are a farmer Mr. Andrews & myself will help you to a sale of forty bushell good potatoes, 200 head of Cabbages, few bushells onions 20 bushell of turnips Carrots & parsnips & few onions, or what you can spare of these articles.

Mrs. Otis desires you would take her in a pail or two of Eggs if they come handy.

We have no News here, but find ourselves alarmed by the burning of Dartmouth. Cruel Men! Are these their olive branches?

Mrs. Otis is miserably sick & weak & am very much distressed with the apprehension that she w[ill] not recover.

Give my Duty & Love to all friends, & send namesake [7] home

[6] In the James Otis MSS. (Mass. Historical Society), III.

[7] Harry's brother, Samuel A. Otis, Jr., born in 1768. He was brought up for a mercantile career, and lived at Newburyport until his death in 1814. The other children of Samuel A. Otis by his first marriage died in childhood.

first oppy, and if he is scandalously ragged as I fear he is let the
shoe maker & Taylor put him in decent kilter.

The forebodings that Mr. Otis expressed for his wife
in the last letter were too well founded. The separation
from her beloved father inflicted on Elizabeth Otis a
wound from which she never recovered. With gentle submission she accepted the course that her husband had
taken, but as her letters show, she remained a loyalist at
heart, inwardly protesting against the course of events
that had placed an insuperable barrier between her husband's family and her own. There was nothing in the new
order of things to make up for the friends she had lost.
Anxiously her husband and children saw depression turn
into poor health and continual illness. A painful confinement coming after long months of sickness hastened her
decline, and on January 22, 1779, she passed away, clasp-
ing her father's miniature to her breast. She was only
thirty-two years old, and left five children. "As she lived
a saint, she died an Angel," wrote her husband to Harrison Gray, who answered: "The tenderness and affection
you had for my dear child, make you stand high in my
Estimation, notwithstanding we widely differ in our political principles."

When the shadow of this calamity fell across his life,
Harry was thirteen years old, and in his last year at the
Latin School. The following summer he entered Harvard
College with the class of 1783,[8] in which his active intellect and charming personality made him a leader in work
and in play. In undergraduate debates he showed unmis-
takable signs of having inherited the oratorical gifts of
his uncle. He was one of the earliest members of the

---

[8] The ages of the class of 1783 at entering ranged from eleven to thirty;
the average was fifteen and a half. See Triennial Catalogue of 1791, in the
Boston Athenæum, containing manuscript notes by President Quincy.

Phi Beta Kappa Society, and graduated first in his class. But Harry Otis could always be counted upon to take part in any sort of mischief. In a letter of his riper years he alludes to "our old College practice, of putting a bullet at the end of a whip, and when we passed near a flock of geese full speed, of throwing it over the neck of one and jerking it into the chaise. When the goose was caught he must be roasted and eaten or the sport was spoiled. No matter whether fat or lean, goose or gander, down he went before Billy Darling's fire." Among his friends and associates in this and similar college sports were several future politicians and statesmen, such as William Prescott, Benjamin Pickman, Prentiss Mellen, and John Welles of Massachusetts; John Dawson of Virginia; Ambrose Spencer and John and Stephen Van Rensselaer of New York.

In an amusing undergraduate letter to the last named, Harry expresses his contempt for the sort of instruction he was privileged to receive at Cambridge:

Boston October 20, 1782.

My dear Stephen,

\* \* \* \* \* \* \* \* \* \* \*

The Subscription is open for the Assembly: may no unpropitious Occurence prevent your coming here and enjoying with your usual Polish, the Pleasures of this Metropolis; — D[awso]n is in Philadelphia: Quiri; if his Eclat is as brilliant as it was amongst us *Yankees*. It is now Vacation and I have a temporary Respite from Pedantry and Logic. May Father Time ameliorate his tardy Pace and hasten the desired Period, when I shall bid adieu to the sophisticated Jargon of a superstitious Synod of pension'd Bigots and ramble in the fields of liberal science. . . .

Your affectionate friend
HARRISON GRAY OTIS.[9]

[9] Manuscript Collection of Herbert Foster Otis, Esq.

A loyal son of Harvard, an authority on the history of his alma mater, has assured me that the epithets applied by Harry to the faculty of 1782 were none too vigorous. The college had fallen a victim to the neglect and decay from which every institution of learning must suffer during periods of social convulsion and civil war. No one then suspected that the greatest intellect in Cambridge belonged to a twenty-one year old graduate of the University of Geneva, from whom Harry and a few of his classmates were permitted by the college authorities to take lessons in French. Since Otis read and quoted French pretty readily during the rest of his life, we may assume that Albert Gallatin was as capable a tutor as he afterwards proved to be a statesman.

The class of 1783 received their degrees from President Willard not long after the welcome news had arrived that war was over, and that all the world recognized the independence of the United States. Otis as the first scholar in the class was assigned the English oration. He naturally chose the recent event for his theme, and, as he afterwards remembered, painted "in somewhat gorgeous colors the prospects unfolded to our country by this achievement of its liberties, and its probable effect on the destinies of other nations."[10] It is a pleasant picture to look back on, — the black-haired, keen-eyed boy of seventeen, pouring forth glowing prophecies of the future, before the grave and reverend dignitaries of college, church, and state. It was the triumphant end of his boyhood, and the beginning of his manhood. He had every advantage a youth of his age could ask. Gentle birth, an alert and active mind, a winning personality, and the heritage of

[10] Address prepared for Harvard Centennial, 1836. Quincy, *History of Harvard University*, II, 662.

*heritage*
*of gut.*

a great name: all were his. Surely no boy was ever launched into the battle of life with more brilliant prospects than Harrison Gray Otis, "the first scholar of the first class of a new nation."

# CHAPTER III

## LAW AND BUSINESS

### 1783–1796, ÆT. 18–31

WHILE at college, young Otis determined to study law. The legal profession was the natural one for him to follow; for, as we have seen, his grandfather and great-grandfather Otis, and his uncle James, had been eminent lawyers in their day. During his junior year, it looked as if Harry might be initiated into the mysteries of the law by James Otis, who had entered one of those lucid intervals that lightened the darkness of his later life. With the return of his old intellect and brilliancy, he seemed so completely restored in reason that the family planned to have him take charge of Harry's legal education, and uncle and nephew had a long and delightful conversation on the subject in the course of a drive from Andover to Boston. But James Otis soon lapsed into his previous state, and died before Harry left college. Samuel A. Otis then decided to give his son the very best legal education that could be procured — at the Temple, in London. This plan, also, fell through, since shortly after his son's graduation the father's business, affected by the general depression following the war, became bankrupt.[1]

[1] The state of business in 1783 was particularly unfortunate for the affairs of men like S. A. Otis, who depended for a livelihood on supplying government, and for speculative enterprises to which peace brought an abrupt stop. A contributing cause of Otis's bankruptcy was the failure of General Joseph Otis of Barnstable, £6000 in his brother's debt, after losing by his mismanagement the estate left by their father, the Colonel. Whatever the cause, this disaster did not injure the reputation of S. A. Otis, for he was elected to the General Court for a number of years, chosen speaker of the House in 1784, and appointed Secretary of the United States Senate in 1788. He held this position through successive administrations, until the day of his death in 1814, without missing,

For Harrison Gray Otis, his father's bankruptcy was a blessing in disguise. It must have been a rude shock to the young favorite of fortune to be thrown on his own resources at the age of eighteen, but it was just what he needed to toughen his character, and develop his self-reliance. He was fortunate in being saved from a legal education at the Temple. Americans of the upper class at the end of the eighteenth century were too much accustomed, as it was, to look to England for everything that was good, without receiving the additional bias of an English education. Nevertheless, young Otis had the best legal education afforded by the time and place, through the generosity of the eminent lawyer and patriot John Lowell, who took him as a pupil into his office without charge, out of friendship to the Otis family. An anecdote afterwards told by Benjamin Bussey, a merchant of Boston, shows how earnestly Otis applied himself to the study of law. Every morning on his way to his shop, Mr. Bussey saw one of Mr. Lowell's office windows decorated by a pair of boots, that evidently belonged to some early riser who preferred to read with his heels higher than his head.[1] Curious to know how early they occupied that position, he arose before daybreak one morning, and, passing before Mr. Lowell's office, found the boots posted at their usual place. On entering the office, he discovered, deep in Blackstone, young Harry Otis, who said he was simply keeping his usual hours for study.

In the autumn of 1783, this diligent student was invited by Mr. Lowell to accompany him on a journey to Philadelphia. Recalling this tour in his old age, Otis wrote:[2]

it is said, a single session. He married in 1782, Mary (Smith), widow of Edward Gray.

[2] Letter of November 10, 1846, to Charles Lowell, in *Historical Magazine*, I, 161.

This afforded me a better opportunity of seeing him [Lowell] in hours of unguarded relaxation from the cares of business than afterwards occurred. The whole journey was a continued scene of pleasant and instructive conversation, and on his part of kind and condescending manners, sparkling anecdotes, and poetical quotations. We came to New York before the evacuation by the British army was consummated. There Mr. Lowell found Col. Upham, aid of Sir Guy Carleton, and Mr. Ward Chipman, judge-advocate, as I recollect, of the British army, — both old acquaintances and early companions. Their interview, after eight years' separation and various fortunes, was most cordial. They introduced Mr. Lowell to Sir Guy, with whom he and my other fellow-travellers dined, with a large and splendid party of military and civilians, into which they had me worked, as an attaché to the Boston delegation; and it seemed to me as brilliant as Alexander's feast. While in New York, Mr. Lowell received the hospitality and attentions of the distinguished citizens who had begun to return from exile. In Philadelphia, among others, he was waited upon by Mr. Robert Morris, who was still in his glory, and regarded in public estimation next to Washington, as the man on whose financial exertions had depended the success of the Revolution. He entertained us, I still hanging as a bob to a kite, at a dinner of thirty persons, in a style of magnificence which I had never seen equalled. I left him at Philadelphia, and went on an excursion to Baltimore for a few days. On my return to Boston, I resumed my desk and books in his office.

After three years' study with Judge Lowell, young Otis was recommended by the Suffolk Bar Association, and sworn in as an attorney. He borrowed a sum of money to buy law books, hired an office, and hung out his shingle. His first client was secured by the lucky chance of being at home while all the other lawyers were out; others came through Mr. Lowell, who turned over to his pupil a part of his business in the lower courts. Thus Otis was enabled to pay his debts by the end of his first year's practice.

The year 1786, in which Otis was admitted to the bar, was a crisis in the history of Massachusetts. The smouldering discontent of the huge debtor class created by the recent hard times flamed out in the western part of the state. Shays's Rebellion, as it was called, had begun; whole counties were in armed insurrection; the courts were forcibly prevented from sitting; local conventions were demanding radical alterations in the government: it seemed to thinking men as if the "goodly fabric, that eight years were spent in raising," was about to be pulled down over their heads. With the situation dangerous even to Boston, the young men of the town formed a new militia company, the "Independent Light Infantry," and chose Harrison Gray Otis their captain. When Cambridge was threatened by an armed body of insurgents in November, the Light Infantry was stationed at the Charles River Bridge, prepared for action, while a troop of volunteer cavalry dispersed the band, and captured its leader. Although Boston was saved from attack, the rebellion was still in full swing in western Massachusetts, where Daniel Shays threatened the Federal arsenal at Springfield. Finally the state government, awaking to the seriousness of the situation, appointed Benjamin Lincoln commander of the state militia, with orders to raise a force to break the rebellion. He called at once for volunteers, and Otis offered the services of his company in a letter of January 27, 1787, to Governor Bowdoin: [3]

May it please your Excellency,

The Independent Lt. Infantry, ready to serve their Country & share the Dangers of their fellow Citizens beg leave to tender their Services to your Excellency upon ye present occasion, and are ready to march at the Shortest notice — & to continue in service untill regularly discharg'd.

Yr Excellency's most obedt Servt

HARRISON G. OTIS — Capt. Indt Lt Infantry.

[3] Mass. Archives, CLXXXIX, 88.

This letter is endorsed: "Capt Otis will proceed with his Company to join General Lincoln and until the junction will be under the command of General Brooks." The company was sent home, however, after advancing no farther than Cambridge, but Otis volunteered his services as aide to General Brooks, and accompanied him through the remainder of the bloodless but successful campaign. He continued to serve in the state militia for a number of years, and in 1789 "The Independent Light Infantry, under Major Otis," headed the cortège that escorted President Washington into Boston.

Taking to heart the advice given his father by James Otis, Harry made his reputation at the beginning of his career. In 1788 he was chosen by the town authorities to deliver the annual Fourth of July oration.— a singular honor for a young man of twenty-three. The oration seems labored and bombastic according to our modern ideas of eloquence. We feel the "scorching rays of supreme majesty," and the "pestilential breath of a despot"; the Americans are "elevated, patriotic, godlike," etc., etc. Otis was evidently a little ashamed of the effusion himself, for on sending a copy to his grandfather Gray, he remarked that these expressions "are as necessary for an oration in this Country, as the Lemon juice for punch." He seems, however, to have pleased his hearers, for one of them, John Quincy Adams, by no means an easy critic of other persons' performances wrote: "The composition and the delivery were much superior even to my expectations, which were somewhat sanguine. It was greatly superior, in my opinion, to that which he delivered when he took his second degree; the only public performance that I had heard before from him." [4]

The bulk of Otis's law practice, at the beginning of his

[4] *Proc. Mass. Hist. Soc.*, 2nd ser., XVI, 433.

professional career, was derived from the questions of admiralty and maritime rights that were always coming up in Boston. One of the most amusing, if not the most important of his cases, was that of Lemon v. Ramsden. Captain Clement Lemon, it appears, had so unsavory a reputation for drinking at sea, that he secured a ship only after signing the following agreement:

Boston December 31st, 1790

Be it Known; I Clement Lemon do hereby Agree to, and with, Thomas Ramsden of Boston Mercht. that if I am seen or known to be disguised with drinking Liquors, or in any wise drunk or disorder'd with drinking during the Voyage now bound on from Boston to Liverpool in the Brigantine Mary Ann and back to Boston — I will forfeit and give up all my Wages or demands I may have against the said Thomas Ramsden or Brigantine Mary Ann. In Witness whereof I have hereunto set my hand and seal this thirty first day of december One thousand seven hundred and Ninety.

CLEMT. LEMON

Sign'd & seal'd in presence of
JOSIAH BACON.

But alas, Captain Lemon became very much "disguised with drinking Liquors" during the voyage, and the good ship *Mary Ann* meandered all over the North Atlantic before it returned to Boston. The captain, nevertheless, sued the owner for the full amount of his wages when the latter, according to the agreement, refused to pay them. Otis was retained as attorney for the defendant, and during the trial produced in evidence of the Captain's condition the following gem of English composition from the mate of the *Mary Ann*. It is addressed to "Mr Thomas Ramsdel Marchant Boston head of the Long Whorf."

March 2d 1791                                         Liverpool
Sir
With the utmost Satisfaction I take this opportunity To In from you that I have Left your Brig and The Reason there off is

upon the aCount of the Capting Who has treated me with very
onsivel [la]ngeage — Nothing but quorling and fighting has
ben on board Sence we have ben out we got here in 37 Days
but more by good Luck then good Conduckd and Now had I a
Long bote I wold not trust him as fare as Castle William in hir.
I Dont say he gets Drunk but I say that he can grink groge as
well as my Self nor due I say he Neckglecks his Duty but he
Loves to Slipe.
I wish your vesel safe home and I am very glad that you have
hir Inshured I have no more Sir But am you humble Sarvent
                                        DANIEL LEWIS.

P S Sir
I wold in from you that the 2 small pigs Died and Capt
Lemon Lost the Dicsy Line [5] and both Leades out of his hand
overboard and then took all the Lead of the hase hole when
there was plenty of bolts and Speaks that wold answer the same
purpose I say Dam such a fellow that Stoes away Cags of Rum
on be none [6] to the oner.

By aid of more direct and grammatical evidence, Otis
won the case for Mr. Ramsden.
A scattered practice added more to Otis's reputation
than to his income, as the following extract from one of
his letters to Harrison Gray, dated January 14, 1790,
indicates:

My business calls me and keeps me so frequently from home
that I am really able with truth to say that I have hardly had
time to sit down and write you deliberately since my last. If
these avocations into the Country were as profitable as they
are troublesome, you would perhaps be reconciled to my apparent negligence, but this is far from true. Our profession in this
Country is not lucrative and I feel already that I am doomd to
a hard life and scanty fortune.

One of these journeys, however, took Otis to New York
in season to witness the first inauguration of a President
of the United States, on April 30, 1789. The ceremony

---

[5] Dipsey (i.e., Deep Sea) Line.          [6] Unbeknown.

was especially interesting to the young man on account
of the important part taken in it by his father, who had
just been chosen Secretary of the United States Senate.
As he stood in the crowd outside Federal Hall, Harry
could see his father, conspicuous among the impressive
group on the balcony, bearing on a crimson cushion the
open Bible on which the President was to take his oath of
office. As the solemn words of the inaugural oath were
concluded, Samuel Otis made a motion as if to raise the
Bible to the President's lips, but Washington gently re-
strained him, and reverently bowed to kiss the book. The
scene impressed itself indelibly on Otis's memory; sixty
years later he wrote: "No one can describe the silent
tearful ecstacy, which pervaded the myriads who wit-
nessed that scene; succeeded only by shouts which seemed
to shake the canopy above them." [7]

Early in the following year, 1790, Otis offered himself
to a young lady whom he had been courting for some time.
In a letter that passed between two of his former college
mates, Timothy Williams and Timothy Bigelow, we get
an unofficial view of this important event in Otis's life:

H. G. Otis is to be married in three months to Miss Sally
Foster — poor girl who has been kept in the twitter of expectation these two years by his attention to her, but never received
an explicit declaration till within a month. In this situation a
girl must possess uncommon fortitude and virtue not to express
or degrade herself in a thousand ways to which she is liable —
court instead of being courted.

Whatever may have been her feelings, the diffidence of
young Otis was probably due more to the lack of the
wherewithal than to lack of courage. Long engagements
were looked upon askance in those days, and a young man
was not expected to declare himself until he was capable

[7] Boston Atlas, October 2, 1848.

of supporting a family. Miss Sally Foster was a beautiful
and vivacious girl of twenty, five years the junior of her
fiancé. She was the daughter of William Foster, a respectable Boston merchant who possessed considerable
wealth, but who had no intention of applying it to supple-
ment the income of his son-in-law.

' The family correspondence regarding the engagement
throws a pleasant light on the formalities of the period.
Mrs. Samuel A. Otis, Harry's stepmother, sent Miss Foster this somewhat qualified approbation of the match:

> Mrs. Otis's love to Miss Foster, & cannot refrain from ex-
> pressing the pleasure she feels in the connection which is like
> to take place, & wishes Miss Foster all possible felicity and
> happiness. — Mrs O. intends to do herself the pleasure of
> Personally testifying her approbation of Mr Otis's choice the
> moment she has reciev'd the form of his Father's consent [of]
> which She's persuaded there can be no doubt.
>
> Mrs O. compliments to Mr & Mrs Foster.
>
> Tuesday Morng. Jany. 12th.

If she was led to expect a chilly reception into the Otis
family by the tone of this letter, Miss Foster was soon
relieved by a gallant epistle from her future father-in-law:

New York Jan 24 '90

Dear Madam

When an old Gentleman writes to a fine young Lady his first
care should be to provide an apology. A declaration of Love
would be worse than none. But dont be alarmed my dear Miss
Forster, for altho' it must be a cold heart indeed that is not
half in love with you at least, I shall not make a declaration,
for many obvious reasons. Love to a very worthy & dutiful
son I may however declare; Nor will it I hope offend your delicacy if I add, I am almost jealous too; For I am convinced you
have engrossed so much of his regard that I must submit to a
transfer. Give me credit for a little candour if I confess it could
not in my opinion have been made to a more worthy object; And

to whom I should with greater pleasure resign the first place in his affections than to, — I had like to have said — *my* Sally. And will Miss Forster permit me at some future time to call her so? I have lost an amiable daughter. In my Harry's wife I can only hope to recover her. You may rely upon the most cordial reception into our family, if you will consent to become one of us, & because we all love Harry, tis impossible to withold our affections from the Lady of his choice, even if it was not one, whose "bland accents" & whose "female attractions steal the hearts of the wise." I can only promise you a continuance of that solicitude for the dear youth, & all that are dear to him, which has invariably attended him from his cradle, & will I have no doubt, go down with me to my grave; On the verge of which, I shall retrospect the pleasing reflection, that he is happy in loving & being beloved, by such an one as yourself. I should say more on this agreable subject but I fear my affectionate heart has already made me too expressive. Permit me to present my kind regards to your good Mamma, and to entreat her entire approbation of a plan of happiness, on which I felicitate at least one family, & to believe me with great sincerity and respect, her &

　　　　　　　　　Your most Humble Sert.

　　　　　　　　　　　　　　　SAM: A: OTIS.

The young couple were married on May 31, 1790, by the Rev. Samuel Parker of Trinity Church. A daughter, the first of a family of eleven, was born to them on June 1, 1791, and christened Elizabeth Gray, after her sainted grandmother. The correspondence of Mr. and Mrs. Otis, which has been preserved almost entire for the forty-six years of their married life, shows that their union was ideal. Perhaps the secret of its success lay in the fact that Mrs. Otis was very like her husband in temperament, and made his interests her own; and that he never ceased to be her ardent lover, as well as her faithful husband.

Shortly after his marriage, Otis's name begins to appear prominently in the accounts of town-meeting debates. We find him, together with James Sullivan and

Dr. Jarvis, arguing in favor of a city charter, at a meeting
of December 30, 1791. Thirty-one years elapsed before
this movement bore fruit, but another matter of local dissension, in which Otis played a prominent rôle, had more
immediate consequences. This was the question of the
legality of theatrical performances. "Stage plays" were
forbidden by an act of 1750, the repeal of which was now
demanded by a more enlightened public opinion. Otis
took at first the contrary side and opposed, at a town meeting in October, 1791, the adoption of a petition to the
General Court to repeal the act in question. "So strong
was his rhetorical power," says Mr. Loring, "that Samuel
Adams lifted up his hands in ecstacy and thanked God
that there was one young man willing to step forth in defence of the good old cause of morality and religion."
Harrison Gray took the trouble to write his grandson
from London:

It affords me great pleasure my child to hear of the Christian
as well as the political opposition you made to the motion in
your Town meeting to petition the General Court for the repeal of the Act against *plays*. If your Legislators have any
regard for the morality of the people, they will not give the
least countenance to the Stage, which by the late Doc. Tillot-
son is called the *Devil's Chappel;* and which is condemned by
the primitive church. The Fathers have given their Testimony
against it; I could quote many extracts from the holy Fathers
condemning plays, but shall content myself with one from
*Chrysostom*, who in his preface to his commentary upon St.
John's Gospel, speaking of Plays and other public Shews says
"But what need I branch out, the Lewdness of these spec-
tacles and be particular in description, for what's there to be
met with but Lewd laughing, but Smut, railing and buffoon'ry?
In a word it is all Scandal and confusion. Observe I speak to
you all. Let none who partake of the holy Table unqualify
themselves with such mortal Diversions."

Although the General Court refused to repeal the prohibitory act, a company of comedians visited Boston the following year, fitted up an old stable with a stage, and advertised their performances as "moral lectures." [8] Thus the situation continued for some time, but on December 2, 1792, while the audience was enjoying a moral lecture entitled *The School for Scandal,* a sheriff suddenly appeared on the stage and arrested one of the actors. The audience became greatly excited, and a party of enraged young men tore down and trampled under foot a portrait of Governor Hancock that hung on one of the boxes. So great was public interest in the affair that the examination of Harper, the arrested actor, was held in Faneuil Hall. Otis apparently had changed his opinion about the nefariousness of stage plays, for he appeared as Harper's counsel, and made a very clever defense on technical grounds. He won his case, the actor was discharged amid loud applause, and thereafter Boston was permitted to enjoy the theatre.

What Harrison Gray thought of this backsliding on the part of his grandson in favor of the "Devil's Chappel," he was careful to keep to himself, for Otis was at that time engaged in the very delicate business of attempting to recover some of the Gray property. [9] The old gentleman, now over eighty years of age, supported himself in London on an annual pension of £200 from the Crown. His property in America had met the same fate as that of most loyalists. The General Court had given him the compliment of fourth place on a select list of twenty-nine

---

[8] The advertisement in the *Independent Chronicle* of November 30, 1792, reads, "This Evening will be delivered a Moral Lecture, in five parts, called Hamlet, Prince of Denmark. . . . End of the Lecture, a Hornpipe. The whole will conclude with an entertaining lecture called Love À-la-Mode."

[9] Cf. S. E. Morison, "The Property of Harrison Gray, Loyalist," *Publications Colonial Soc. of Mass.,* xiv.

"Notorious Conspirators," whose estates were confiscated, and by the end of the Revolution all his real estate, to the value of about £2000 lawful, was long past recovery. In addition to this loss, however, there were outstanding debts owed to him in Massachusetts to the amount of £8036 lawful. Here young Otis was able to effect something, although with endless trouble and small profit. There were no legal impediments in the way of collection, but public opinion was so hostile to the loyalists that few juries would give a verdict in their favor. The very fact of Otis being retained by Tory clients, if generally known, would have been fatal to his political aspirations. Altogether it was a very ticklish business, requiring all his resources of cleverness and tact. Otis, nevertheless, persisted in it, out of a sense of justice and family duty, and was afterwards able to boast that he saved more from his grandfather's fortune than had all the other agents of Boston loyalists put together. His usual method, when forced to resort to a lawsuit, was to procure an assignment of the debt from his grandfather to himself, so that the jury could not be appealed to on the ground that the creditor was an outlawed Tory.

One item in the list that gave him more trouble than all the rest was a debt of £956 16s. 5d. sterling due from John Hancock. This sum was lent to the patriot leader by Treasurer Gray before the Revolution as an advance on his salary, when there was no money in the treasury to pay it. Otis was obliged to proceed in this case with more than ordinary caution. Hancock wielded so great an influence in Massachusetts that even the Harvard Corporation dared not press him hard for the settlement of his long outstanding accounts with the college. If Otis went to law, this powerful debtor could easily have procured an act from the General Court permitting him to tender the sum to the Commonwealth in paper money; he might even have blasted Otis's reputation. During four years, from 1789 to Governor Hancock's death in 1793, Otis wrote him letter after letter, danced attendance in his waiting-room, received appointments only to have them broken on the plea of illness, but never succeeded in securing a direct reply, oral or written, to his demands. "I have taken such unwearied pains with regard to this debt for years past," Otis wrote his grandfather at one time, "I have experienced such disappointment deceit & falsehood, that I have almost despaired of receiving a farthing." Finally, in 1795, after both John Hancock and Harrison Gray were dead, Otis recovered two thirds of the original debt by a clever move against the Governor's widow. She became engaged that year to Captain Scott, who commanded a packet ship between Boston and England. "As all former arguments had failed," Otis wrote Harrison Gray, Jr., "it occurred to me that some advantage might arise from the intended connection of Mrs. H and Capt Scott, especially as an idea prevailed of her intention to accompany him to England. I therefore gave intimation, which I knew would reach her ears, of a determination to prosecute for the debt in England, if Mr. Scott should ever be found there after marriage, and this suggestion though it could never have been executed, very unexpectedly produced its effect, and induced the parties concerned to hearken to terms of accommodation."

Meanwhile, Boston was recovering its ancient prosperity. The population, which decreased from 15,500 in 1770 to 10,000 in 1780, owing to the loyalist exodus and the hardships of war, rose to 18,000 in 1790, and to 24,000 in 1800. With commerce and business of every sort expanding rapidly, Otis was not one to be left behind in

such a movement. Samuel Breck, in his *Recollections,*
gives a pleasant picture of Otis in 1792, toiling away at
his profession. He borrowed a thousand dollars, it seems,
from Mr. Breck, and on repaying it, told him that "the
utmost extent of his desires as to riches was to be worth
ten thousand dollars," certainly a very moderate ambition. "It has pleased God to allow us a very full measure
of domestic felicity hitherto," Otis wrote in December,
1792. "We have two fine children, one of each sex; my
affairs have been prosperous beyond my most sanguine
expectations, and I have a full share of business."

When his political career began in 1796, Otis had already risen to a leading position in the bar of Suffolk
County, which, though small in numbers, was rich in
talents. Such men as Theophilus Parsons, Christopher
Gore, James and William Sullivan, Samuel Dexter, William Prescott, Josiah Quincy, and John Lowell, Jr., were
Otis's brother lawyers and competitors; all but the first
three were within a few years of his age. Parsons, Dexter,
and Otis were the acknowledged leaders in the period between 1795 and 1815. Each excelled in some one quality:
Parsons in learning and intellect, Dexter in reasoning
power, and Otis in eloquence, tact, and personality. It
would be difficult to say whether his power of graceful
oratory or his capacity for making every one his friend,
was his greater asset as a lawyer. The rich and varied vocabulary at his command was the despair of his rivals.
When Chief Justice Shaw heard that Noah Webster was
about to issue a dictionary containing three thousand
new words, he exclaimed, "For heaven's sake, don't let
Otis get hold of it!" [10]

[10] N. S. D.'s "Recollections of the Boston Bar," in *Historical Magazine*
n. s., VIII (1870), 185. Fisher Ames, in his oft-quoted letter on the Suffolk Bar
in 1800 (*Works,* I, 300), says, "Otis is eager in the chase of fame and wealth,

At this period the Boston Bar was composed almost exclusively of members of the leading Federalist families, and, owing to the small numbers and the close personal friendships that existed among the lawyers and the judges, there was an informality about the procedure that would now be impossible. Otis was allowed free rein for his oratory, until his friend and colleague Theophilus Parsons was elevated to the supreme bench of the Commonwealth in 1806. The new Chief Justice started out with the idea of shortening the length of trials, which had become a crying abuse. Many were the flowers of eloquence about to blossom from Otis or Lowell or Prescott, that his ruthless authority nipped in the bud. A story is told of one case, in which Judge Parsons broke in on Otis's argument with, "Brother Otis, don't waste your time on that point, there is nothing in it." Otis stopped, bowed to the bench in a somewhat surprised manner, and went on to another point. After a moment: "Nor in this either, Brother Otis; don't waste your time." Otis bowed once more, and took up a third point, only again to be interrupted. "I regret to find myself, your Honor, unable to please the Court this morning," he remarked with some asperity. "Brother Otis," replied the Judge, with his most winning smile, "you *always* please the Court when you are *right*."

Before he was thirty years old, Otis not only had achieved this enviable reputation as a lawyer, but also had laid the foundation of his fortune by wise investments in real estate. His largest and most profitable venture was the purchase of the Copley Pasture in 1795. Early in that year he was appointed one of a committee to procure a

and, with a great deal of eloquence, is really a good lawyer, and improving. He, however, sighs for political office — he knows not what; and he will file off the moment an opportunity offers."

site for a new State House in Boston. The committee
found by far the best situation to be the so-called "Governor's Pasture," near the top of Beacon Hill, and just
above the Boston Common. This land they purchased
for the Commonwealth from Governor Hancock's heirs,
and there the present State House was built. Meanwhile
Otis had opportunity to observe that the building of the
State House would give prestige to Beacon Hill, and make
its southwestern slope, facing the Common and the Back
Bay, an ideal residential district. The entire slope at that
time was an upland pasture, encroached upon only by the
Hancock mansion and one or two wooden dwellings. Except for the Hancock estate, it was the property of John
Singleton Copley, the celebrated Boston painter. Since
Copley had resided in England for twenty years, his property was in the hands of an agent, who, on being approached by a syndicate formed by Otis, was injudicious
enough to sign a bond for the sale of the entire Beacon
Hill estate at the rate of a thousand dollars an acre.

When he heard of this transaction, Copley disavowed
his agent's act, refused to execute the deed, and sent his
son (afterwards Lord Lyndhurst) to Boston in order to
break the bond. But the future Lord Chancellor of England found that young Mr. Otis had taken care of all the
technicalities. The contract was binding, and Copley was
forced to convey the property to Otis *et al.* for the stipulated sum of $18,450. But the matter did not end here.
Since no deeds to Copley could be found, one claimant
after another came forward during the next fifty years to
contest the title of the Mount Vernon Proprietors, the
name under which Otis and his colleagues had incorporated themselves.[11] These efforts were unsuccessful, how-

[11] The original purchasers were Otis and Jonathan Mason (each a three-
tenths interest) and Joseph Woodward and Charles Ward Apthorp (each a two-

ever, and the old pasture proved a veritable gold-mine for its purchasers. It covered the territory now bounded by Beacon Street, Walnut Street, a line drawn diagonally from Walnut Street to Louisburg Square, Pinckney Street, and the Charles River. Originally over eighteen acres, this tract amounted to almost as much again when the mud-flats at the foot of Beacon Hill were filled in. Before Otis died, the whole territory, exclusive of the flats, was covered with first-class houses, and the Copley Pasture had become, as he foresaw, the fashionable residential district of Boston.

Otis did not confine his speculations to real estate; he was interested in one or more of the Western land companies of the period, and in wild lands in Maine and Georgia. By 1796 he had built himself a substantial brick dwelling, still standing, on the corner of Cambridge and Lynde Streets, and had accumulated considerable property for a young man who eleven years before had none. Assured of a steady income sufficient to support his family, Otis was ready to enter the field of national politics.

tenths interest). Woodward and Apthorp soon sold out to Benjamin Joy. For the whole Copley affair, see articles by "Gleaner" (N. I. Bowditch), reprinted in the *Fifth Report of the Boston Record Commissioners*, 147–171. The Otis papers give many additional details. It appears, for instance, that Copley received from the Proprietors almost a thousand guineas in addition to the original price, in return for furnishing evidence in regard to his title.

# CHAPTER IV

## A HAMILTONIAN FEDERALIST

### 1794-1796, ÆT. 29-31

It was in the nature of things inevitable that Harrison Gray Otis should take up politics as a profession. He was especially fitted for it by heredity, education, and character. In New England during the eighteenth century, as in Old England, social position and political success were almost synonymous. Some one or other of his ancestors had been in public life since 1688, and few families in the United States had played a more important part in the Revolution than his. Men were inclined to look favorably upon him for what his grandfather, father, and uncles had done in the great cause of independence. Young Otis, moreover, not only inherited the name, but the characteristics of his ancestors that win success in politics. He possessed the gift of eloquence, which was then a far more important factor in a politician's equipment than it is to-day, and also the very essential qualities of tactfulness and popularity. However, since in his day, as now, a public career was unremunerative to honest men, it was necessary for him to provide for the support of his family, before he could enter politics. With the accomplishment of that task, in 1796, came the opportunity.

In order to understand Otis's position at the outset of his political career, we must glance briefly at the political situation in the last decade of the eighteenth century. One party, the Tories, had been eliminated from the American political system by the Revolution; the triumphant Whig party then split into Federalists and Anti-Federalists on the question whether the Constitution of 1787 should or should not be adopted. Once the Constitution was ratified, the Anti-Federalists were eliminated — not, like the Tories, by bodily removal from the country, but by reconciliation with the new government. At this stage came a new division which the framers of the Constitution, in defiance of all human experience, had hoped to avoid. The separation was none the less inevitable, for the same divergent political tendencies remained in the people after 1788 as before. Opposition to the triumphant Federal party, developing as Hamilton unfolded his wonderful system, found a leader in 1790 in the person of Thomas Jefferson, farmer, scientist, diplomat, and philosopher, fresh from Revolutionary Paris. We may fix the date of Jefferson's return — March, 1790 — as the birth of the two national parties that occupied the stage for the next quarter of a century: the Federal or Federalist party,[1] under the lead of Hamilton, and the Republican or Democratic party [2] under the guidance of Jefferson.

To Hamilton's standard flocked the mercantile, non-agricultural classes throughout the Union, who were interested in a strong and efficient government, sound finance, and a vigorous foreign policy. The principles of Federalism appealed also to men who had the common sense to see that the country had enjoyed an excess of

[1] Both terms are correct; throughout this work I have employed the former, which was more generally used at the time. The official name of the party was "Federal Republican."

[2] According to the custom of the time, I have used both terms interchangeably for the party of Jefferson. "Republican" was the term preferred by the party itself, as it was implied that the Federalists were monarchists; "Democratic," at first a term of opprobrium, was accepted by the Jeffersonians as early as 1795. (See *Independent Chronicle*, May 14, 1795.) The Federalists also called the Jeffersonians "Anti-Federalists," but this term is properly applied only to the party that opposed the Constitution of 1787.

liberty; that consolidation and strength were necessary to preserve the Union. Jefferson, on the other hand, united and typified the agricultural classes, which looked with suspicion on financial schemes they did not understand, and saw in the Hamiltonian system only an attempt to corrupt the government and to pave the way for a monarchy. He also represented the idealists, the theoretical democrats of the period, who had sublime faith in the fallacious theory of Jean-Jacques Rousseau, that a weak and decentralized government was the best safeguard of liberty. Persons like Samuel Maclay and Elbridge Gerry, who, morbidly suspicious of tyranny, saw indications of a deep-laid monarchical plot in Washington's dignified aloofness, and in John Adams's love for titles and trappings, naturally followed Jefferson.

Many of the differences between the Republicans and the Federalists were only those of "Outs" and "Ins," and were mutually exchanged after the Republicans had tasted the sweets of power, and Federalists the dregs of defeat. But there was between them a fundamental cleft which was summed up in radically opposite opinions of their leaders. As Henry Adams has said in his *Life of Gallatin:* "Mr. Jefferson meant that the American System should be a democracy, and he would rather have let the world perish than that this principle, which to him represented all that man was worth, should fail. Mr. Hamilton considered democracy a fatal curse, and meant to stop its progress." [3]

Federalism made its widest appeal in the more thickly settled parts of the country, along the seacoast and navigable rivers, where commerce took precedence over agriculture, and the wealthy classes had long been in control of politics. The strength of Republicanism lay in the more

[3] *Life of Gallatin*, 159.

Essex Junto ultra-consv [illegible]
- hard-headed [illegible]
refused compromise [illegible]
distrusted Fr. Rev. [illegible] the start.

stronghold
Fed.
① commercial
interest
② conserv.
react. to
[illegible]

Congressional

remote agricultural country, and it spread with the western advance of the frontier. Massachusetts from the first was a stronghold of the Federal party, owing to the prevalence of commercial interests in the eastern half of the state, and to the conservative reaction that set in after Shays's Rebellion.[4] Both parties, however, united in the support of John Hancock for Governor until his death in 1793, and of Samuel Adams until 1796. The Federalists generally controlled the state legislature, and their nominees were elected from 1790 to 1794 in all districts except Hampshire County (the old stamping ground of Shaysism), Middlesex County (in 1794), and the Cape. James Bowdoin, Fisher Ames, Theodore Sedgwick, and Samuel Dexter were at this period the most popular leaders of Massachusetts Federalism. But from the first there stood out from its ranks a clearly defined group which often dominated it, and which maintained its importance as long as the party existed. This was the famous Essex Junto. It was composed chiefly of hard-headed merchants and lawyers of Essex County, where mercantile and maritime interests were even stronger than in Boston. Stephen Higginson, George Cabot, and Theophilus Parsons were its earliest leaders; Timothy Pickering was an influential member, even when absent from Massachusetts, and a few Boston Federalists, such as Fisher Ames, Timothy Bigelow, Christopher Gore, and John Lowell, Jr., afterwards became identified with the group. This Essex Junto, the ultra-conservative and ultra-sectional wing of the party, refused all compromise with democracy, distrusted the French Revolution from the very start, failed entirely to sympathise with the South and West, and, in short, was blind to the fact that the world had moved forward since 1775 and 1789. Otis happily characterized the

[4] A. E. Morse, *The Federalist Party in Massachusetts to 1800.*

group when he wrote Josiah Quincy, in 1811: "There is not one of these sworn brothers who is, or ever was, a politician, or who ever had what old John Adams calls the tact of the feelings and passions of mankind; but they are men of probity, of talent, of influence, and the Federal party may say of them, *Non possum vivere sine te nec cum te!"* [5]

Otis naturally joined the Federal party. He had seen with his own eyes, in Shays's Rebellion, the dangers of a minimum of government and an excess of democracy. His professional and business connections with the mercantile classes in a great mercantile centre made it to his interest that the finances of the country should be on a sound basis. His appointment, in 1796, as a director of the Boston branch of the United States Bank further identified him with the interests which formed the backbone of the Federal party. Most important of all, he was by birth a member of the native aristocracy. In the Revolution the larger portion of that class was Tory; but families like the Otises who joined the patriot cause abandoned none of their conservative principles. They had fought for independence from Great Britain, not independence from government and social restraint, and consequently they expected the wheels of democratic evolution to stand still in 1783. "You and I did not imagine, when the first war with Britain was over, that revolution was just begun," Otis wrote an old friend, half a century later. Young Copley, the future Lord Lyndhurst, wrote from Boston in 1796: "The *better* people are all aristocrats. My father is too rank a Jacobin to live among them."

The two great parties crystallized on the question of the nation's attitude toward the struggle between Revolutionary France and the rest of Europe: the Federal-

[5] Edmund Quincy, *Life of Josiah Quincy*, 242.

ists became zealous champions of England; the Republicans, of France. In 1793 the issue was first squarely presented, by the announcement that war had broken out between Great Britain and the French Republic, and that Citoyen Genet, minister of the French Republic to the United States, intended to use this country as a French naval base against England. President Washington, in his famous proclamation of April 23, 1793, met the situation by a declaration of neutrality, and a refusal to permit either belligerent to use United States ports as bases for privateering. Later in the year came the news that both England and France, at the outset of the struggle, had issued severe and illegal edicts, subjecting to capture and spoliation the neutral commerce of the United States. This problem of foreign relations remained unsolved until the close of the War of 1812 and of the Napoleonic epoch.

Washington's policy of neutrality was entirely distasteful to the Republicans, and satisfied the Federalists only for a brief period. Jefferson's party let itself be carried away by its enthusiasm for the militant French Republic, and made the cause of Citoyen Genet its own. Within a week of his arrival at Philadelphia the Democratic Club was founded, on the model of the Jacobin Club of Paris, and like the parent institution it helped to form a chain of clubs throughout the Union. These societies carried on a lively abuse of Washington for his neutrality policy, denounced the Federalists as hirelings of Britain, and by intimidating judges thwarted the administration in its attempt to preserve neutrality. The "Constitutional Club" in Boston encouraged the French consul to defy a United States marshal, and even instigated the frigate *La Concorde* to a piratical attack on a merchant vessel owned by Federalists.

Conduct such as this, added to the course of the French Revolution itself, and their close mercantile relations with England, drove the Federalists into as strong sympathy with Great Britain as the Republicans expressed for France. In the earlier phases of the French Revolution the Federalists yielded nothing to the Republicans in their enthusiasm for this great movement. It was considered a triumph of American revolutionary principles; the officers who had fought for the colonies were among its leaders; Valmy and Jemappes were hailed as another Bunker Hill or Saratoga. But when Louis XVI, the friend of America, was executed, when the Reign of Terror commenced, when property, religion, and morals were no longer respected, conservatives felt that the very bases of society were threatened. The manifestations of Democratic clubs on this side of the water, and the Whiskey Rebellion in Pennsylvania, which Washington himself attributed to their influence, made the Federalists believe that similar excesses were possible in this country. Otis thus expressed the sense of his party in a letter to his wife: "Should Great Britain be compelled to yield, it is my opinion that our liberties and independence would fall a sacrifice. She is the only barrier to the dreadful deluge, and when that is broken down, it will be time for us to prepare to be good and dutiful subjects to the French." On the other side, a Republican newspaper of Boston announced, and doubtless believed, that: "If Britain is victorious, the United States will be as a *Republic* annihilated."[6]

In like manner foreign events and foreign issues continued to dominate American politics, until the War of 1812 brought an end to this political and intellectual thralldom. The settled and influential portion of the

[6] *Independent Chronicle*, October 27, 1796.

United States was far nearer to Europe in thought than
to its own hinterland, and was overpowered by the immen-
sity of the European struggle. Federalists and Republicans alike believed that their country's fate depended
on the issue of events across the Atlantic. The newspapers
devoted the greater part of their space to foreign news,
and much of the remainder to pithy applications of it to
home politics. French ministers interfered in presidential
elections, and Federalist leaders unbosomed their plans to
envoys of Great Britain. Politically and intellectually,
the American people until 1815 were in the colonial epoch;
their politics were but a shadow of the great drama across
the Atlantic.

Although Otis was not able to devote his entire time
to politics before 1796, he took part in contests with the
local Democracy for several years previous. Boston was
always a Federalist town. The lawyers and merchants
almost without exception belonged to that party, and as
many of them had been popular leaders in the Revolution,
they carried a majority of the people with them. Boston
was strongly in favor of the ratification of the Constitution in 1788, and, when the issue was drawn between
Hamilton and Jefferson, elected to Congress Fisher Ames,
one of Hamilton's closest friends and allies. The local
Democracy, however, made up in noise and activity
what it lacked in strength. It possessed, in Dr. Charles
Jarvis, a member of Otis's class of society, and in Benjamin Austin, a ropemaker, whose rabid essays over the
signature "Honestus" were much dreaded, two leaders
of great ability.

Otis was instrumental in preventing the town from
falling into Democratic hands on a memorable occasion
in 1794. The Federal party that year was much embarrassed by the policy of Great Britain toward the

United States. The British government continued to hold its Western posts, now in American territory, and British privateers and prize courts were sweeping American commerce from the seas. James Madison, the Republican leader in Congress, introduced seven resolutions on January 3, 1794, providing for retaliation on British commerce. This plan did not meet the ideas of the seaboard merchants who controlled the Federal party. Since about seven eighths of their trade was with Great Britain, they preferred to enjoy it on her terms rather than risk losing the whole by retaliation,—an attitude that they steadily maintained for the next twenty years. The excitement in Boston over Madison's resolutions was intense. Jarvis and Austin, reviving a custom of Revolutionary days, called a town meeting "to take the sense of the inhabitants." They hoped, by playing on the old hatred of England, to overrule the mercantile interests, and procure resolutions requesting the Massachusetts Congressmen to support Madison; they very nearly succeeded. The town meeting, begun at ten in the morning of February 24, adjourned, owing to the crowd, from Faneuil Hall to the Old South at three, lasted there until after dark, and adjourned until the next day. Only at one in the afternoon of the 25th did the Federalists succeed in wearing out their opponents, and in securing an indefinite postponement of the whole matter. After the affair was over the *Centinel* remarked, "We cannot omit mentioning in a particular manner, Mr. Otis, who took a conspicuous part in the course of the debate, in opposition to the Report. His fellow citizens did justice to his abilities, and eloquence"; and Christopher Gore wrote Senator King of New York, "It is said that we owe very much to Eustis, Jones & Codman and Lyman. Otis also took a decided part and greatly aided the cause of good government &

order." [7] Although this is the first recorded instance of Otis's entering the political arena, the language of both reporters indicates that it was not his first performance.

In recognition, doubtless, of his part in this exhausting contest, Otis was given in 1794 and 1795 a place on the Federalist ticket for the "Boston Seat," *i.e.*, the town's quota of Representatives in the General Court. On both occasions the Federalist ticket was defeated. This result, also, was due mainly to the influence of foreign affairs. Between the town meeting of February 24 and the State elections in May, 1794, news arrived of a fresh British decree against neutral commerce, even more outrageous than the previous ones, and of Lord Dorchester's inflammatory speech to the Indians of the Northwest. The Federalists, for refusing to take retaliatory measures against Great Britain earlier in the year, were naturally discredited.

Meanwhile, President Washington had averted almost certain war by sending John Jay to London. All was suspense until the result of his negotiation should be heard. Otis described the situation in a letter of November 15, 1794, to his uncle, Harrison Gray, Jr.:

We have just passed through the turbulent period of the election of members for Congress. Strenuous exertions have been made by the anti-federal faction throughout the Union, but generally without success. Mr. Ames is reelected here, and the Friends to peace and good order are greatly encouraged by the appearance of our public affairs. Much however you are sensible depends on Great Britain. The moderate and respectable part of the Community wait with patience and anxiety the result of Mr. Jay's mission; but should justice be denied to our claims, I think a very general sentiment of indignation & spirit of resentment will prevail here among all classes of people & produce a rupture between the countries.

[7] C. R. King, *Life and Correspondence of Rufus King*, I, 547.

In July, 1795, the text of Jay's treaty was made public, and, as Henry Adams has said, "threw a sword into the body politic." A howl of rage followed the news through the country, and effigies of John Jay went up in smoke all the way from Maine to Georgia. The treaty was indeed humiliating, and all parties at first united in condemning it. At a crowded town meeting in Faneuil Hall on July 10, not a single vote was registered in its favor. George Cabot, of the Essex Junto, was willing to swallow the treaty whole, but he had to attend Harvard Commencement to find sympathizers.[8] Gradually, however, the conservative elements came to see that Jay's treaty was better than none, and that the only alternative to accepting it was war. When Washington finally signed the agreement, without the objectionable article forbidding the United States to export molasses or cotton, the Federal party to a man approved.

But the last chance to defeat the Jay Treaty had not expired. The House of Representatives, through its power to defeat the necessary appropriations to carry it into effect, held a veto over the treaty; and under the lead of Edward Livingston and Gallatin, a determined effort was made by the Republicans to exercise this prerogative. The Boston Federalists, seeing another crisis at hand, called a town meeting for April 25, 1796. Dr. Jarvis, the Democratic leader, opened the debate. Then Otis made such a speech that it seemed "a new and frightful planet blazed through the darkness, and dispelled the clouds." At his conclusion Bishop Cheverus, the gifted Catholic prelate, "threw his arms around Otis, and while tears were streaming down his cheeks, exclaimed: 'Future Generations, young man, will rise up and call thee blessed!'"[9] Such is the traditional account of Otis's

[8] H. C. Lodge, *Life of George Cabot*, 80.      [9] Loring, 308.

speech. Unfortunately the only contemporary report of it is in the *Independent Chronicle*, which, as a leading opposition journal, attempted to depreciate the "new and frightful planet." According to its account, Otis began by painting the horrors of the war that would be necessary to drive the British forces from the Western posts if the treaty was blocked — the same line of argument followed by Fisher Ames in his celebrated oration three days later. After a rejoinder by Benjamin Austin, and a general discussion, "Mr. Otis concluded the debate," to quote from the *Chronicle*, "by a very pathetic eulogy on the President, and a very illiberal reflection on Mr. Gallatin, who Mr. Otis said was the *leader* of the majority in Congress. Shall we (said Mr. O.) join a vagrant foreigner in opposition to a Washington; a foreigner who to his knowledge ten years ago came to this Country without a *second shirt to his back?* A man who in comparison to Washington is like a Satyre to a Hyperian?"

No doubt Otis's attack on Gallatin was delivered in rather vigorous language, for in those days gentlemen seldom permitted the amenities of private intercourse to dull the acerbity of political controversy. Gallatin, moreover, was regarded by Federalists as a low foreign-born adventurer, the instigator of the Whiskey Insurrection, and the connecting link between the American and French Jacobins.

> "Bold convicts lend their aid in every state,
> *Genevan* ALBERT and *Hibernian* MAT" —

runs a bad verse in the *Jacobiniad*, in reference to Gallatin and Lyon. Still, we are glad to find that Otis was a little ashamed of his reflection on the size of his old tutor's wardrobe, and had the courage to risk his party's disapprobation by apologizing to Gallatin after they had met in Philadelphia.[10]

Otis's "Second Shirt Speech," as his effusion was called, was widely commented on by newspapers of both parties. Immediately after its conclusion, a vote of confidence in Washington's administration had been proposed, and carried by a vote of about 2400 to 100. This was a personal triumph for Otis; he had met Democracy in its citadel, the assembly of the people, and had conquered it by his eloquence. Immediate recognition came from his party; on May 26, 1796, the President commissioned him United States District Attorney for Massachusetts. Having higher objects in view, Otis refused to accept this appointment, but consented to act under it temporarily until a successor could be procured.

The eloquence of this speech was not wholly responsible, however, for the change of sentiment in Boston. The same phenomenon was taking place throughout Massachusetts. In response to a circular letter of the Federalist leaders in Boston, almost every town in the state memorialized Congress to carry out Jay's treaty. This notable increase in Federalist strength was due partly to a conservative reaction against the excesses of Democratic clubs and mobs; partly to the efforts of the orthodox clergy, who for two years had been preaching Federalism in and out of the pulpit. In the spring elections to the General Court, the Federalists regained their hold on Boston. Otis and the entire Federalist ticket were elected to the House of Representatives by a strong majority.

The next autumn came Otis's opportunity for further advancement. Fisher Ames, who had represented the First Middle (Suffolk) District in the first four Congresses, decided to withdraw from politics, and regarded

[10] *Chronicle*, July 27 and August 3, 1797. Cf. below, p. 77.

Otis as his most promising successor. The *Centinel* announced on November 2: "The Federalists are determined to be united on Hon. Tho: Dawes for an elector, and Harrison G. Otis for a Representative. They give this early information that our brethren in the middle district may know unequivocally who are considered in the capital as real Federal characters." In behalf of James Bowdoin, the opposition candidate, Otis was attacked in the *Chronicle* for his "Second Shirt Speech" on Gallatin, and accused of being "a mere AUTOMATON of funds, banks, and land-jobbing speculators." But on November 7, 1796, when Massachusetts as a whole cast her ballot for John Adams for President, the First Middle District elected Harrison Gray Otis to Congress, by a substantial majority.[11]

[11] This district included *Boston, Roxbury, Dorchester, Dedham, *Weston, *Brookline, *Newton, *Needham, *Natick, *Sherburne, Hopkinton, Holliston, Sharon, *East Sudbury, Medway. Those marked * gave Otis a majority. In the *Chronicle* for November 10 appeared accusations that over four hundred of the votes for Otis were given by "British residents, refugees, etc."; but these charges were successfully refuted. A. E. Morse, *Fed. Party*, 163.

# CHAPTER V

## THE FRENCH PERIL

### 1796-1798, ÆT. 31-33

OTIS's congressional career, from 1797 to 1801, covered a period when the neutrality and the independence of the United States were threatened by the American policy of the French Republic. Nineteen twentieths of the congressional business during this period concerned directly or indirectly our French relations. It will be necessary, therefore, to enter into the policy and aims of France in order to understand the attitude of Otis, as a Federalist Congressman.

From the date of the publication of Jay's treaty with Great Britain, relations between the United States and France went from bad to worse. That agreement was a blow to French influence in the United States, since it gave England privileges to which France considered herself alone entitled by virtue of the treaty of alliance of 1778, and it violated in several respects the French construction of that document. The principal French objection to the Jay Treaty, however, was that it settled difficulties between the United States and England which the French Republic counted upon to produce hostilities. Protests and threats having failed to prevent its ratification by the Senate, France attempted coercion of the United States through commerce-destroying. Beginning in July, 1796, the Directory promulgated a series of outrageous decrees against neutral commerce; and under their authority French privateers began to capture, and

French prize courts to condemn, every American vessel bound to or from ports in the British Empire. By the month of June, 1797, over three hundred captures had been made, many of them attended by atrocious cruelty to the American crews.

When these aggressions began, President Washington recalled the minister to France, James Monroe, a friend of Jefferson who had proved himself incapable of caring for American interests, and appointed in his place Charles Cotesworth Pinckney, a moderate Federalist of South Carolina. But the French Directory took leave of Monroe with threats and insults, refused to receive his successor until the "grievances" of France were redressed, and on February 3, 1797, threatened Pinckney with arrest if he remained in Paris.

As a result of the continued depredations on our commerce, and the threatening attitude of the Directory, President Adams summoned the Fifth Congress to a special session in the spring of 1797. Otis was present at the first quorum, on May 15. Philadelphia was then the national capital, and Congress Hall, a plain brick building adjoining Independence Hall, was the scene of Otis's political activities during the next three years. That portion occupied by the House of Representatives is unpleasantly described by a contemporary as "A room without ventilators, more than sufficiently heated by fire, to which is superadded the oppressive atmosphere contaminated by the breathing and perspiration of a crowded audience."[1] At its full strength, the House of Representatives numbered one hundred and six members. Among those prominent in his own party, Otis found the veteran Jonathan Dayton of New Jersey, who was elected Speaker, James

[1] Letter of Thomas Pinckney, March 4, 1798, in his *Life*, by C. C. Pinckney, 180.

A. Bayard of Delaware, Roger Griswold, the future war governor of Connecticut, and from the same state Chauncey Goodrich, future colleague of Otis in the Hartford Convention. South Carolina sent a small but most notable Federalist delegation, — William Smith of Charleston, Robert Goodloe Harper, and John Rutledge, Jr. The two last, recent converts to Federalism, embraced, like most converts, the most extreme doctrines of their new party. Harper, who had already served two terms, was now the ablest debater and pamphleteer on the Federalist side of the House, and Rutledge, elected in 1796 as a non-partisan, turned Federalist, like many South Carolinians, after the insulting rejection of his fellow-citizen Pinckney by the Directory. Both were men of Otis's age and tastes; they became his lifelong friends, and like him, never deserted the Federal party.

Prominent among the "Jacobins"[2] in the Fifth Congress were John Nicholas and William B. Giles, two veteran parliamentarians from Virginia; Nathaniel Macon of North Carolina, serving the fourth of his fifteen terms in Congress; Edward Livingston, future lawgiver of Louisiana, representing his family interests in New York; and the ablest man in the House, Otis's old tutor of the single shirt, Albert Gallatin, whose Genevan origin was still betrayed by his accent. Besides the members affiliated with Federalism or Republicanism, there was a handful of new and unattached backwoods members, whose support was ardently wooed by both sides.

Otis served in Congress during one of the most intense periods of party feeling that the country has ever passed

[2] This term was applied to the Republican party by the Federalists in 1793, on account of their opponents' attachment to the cause of the French Revolution. It remained in current use until 1815. Jefferson, in retaliation, coined several nicknames for the Federalists, such as "Anglomen," "Monocrats," etc., which never became popular.

through. The principles of the two parties were opposite
and irreconcilable; the one believed in a government by
the upper classes, the other, in a government by the people;
the one feared French influence and democracy, the other,
monarchical plots and aristocracy. To all this contention
was added a rigid social cleavage. Members of the two
parties studiously avoided each other on the street and
in society: there were Republican taverns and Federalist
taverns; Republican salons, and Federalist salons.[3] Outside the halls of Congress, party warfare raged in the partisan press, with a violence and bitterness of language
that the good taste of a later epoch has proscribed. Benjamin Franklin Bache was still conducting the *Aurora*,
which had spared not even Washington from its torrents
of abuse and filth, and William Cobbett paid him back in
kind through the columns of *Peter Porcupine's Gazette*.
After Monroe returned from France, his acrimonious
correspondence with Pickering, and his dishonorable
disclosure of the Reynolds affair in order to tarnish
Hamilton's reputation, added more fuel to the flames of
party hatred.

The first business before the House was to draw up an
answer to the President's speech. During the Federalist
period the President always delivered his opening message in person, and each house went in a body to his residence to present a reply. This graceful custom was happily done away with by Jefferson, for the framing of a
suitable reply, in times of high party feeling, wasted several weeks. In this instance, the debate over the Answer
of the House lasted until June 3. When the Committee
on the Answer brought before the House a draft that fully
responded to the President's sentiments, Nicholas of Virginia immediately proposed an amendment to it, to the ef-

[3] See chap. IX.

fect that, "we flatter ourselves that the Government of
France," by its dismissal of Pinckney, "only intended to
suspend the ordinary diplomatic intercourse" in favor
of "extraordinary agencies," and that a disposition
to remove the inequalities of treaties would produce
the desired accommodation. In other words, that all
the demands of the French government should be
obeyed.

Words like these made the Federalists' blood boil, and
precipitated a vigorous debate. Otis, as a new member,
was not expected to take part, in spite of his reputation for
eloquence. "His talents will distinguish him," wrote his
predecessor, Fisher Ames, [4] "and I hope he will be careful to wait patiently in Congress until they do; but he
is ardent and ambitious." Such was the case. Young
Harry Otis, burning with anti-Jacobin fire, refused to
remain in the background, and on May 23, 1797, just a
week after the session began, delivered his maiden speech
on the Nicholas Resolution: [5]

[4] *Works*, I, 202.
[5] *Annals of Fifth Congress*, 103–108. In quoting speeches made in Congress,
I have transposed them, for the sake of clearness, to the first person and the
present tense. Otherwise no liberties have been taken with the text as given in
the *Annals*, and omissions are always indicated. The *Annals* are the best reports of the debates we have, although neither impartial nor accurate. The following letter of March 29, 1798, from Joseph Gales, the editor, to Otis throws
light on the method of reporting:

"Sir: When you presented me with a Five Dollar Note some days ago for
the extraordinary trouble which you thought I had had on your account, I
then doubted whether I ought to receive it. It was the first time I had ever been
offered any money for any thing which I had done in the business of debate
taking. I now believe I ought not to have received it, and therefore return it,
that I may not, at the same time that I am charged with *Partiality*, be charged
also with *Ingratitude*.

"In answer to your Note, I can only say, that I have now an injunction laid
upon me by my Employers to bring every day's business into one paper. Of
course, after I come from the house, I have to write an account of the proceedings of that day before I sleep, or at least before I come to the house next day.
If you, therefore (or any other member, for I cannot accuse myself of any partiality) speak very late in the sitting, and when I come to your observations,

The present is not an ordinary occasion, and the situation of the country requires that the Answer shall not be a spiritless expression of civility, but a new edition of the Declaration of Independence. . . . For my part, I conceive that all party distinctions ought now to cease; and that the House is now called by a warning voice, to destroy the idea of a geographical division of sentiment and interest existing among the people. My constituents and myself are disposed to regard the inhabitants of the Southern States as brothers, whose features are cast in the same mould, and who have waded through the same troubled waters to the shore of liberty and independence. . . .

The injuries sustained by us are of a high and atrocious nature . . . If any man doubts of the pernicious effects of the measures of the French nation, . . . let him inquire of the ruined and unfortunate merchant, of the farmer whose produce is falling, and will be exposed to perish in his barns. Where are you sailors? Listen to the passing gale of the ocean, and you will hear their groans issuing from French prison-ships!

There was a time when I was animated with enthusiasm in favor of the French Revolution, and I cherished it, while civil liberty appeared to be the object: but I now consider that Revolution as completely achieved, and that the war is continued — not for liberty, but for conquest and aggrandisement, to which I do not believe it is the interest of this country to contribute.

Otis then made an unjustifiable argument for severer measures against France than those taken against Great Britain in 1794, on the ground that the British were stimulated to annoy our commerce through an apprehension that we were united with France against them, and the French, by a belief that we were divided in their favor.[6]

my time is expired, I must abridge what you have said very materially, in doing which it cannot be expected that I should be very correct.

"In future, however, since you have desired it, I shall omit what you say altogether, if I cannot give anything like a complete sketch of your sentiments."

[6] This was a common argument of extreme Federalists. "I debit the French and American Jacobins with the whole loss by British spoliation." J. Lowell, *The Antigallican*, 26.

He stigmatized the resolutions offered by Nicholas as "an absurd and humiliating apology." He then proceeded to argue for measures of defense, first tearing up the opposition doctrine that defensive measures could justly be construed by France into acts of hostility: — "If negotiation fail, will the French give us time to equip our vessels, fortify our ports, and burnish our arms, in order to show us fair play?" — and concluded with a grand burst of rhetoric:

The tide of conquest has deluged Europe; it may swell the great Atlantic and roll towards our shores, bringing upon its troubled surface the spirit of revolution, which may spread like a pestilence, possibly in the Southern States, and excite a war of the most dreadful kind — of slaves against their masters, and thereby endanger the existence of that Union so dear to my constituents, and the separation of which would be as painful as the agonies of death.

This speech of Otis gave him a national reputation for oratory. Judge Iredell wrote Oliver Wolcott, the Secretary of the Treasury: "Mr. Otis' speech has excited nearly as warm emotions as Mr Ames' celebrated one, on the treaty. It does indeed the highest honor to his patriotism abilities and eloquence, and I confess, much as I expected from him, far exceeds my expectations."[7]

Otis's maiden speech was not simply a display of rhetoric; it was his confession of faith as a steadfast member of the Federalist party, and an indication of that party's opinion of French policy. Before proceeding further, let us take advantage of our remote standpoint to ascertain what the American policy of France in 1797 really was, and how far Otis's analysis was correct.

The successive French governments from 1793 to 1800 constantly aimed to incorporate the United States into

[7] Gibbs, I, 543.

the French system of alliances. France needed the provisions and produce of the United States for herself and her West-Indian colonies; she demanded as a right, under the treaty of 1778, the use of American ports for naval bases against Great Britain; she hoped to use the potential naval strength of America to increase her own. In pursuit of these ends the French government had three different methods. The first, commerce-destroying and bullying diplomatic correspondence, had its effect; but the Directory knew that mere brutality would be insufficient to keep in tutelage a republic separated by three thousand miles of ocean from the armies of Bonaparte, Jourdan, and Moreau. The real danger of the French policy lay in the two other weapons, of which the first was intervention in American politics, — that we shall consider presently, — and the second, the recovery of her ancient territory in North America. The possession of Louisiana and Canada would render France and her colonies independent of the United States for provisions, and draw a French cordon about the United States that would check its expansion, threaten its western territory, and make it as much a tributary to French policy as Belgium or Holland. From 1796 to 1800 the French government was pressing Spain to cede it Louisiana, a policy which finally succeeded in 1800, and as an alternative, in case negotiation failed, French agents were sent into Vermont, Georgia, and the trans-Alleghany region, to stir up sedition against the United States, and to start filibustering expeditions against Spanish and British America.[8]

[8] F. J. Turner: "The Diplomatic Contest for the Mississippi," *Amer. Hist. Rev.*, x, 249–79, with bibliography in footnotes. This policy was constantly urged on the French government by the successive ministers at Philadelphia. *1903 Report of the American Historical Association*, II, 566–70, 929, 1015–77 *passim*.

By the time the Fifth Congress assembled, the Federalist leaders had a fairly correct idea of the different lines of French policy;[9] their only mistake was in overestimating the final goal toward which it was tending. Chiefly conducive to their belief were the current events of Europe, which seemed full of ominous lessons for the United States. Almost every European mail brought news of some fresh aggression of France on a neighboring country. One after another, the ancient governments of the old world had fallen victim to French intrigues, in alliance with a French party at home. By the time that the Fifth Congress assembled, France, by these methods, had annexed Belgium, and secured an absolute control over Holland and Genoa. The news of Napoleon's partition of Venice, which arrived during the first session, and the sad tale of Switzerland's subjection, which reached America in the summer of 1798, both demonstrated the fate of republics that could not or would not defend themselves against French force and intrigue.[10] The

[9] The designs of France on Louisiana and the West were known through Monroe; and the movements of French agents in the Western country were regularly reported to the government, and through it, to the press. B. C. Steiner, *James McHenry*, 259, 263, 264, 272; Gibbs, I, 350 *et seq.*, 548, 551.

[10] See the application of these events to the United States, in Hamilton's "Warning" (*Works*, VII, 619, 624-27), and R. G. Harper: *Observations on the Dispute between the United States and France, addressed . . . to his constituents*, May, 1797. This pamphlet, which appeared shortly after the meeting of the Fifth Congress, was most influential in forming public opinion. It ran through at least seven American, fourteen British, one French, and one Portuguese, editions. Otis, in his *Letter to William Heath* (p. 24), reminds his readers of the "fearful fate of other countries, the blood stained revolution of Geneva, the incorporation of Belgium, the subjugation of Holland, the divisions of Italy, the sale of Venice, the commotions of Switzerland, and their known designs on Louisiana and the Floridas." Chauncey Goodrich wrote John Treadwell of Connecticut, June 6, 1798: "In some of the late papers I have forwarded to Mr. Gordon, is told the melancholy tale of miserable Switzerland. It seems to have been written by some friendly spirit to admonish us." *Treadwell MSS.*, Connecticut Historical Society. The most cursory perusal of the correspondence of other Federalist leaders will yield many similar statements.

French spoliations on our commerce, the machinations of French ministers with the Democrats, and the presence of French spies, all pointed to similar intentions on the part of France toward the United States; and by the middle of 1798 most Federalists, from Washington down, believed that the French Directory would invade the United States from Santo Domingo, raise a slave insurrection in the South, and seek to set up a vassal republic west of the Alleghanies or south of the Potomac.[11]

Otis helped to spread this belief through his first political pamphlet, a published letter to General William Heath of Roxbury, dated March 30, 1798:[12]

[I expect that the French Republic will proceed] to last extremities against this country, whenever she shall be at leisure for this purpose, and shall be confirmed in the belief that our internal divisions, and blind infatuation in her favor, will enable her, if not to conquer, at least to divide the Union. . . . War is not the most effectual instrument, nor the first which France employs in the manufacture of the rights of man: Spies, emissaries, exclusive patriots, and the honest but deluded mass of the people, are the tools with which, in other countries, she carves revolutions out of the rough material. The Generals and soldiers are reserved to give the finishing stroke. . . . Can you, Sir, seriously doubt of their hopes and expectations that Georgia, the Carolinas and Virginia will pass under their yoke? That they have an eye upon a *Cis Apalachian* as well as upon a *Trans Apalachian* Republic?

[11] See Mason's letter to Otis of March 24, 1798, following chapter VI; leading articles in the *Columbian Centinel*, February 3, 1798; Sparks's *Washington*, XI, 248; J. C. Welling, *Addresses, etc.*, 279. Timothy Pickering, the Secretary of State, wrote R. G. Harper, March 21, 1799, that he had received authentic information of a projected French invasion of the South from Santo Domingo under General Hédouville, to be preceded by negro emissaries to arm the slaves. Pickering MSS., X, 502.

[12] General Heath, a Revolutionary veteran, had acted as chairman of a Roxbury town meeting, which drew up a petition against permitting merchant vessels to arm in their defense, a measure that was then under discussion in the House. See Heath's letter accompanying the petition, and Mason's letters, following chapter VI.

What reason can be assigned to make it probable that we may rely upon an exemption from this general deluge? . . . Already their Geographers, with the scale and dividers, mark out, on the Map of America, her future circles, departments and municipalities. Already their Buonapartes and Bernadottes, are planning future triumphs; *here* with the army of the Mississippi and Ohio; *there* with the army of the Chesapeake and Delaware. — Remember, Sir, things much less probable have come to pass.

Extravagant as it may seem at this distance, Otis's prophecy of a French invasion was then quite within the bounds of possibility. France, by the Treaty of Campo Formio, in October, 1797, was at peace with all the world but England. Her boundaries were extended to the Rhine, the Alps, and the Pyrenees, and vassal republics beyond acknowledged her control. By March, 1798, the American press had already announced that a huge *Armée d'Angleterre* was being mobilized at Boulogne. Should England fall before the all-conquering Bonaparte, whose turn would come next? That Otis's apprehensions on this subject were genuine, and not published merely for political effect, is shown by a letter to his wife of March 14, 1798:

The state of the country is alarming and if the Southern States do not change their representation, or that Representation change their measures, that part of the country will be lost, and the Eastern States will be compelled to take care of themselves. My principal hope is that the affairs of Europe cannot long remain in their present posture; but who can calculate the event. Should Great Britain be compelled to yield, it is my opinion that our liberties and independence would fall a sacrifice. She is the only barrier to the dreadful deluge, and when that is broken down, it will be time for us to prepare to be good and dutiful subjects to the French. I still trust that the Providence which has protected will still preserve us to steer thro the surrounding difficulties, without being overwhelmed.

Otis alludes to the Southern States in this letter because that section of the country, which would have been the first to suffer from a French invasion, was represented in the Fifth Congress almost wholly by Republicans,[13] who were opposing the simplest measures of defense against France. Since the beginning of our difficulties with France, Jefferson's party had taken sides against its own government. So consistent had been this attitude that most Federalists suspected the existence of a good understanding between the French and American Jacobins. Otis remarked in debate, on March 2, 1798:

If my private sentiments are required, I am ready to profess my sincere persuasion that our difficulties with France are not to be imputed to any one man, but to a desperate and misguided party, existing in the bosom of our own country, who are in league with other bad citizens resident in France, and with the French nation; and I have no doubt that regular information and instructions are conveyed from this country to influence the measures of the Directory, and impede our attempts to negotiate with success.

Otis was right. The difficulties with France would have been of short duration, had not the blind infatuation of Jefferson's party for France encouraged the rulers of that country to use them as instruments to keep the United States in tutelage. Many Democratic leaders, moreover, were not unwilling to attain power through the good offices of France. We now know that the French ministers in Philadelphia maintained what to-day would be called a lobby in Congress, both receiving inside information from Jefferson and Republican Congressmen, and ordering the defeat of legislation unfriendly to French interests. Minister Adet took an active part in

[13] Only eight of the thirty-eight members from South of the Potomac were Federalists.

the election of 1796 in behalf of Jefferson. During the previous summer he made a tour of New England, in the course of which he "raised the courage" of the local Democrats, assured them that "France would never abandon them," while they in turn urged France to continue its policy of commerce-destroying in order to make the merchants support Jefferson. He even published letters in the *Aurora*, giving the American people to understand that they must elect Jefferson or prepare for a French war.[14]

When the Fifth Congress assembled, then, Otis and his Federalist colleagues were face to face with a momentous problem. The French government, through attacks on our commerce, through designs on our territory, through intervention in our politics, was aiming to make the United States a French dependency. Yet the French party was so strong, and public opinion so favorably inclined toward France, that the task of resisting the great republic seemed well-nigh hopeless.

[14] *1903 Report of the American Historical Association*, II, 912-1081, *passim*.

# CHAPTER VI

## THE CRISIS OF 1798

### ÆT. 32

WE left the Fifth Congress at the commencement of its first session, on May 23, 1797, with the Federalist side of the House applauding the last burst of rhetoric in Otis's maiden speech. After another week of debate, the apologetic amendment offered by Nicholas to the Answer of the House was defeated, and the Answer itself delivered to President Adams with all due ceremony. Congress was then ready to begin the real business of the session.

As Otis probably knew, the mighty personages in his party had already decided on a programme, in the execution of which he was expected to aid. Alexander Hamilton, who generally decided these matters in New York, by request of the President's cabinet, thoroughly appreciated the delicacies of the situation. The Republican party and press were noisy in their defense of French spoliations and insults. It would, therefore, have been folly for the Federal party, with its slender majority, to rush the country into war. Hamilton decided that a second attempt should be made to settle the dispute peaceably, by sending three envoys extraordinary to Paris, and that Congress in the mean time should put the country in a state of defense.[1] If the Directory were willing to negotiate decently, peace would be preserved, and the Federal party would receive the credit; if the new mission were treated as Pinckney had been, the

[1] Cf. B. C. Steiner, *McHenry*, 213-15, with John Adams, *Works*, VIII, 540.

country would be prepared for war, and the French
party would be discredited.

Congress was expected to act, and to act with a vigor
of tone which was noticeably lacking in its predecessor.
The President sounded the proper note in his opening
message, recommending an increase of the army and
navy, the reorganization of the militia, and permission
for the merchants to arm their vessels. All went well at
first, and the Answer of the House to the President was
as high-toned as the most ardent Federalist could desire.
But it was found impossible to carry out the President's
recommendations. In the Senate a sufficient majority
existed, but in the House, party Federalists and party
Republicans were almost equal in numbers. The balance
of power rested with a group of moderate Federalists, led
by Dayton, the Speaker, who were unwilling to take even
simple measures for precaution.

That this situation occurred was no fault of Otis. It
appears from a letter of Stephen Higginson to Timothy
Pickering that the Essex Junto held Otis's character at
little value, and expected him to become one of Dayton's
trimmers.[2] They were entirely mistaken in their judg-

[2] "Mr. Otis who succeeds Ames will not be his equal in any view, & it may
be very uncertain in some cases how he will act. he is a seeker of office, his ambition has no bounds and whoever can offer him the best station for honour and
profit will have him. at present he thinks, I believe, that his best chance is
from the Government, and whilst he conceives his interest connected with and
dependent upon Them, he will be on your side, saving such variations as he
may think essential to his standing so fair with opposition, as to keep a way
open to join them whenever he shall think it for his interest. —
"I think it important & right to say thus much to you, about Mr. O: because his being elected by the friends to Government may otherwise give you
too much confidence in him. It is true we united in supporting his election,
because we could united in no other, and believing that his looking to Government for promotion would keep him in the main steady and right. if you can
keep up his reputation, you may derive some Aid from him at times, as he has
some popular talents; but he is not a man of much application or a very strong
mind, of course can never be a good Sheet Anchor." Boston, May 11, 1797,
*1896 Report of the American Historical Association*, i, 798.

ment. Otis, who was tireless in debate, proved a tower of strength to his party. He made it his particular duty to answer Gallatin's able speeches — "to ferret him in his retreats, and to strip his designs of the metaphysical garb which conceals their turpitude," as the *Centinel* put the case. Far from being a trimmer, he stood out with his young Carolina friends, Harper and Rutledge, in favor of war preparations.[1] He did all in his power to pass measures to permit the arming of merchant vessels in their defense, to increase the navy, and to create a provisional army, — bills which were defeated by the combined votes of Jeffersonians and moderate Federalists. The net result of the session was a loan of $800,000, a beggarly appropriation for fortifications, a slight increase in taxes, and an act for the completion of the three frigates, *Constitution*, *President*, and *United States*, whose keels had been laid down in 1794.

The failure of such men as Jefferson, Madison, and Gallatin to see that their policy tended inevitably to make their country a French dependency, can be understood only through their political theories and their interests. As representatives of agricultural districts they were indifferent to the commercial depredations of France. Jefferson, indeed, considered the carrying trade an illegitimate business, that deserved to be pillaged by French privateers. The childlike confidence of his party in the good faith of France, whose policy, they yet be-

[1] A Philadelphia letter in the *Chronicle* of June 22, 1797, announces the "melancholy fate of poor Smith, Harper, and Otis." — "About ten or fifteen days ago these gentlemen were seized with a violent delirium — the Gallophobia" and became "especially outrageous when the French Republic was mentioned." They raved about "magazines, cannon, bombs, gallies, frigates, and a land tax. . . . They are all now a little more composed, owing to some Buonaparte Pills which happily arrived in the ship Chronicle." The "Buonaparte Pills" meant the news of Napoleon's pursuit of Archduke Charles across the Alps, and the peace of Leoben.

lieved, was still actuated by the anti-monarchical propaganda of 1792, made them willing to swallow her arrogance and insults. Above all, they feared that the Federalists, under cover of a French war, would ally themselves with Great Britain to crush out liberty in both France and America. Republican fears of an Anglo-Federalist despotism were quite as strong as Federalist fears of a French invasion. Hence we find Jefferson and his party at every opportunity seeking to limit the power of the Executive;[4] and, because war would necessarily tend to increase the power of that arm of the government, they feared war above all things. Their refusal to coöperate with the government in strengthening its military and naval armament is thus not very surprising, especially when we consider that the opposition party in England was then acting in precisely the same manner, and that the Federalists, when conditions were reversed ten years later, acted in precisely the same manner in their turn.

The same state of affairs continued through the winter months of the second session of the Fifth Congress. The President's opening address, of November 23, 1797, renewed his recommendations of the previous session. Otis was appointed chairman of the committee on the House reply, and announced to Mrs. Otis, on November 27:

Inclosed is a printed copy of the *reported* answer of the house to the President's speech. You may show it to your friends, but the Printers must not have it untill it has passed the House. I was Chairman of the Committee and drew the

[4] They opposed, for instance, the passage of general appropriation acts, which was the custom under Federalist administrations, and of appropriating lump sums for forts, or army and navy, or foreign intercourse, to be used at the President's discretion. The practice of small detailed appropriations, so conducive to log-rolling and jobbery, sprang up in Jefferson's administration.

answer; and tho I have studiously avoided all hard expression, and endeavored to make it as palatable as possible, I expect that some of the pack will growl and oppose.

Otis proved an able conciliator, for, as he later wrote his wife, his report of the Answer was "adopted unanimously, with only the change of a *single* word, so that we were in luck at least, to save a fortnight's squabbling." Much time was doubtless saved, but time was what the Fifth Congress could best afford to squander. Everything hung fire awaiting news from the envoys in Paris. By the experience of the previous session, the Federalist leaders had learned that no spirit could be expected from Congress without some fresh provocation from France, and consequently they made little attempt to push through a scheme of defense. Otis wrote his wife on December 3:

Congress will do no business of an important nature untill some intelligence is received respecting the probable issue of the negotiation with France. What this will be it is extremely difficult to determine. Their councils are not governed by those settled principles which lead them to respect the rights of others or even to consult on all occasions their own interest.

I cannot however think they will be so infatuated as to widen the breach. This conduct without serving them would probably alienate forever our affections, our prejudices, & what is of more consequence our trade & at the same time strengthen their enemy and rival. And on the other hand, they do not seem to be in a temper to confess errors or repair injuries. Perhaps they will attempt a temporising policy, talk plausibly & try to amuse without adopting any definite measures. I hope however there is yet a spirit in this country to resent and to baffle such intrigues.

The same feeling of suspense is shown in a letter to Otis, dated December 4, 1797, from Jonathan Mason, Jr., of Boston. Since Mason was then a member of the Governor's Council, and one of the leading Massachusetts

Federalists, his letter may be taken, in a certain sense, as Otis's party instructions:

The Presidents speech is esteemed for its principles; The Friends of *decent cloathing*, take exceptions to it. We do not anticipate much from the present Session — do no harm & you will satisfy your constituents. That our Commerce is to remain a prey to our Republican Friends on the other side, seems to be the general sentiment, & the probability of an amicable adjustment is wholly given up. You individually are to stand at your Post, *firm* — I mean by that word — industrious, constant, decisive, complaisant, always to be found by your Party, & never to retreat. These points with talent will carry you to your wishes, & insure the confidence of your friends, which at all events must be inspired & maintain'd. Shall I tell you, that I wish you had never apologized to G—— [5] that in the comment of your friends upon that part of your conduct, it has been deemed an error, & that it was giving to the rascal the possibility of construing it into a Triumph. It is not doubted that it was handsomely done, & not from any improper personal motive, but a laudable solicitude to effect what cannot be in its nature effected — a successful attempt to please every body. I mention this that in future, *after reflection* you may push straight forward. I mention it, that it may help you, for I conceive it an immense advantage, that a person in a conspicuous active, responsible situation, should know the opinions of his own friends, & those who wish him well—as such you will accept it.

Amid this excitement over foreign affairs, one act of the second session, which marked a new step forward in humanity, passed unnoticed. This was a law abolishing imprisonment for debts to the federal government. Otis was chairman of the committee that reported the bill, and acted as its sponsor before the House. [6]

The dull march of routine business in the winter months was not, however, without its amusing incidents. In

---

[5] Gallatin. — a reference to Otis's apology for his "Second Shirt" speech.
[6] *Annals of Fifth Congress*, 3734. Otis's report in favor of the bill, is in *Ibid.*, 1796.

January, 1798, occurred the famous Lyon-Griswold affair. Matthew Lyon of Vermont, an ill-bred little printer of Irish birth, was of all the "Jacobins" in Congress the most obnoxious to Federalists.[7] During the Revolution, Lyon had been cashiered — unjustly, it seems — for cowardice, and punished by being compelled to wear a wooden sword as a sign of disgrace. On January 30, 1798, before the session for the day commenced, Lyon, in conversation with some other member, began to boast of the political revolution he would create in Connecticut, could he bring his printing press thither. Roger Griswold of Connecticut inquired sarcastically whether he would also bring his wooden sword with him. Lyon replied by spitting full in Griswold's face. The Federalists then demanded Lyon's expulsion from the House as the only proper punishment for so flagrant a breach of decorum, but he was stoutly defended by his party on the pretext that the spitting took place before the House was called to order. In the debate that followed, Otis made a long speech in favor of expulsion, remarking that "He would challenge anyone to show so shameful an act of assault and battery committed without provocation at any former period, or in any country, . . . it would not be suffered in a brothel or in a den of robbers!" To his wife he wrote: "Was anything so infamous ever heard of before? Yet I expect the whole party will stand by to protect him, & in that event we cannot expel him; a concurrence of *two thirds* being necessary for this purpose." Such was the case; the vote was strictly on party lines,

[7] At the beginning of each session, Lyon asked to be excused from waiting on the President with the rest of the House to present the Answer, because he found that the ceremony smacked of royalty. On one of these occasions, "Mr. Otis said, as the Lyon appeared to be in a savage mood, he would recommend him to be locked up while the House proceeded to the President." J. F. Mc-Laughlin, *Matthew Lyon*, 224.

*fracas in Co.*

52 to 44, an insufficient majority. According to one of
Otis's letters, the Republicans' motive in thus shielding
Lyon, was "merely to avail themselves of his *vote* hereafter, while they acknowledge that he was deserving of
expulsion. This among other traits serves to shew the
character of the party and their disregard of all principle
& decency, but as they have rope enough it is to be hoped
they will hang themselves."

Expulsion having failed, Mr. Griswold took the law into
his own hands, and at the next appearance of Lyon in
the Hall of Representatives, he attacked him with a stout
club. Lyon grasped the Congressional fire-tongs to defend
himself, and the two men rolled over and over upon the
floor, striking at each other, until some other members
pulled them apart by the legs. The House was then
called to order, but, as the combatants renewed their
scuffling at intervals during the session, it finally adjourned on Otis's motion.

By this affair, Griswold put himself on a level with
Lyon. The Federalists apparently held a caucus to consider the matter,[8] and most of them, including Otis, voted
against a motion to expel and to censure both combatants,
since they felt that Griswold's retaliation was justified.
The Federalists must therefore share with their opponents
the responsibility for leaving unpunished the first of these
disorderly affairs in Congress, which subsequently became far too frequent.

The Lyon-Griswold fracas was a somewhat extreme
expression of the temper of this Congress. While awaiting
news from France, members of the two parties gave vent
to their feelings in long debates on minor topics, filled with

---

[8] "The unfortunate controversy between Griswold and Lyon has obliged me
to attend a meeting of some members this evening." Otis to Mrs. Otis, February 18, 1798. I take this to be an allusion to the congressional caucus.

recriminations and bitter personal attacks. Giles of Virginia on one occasion accused the Federalists of a determination to make war on France at all costs. When Otis stigmatized these remarks as "bold, ungraceful, and disgraceful," Giles replied that "neither Mr. Otis, nor any other gentleman, durst make that assertion in any other place." A rumor, which gave much anxiety to Otis's family and friends, reported that a duel between Otis and Giles, resulting in the former's death, had followed this exchange of pleasantries; but, since the so-called code of honor was no part of Otis's New England upbringing, the affair went no further than words.

Finally, on March 4, 1798, the long-expected dispatches from the three envoys in Paris arrived. The bulk of the papers being in cipher, the President communicated to Congress but the one dispatch in which the cipher was not used. This document, dated at Paris, January 8, 1798, announced that no hope existed of the envoys being officially received by the Directory, and that a new decree, subjecting to capture any neutral vessel carrying in whole or in part British goods, had passed the Council of Five Hundred. The Federalists now felt that the time had come for a fresh attempt to put the country in a state of defense. Only with great difficulty, however, were they able to pass such an essential measure as the equipping of the *Constitution*, *President*, and *United States*. That public spirit had been gradually evaporating during the long period — almost a year now — since Pinckney's dismissal and the beginning of the spoliations, is clear from Otis's letter of March 8: "There seems to be a great want of public spirit among the people, and I should doubt if there be a majority in our own house to adopt those vigorous and decisive measures which to me appear necessary."

On March 19, the President announced that, after an

examination and mature consideration of the dispatches, he could perceive no ground to expect the objects of the mission could be "accomplished on terms compatible with the safety, honor, or the essential interests of the nation." He therefore renewed a second time his recommendation to defend our coasts and commerce, and to act with "zeal, vigour, and concert, in defence of the national rights." If the Federalists expected, however, that this definite announcement of the Directory's refusal to negotiate would shake the Franco-Jeffersonian alliance, they were entirely mistaken. In the House debates that followed the President's communication, the administration was accused of insincerity, deception, and a desire to dragonnade the country into war with France and a British alliance. The Republican press echoed these sentiments. In this dangerous crisis, Jefferson wished his followers to bring about an adjournment of Congress, in order to gain time to allow the French invasion of England — an event which he ardently desired — "to have its effect here as well as there." [9]

This attitude placed the Federalists in an awkward dilemma. Otis, for instance, who had a fairly accurate knowledge of the dispatches on March 22, knew that their publication would silence and discredit the French party; but such a course, he perceived, might not only endanger the lives of our envoys in Paris, but prove a bar to future diplomatic negotiations.[10] Meanwhile the opposition was calling for publication, foolishly confident that it would expose a Federalist bluff. For a time the Federalists resisted, but they found the temptation to disclose the information too strong. "We wish much for the papers," wrote Jonathan Mason from Boston. "The Jacobins

[9] Jefferson, *Works*, IV, 222.
[10] See his letter of March 22 to Jonathan Mason, at end of this chapter.

want them. And in the name of God let them be gratified;
it is not the first time they have wished for the means of
their destruction." On April 2, Harper introduced a resolution asking for the papers, and on the following day the
President sent down to the House the famous "X. Y. Z.
dispatches."

When a few days later the entire correspondence was
published, the people were at last given a first-hand view
of the methods of French diplomacy. None of the American grievances had been redressed; the French spoliations
continued as before; and after a three months' residence in
Paris, the three envoys were still refused an official reception by the Directory. Instead, they had been persistently
informed by go-betweens (whose names, in the published
dispatches, were discreetly represented by the letters
X, Y, and Z) and by Talleyrand himself, that as an
indispensable preliminary to negotiation the American
envoys must make a loan of $250,000 to the French gov-
ernment, pay over a similar sum as a *douceur* for the
Directors' pockets, and apologize for certain "unfriendly"
expressions in the President's first message to the Fifth
Congress. America was threatened with the fate of Venice, and the envoys assured that the Directory was possessed of the means, "through the French party in America," of throwing the blame of the rupture on the Federalists. No set of documents could have served better to
open the eyes of the people to the methods and aims of
French policy, and to wean away their affections from the
French defenders and apologists. Yet the X. Y. Z. dispatches told nothing of the real danger that then threatened the United States from France. Talleyrand and the
Directory were not aiming to drive the United States into
war, as the Federalists supposed, for they were almost
entirely dependent on the United States for provisioning

their colonies. They were simply temporizing, while they carried on negotiations at Madrid for the cession of Louisiana, the possession of which would attain the objects of the Republic's American policy.

The undiplomatic methods by which Talleyrand played his game with Pinckney and his colleagues, is explained by the situation of the French government, when the three American envoys presented their claims. Barras and the terrible triumvirate, supreme over their domestic opponents by the *coup d'état* of the 18 Fructidor,[11] secure in their grip on Italy and the Rhine by the Treaty of Campo Formio, were at that time on a pinnacle of power and arrogance. They had severed the peace negotiations then pending with Great Britain and Russia, and expelled the Portuguese minister from France. *Coups d'état* were being hatched to "fructidoriser" the neighboring republics.[12] Talleyrand's insolent demand for bribes and tribute from the American envoys was due to this overweening arrogance of his government, and to its appetite for plunder. Accustomed to sell its friendship to the smaller states of Europe, it made the mistake of applying these methods to a nation out of the reach of French armies.

The X. Y. Z. dispatches, published and spread broadcast through newspapers and pamphlets, produced a revolution in American public opinion. As the news spread from Philadelphia, a spontaneous clamor of patriotism

[11] By the *coup d'état* of the 18 Fructidor, An. V (September 4, 1797), the "Amis de la Paix," who wished to reverse the policy of France toward neutral nations and make peace with England, were *épurés* from all branches of the government by the triumvirate of militant Directors, Barras, Rewbell, and La Revellière-Lépeaux. This event really ended any chance of the American mission procuring justice from France.

[12] A. Sorel, *L'Europe et la Révolution Française*, v, 225–30, 294–96. Rufus King wrote from London (*King*, II, 294) that the Directory hoped to pull off an 18 Fructidor against the Federalists. The Portuguese incident was well known to the American government; and as Portugal had purchased her treaty, the lesson was obvious. Hamilton, *Works*, VI, 275; Steiner, *McHenry*, 285, n.

burst forth in every part of the country. "Millions for
defense, but not one cent for tribute!" became the popular cry; "Hail Columbia," and "Adams and Liberty,"
the national anthems. The Federal party to a man, and
thousands among the former followers of Jefferson, hastened to sign memorials and addresses tendering the government their confidence.[13] Volunteer companies were
formed; flags embroidered and presented; Talleyrand
hung in effigy; war vessels purchased or built by popular
subscription. It was one of the few occasions between
1792 and the War of 1812 when a majority of the American people showed a "manly sense of national honor, dignity, and independence." [14] Yet the enthusiasm was not
universal. Though deserted by the voters, though dismayed and disheartened, the Republican leaders stuck to
their guns. With a consistency that would be admirable
but for its anti-patriotism, they continued to preach submission to all-powerful France, our "magnanimous ally";
they even made desperate efforts to prove that Messrs.
X., Y., and Z. were a set of unauthorized swindlers, having no connection with the French government; and they
warned the people that Federalist policy spelt British alliance and monarchy.[15] But Jefferson was deposed from
his pedestal, Adams and Pinckney and Marshall were the
heroes of the day. For the first and last time in its his-

[13] A delightful example of the effect of the X. Y. Z. letters is given in a letter
from the Rev. John Murray of Boston to John Adams, June 19, 1798: "Thanks
be to God, that in the greatness of his goodness he has made our enemies instrumental in uniting the good people of these states, more than ever I expected to
have seen them in my day. For a long season my heart was pained, on not
being able to count in my Congregation (as large as any in this Town) as many
Federalists as states in the Union — now, thanks be to God, and our good Ally,
I find converts multiplying every day — it is the Lord's doings and it is mar-
vellous in our eyes." Adams MSS.

[14] Quoted from the President's Message of December 8, 1798.

[15] Madison, *Works*, II, 134; Jefferson, *Works*, IV, 275; Tucker, *Jefferson*,
II, 43.

tory the Federal party found itself popular. The people felt with justice that the administration had pursued the policy of conciliation to the utmost limit permissible for a nation that desired to be called free and independent; that defense by force of arms was necessary to preserve the national honor and integrity.

By his conduct during this period Otis had won the approbation of the wise men of his party. Fisher Ames wrote him, on April 23, 1798:

Your speech was good, but your letter to General H[eath] better than good; it is excellent — useful to the public, reputable to you; and the strokes *ad captandum* are so blended with irony, that Roxbury vanity must be flattered and humbled at the same time. I write in confidence, and I should despise the thought of flattery. Rely on it, your friends exult on the perusal of the letter. You must not talk of fees, nor of being weary of well doing. The enlistment is such, you cannot return to private life yet, without desertion. I hope and trust your task will be in future less irksome, and more will help you. Folly has nearly burnt out its fuel, I mean the French passion; and the zeal of good men must be warmer and more active than it has been or we sink. It is too late to preach peace, and to say we do not think of war; a defensive war must be waged, whether it is formally proclaimed or not. That, or submission, is before us.[16]

Although not yet thirty-three years old, Otis had risen to the position of first lieutenant to Harper's captaincy of the House majority. So far his work had been uphill; it was now crowned with popular sanction and confidence. On Otis, then, as much as on any member of the Federal party, rested the responsibility of retaining this confidence, by a policy at once firm and spirited, yet respecting the prejudices of a people trained to fear strong government.

[16] Ames, *Works*, I, 228.

## LETTERS, 1797-98

### JONATHAN MASON, JR., TO OTIS

Boston Decr 24, 1797

My dear Sir. —

I am to beg your attention, by the request of the Directors of our board, to a grant which they have asked for, for the purpose of building a Bank house in Boston, & which is to be agitated at the Stockholders Meeting on Wednesday next.[17] You know the inconvenience of the one at present used for that purpose, It is indecent, out of repair, filthy & disreputable. The Vaults are too small, the sun never enters any part of it, it is cold, damp, & in short in every view impossible longer to carry on and transact the business there. The Transactions of the Bank, are daily increasing. The other states have been indulged in similar requests, & to a much larger amount.   -

We hold in this state permanently, *a full* proportion of the stock of the Bank — & the seat of Government out of view have the same rights to accomodation, as they have at Philadelphia.

One other reason, I may mention to you — a handsome building, will help your Town & its Mechanicks. Eno' upon that Subject. . . .

We do not like appearances at Philadelphia, tho you have not yet been bro't to open Combat French interest is not drove from your house, by French cruelty, perfidy, & injury. On the contrary it seems to be ingrafted into the blood of you. We wish much for important news from France, & that their Conduct to this Country may be unequivocal, that the strength of its Government may be fairly tried the present session. If we are to Fight them at last, we had better know it now — & there seems to be a universal Wish, that our Commissioners either may be sincerely received, respected & satisfyed, or treated in such manner, as will preclude even Comment. . . .

[17] Otis and Mason were both directors of the Boston Branch of the United States Bank.

JONATHAN MASON, JR., TO OTIS

Boston Febry 19, 1798

\*   \*   \*   \*   \*   \*   \*   \*   \*   \*   \* ]

People in general fear the issue of Lyon's indecency, that your House have made a political question of it, & that your Skulls will be safe, in exact proportion to the strength of your party. You have the honor of outdoing the National Convention, & are in a fair way of becoming an assembly of gladiators. What with Randolph, Blount, Monroe, Lyon & such rascals, in a few Years, I think we shall need great effrontery to defend the American Character. Griswold I think has a difficult task. The world say he must beat him either in or out of the House. One or the other for his own sake — but if you fail of the question upon the expulsion, *in* the House, for yours — I mean your party — for you must have a champion. In any event I feel grieved that the saliva of an Irishman should be left upon the face of an American & He, a New Englandman. My good Father Powell says, that if Griswold had been in the presence of the great God himself, he ought to have taken his revenge upon the spot, & beat his brains out. He ridicules the idea of Griswold's bravery. I pray Heaven he may be disappointed.

Things seem at such a crisis. Good men differ upon the subject *of arming.*[18] They think that Individuals may take undue advantages of the Power & that Foreigners will abuse it under our Flag. Wm Gray Jr seems to be much against it. The depredations have already been great, & it is his opinion that some decided step respecting this Country cannot be at a great distance — that we had better be patient & not irritate. That a revolution in their councils may essentially alter their conduct, & that should the Power be granted, the trade will not pay the expense, & of course very few would take advantage of it. On the other hand, it has very respectable advocates with us, & they say, that it will protect our citizens & their property, & will not alter the Conduct of France towards this Country, provided she is disposed for Peace — & if she is not, the refraining from

---

[18] That is, permitting merchant vessels to arm in their own defense — the question that brought out Otis's *Letter to General Heath.*

arming will be of no consequence. For my own part, I wish that Prudence & reflection & Judgement may precede every step taken & after that, these taken, may be pursued with energy. I feel willing to bear for a time, but I think we ought not to be bore down, with insult, & that it behoves us, if we suffer ourselves to be spit upon, as Griswold has, to show the world that if we are cool, we are decidedly brave — at the expence of our existence as a nation. . . .

God bless you. I wish you well & I beg that in no event, you will differ from your party, but stand by them.

Yrs sincerely<br>J Mason Jr

### GENERAL WILLIAM HEATH TO OTIS[19]

Roxbury March 21st 1798

Sir

The People in this quarter exceedingly alarmed at a report that Congress were about granting liberty to the merchants to arm their private vessels by authority. The Inhabitants of this Town on a *very short* notice assembled on Yesterday and in an Uncommon full meeting, — never did I for the forty years that I have been on the stage of action, see a meeting more attentively and solemnly engaged, or more Unanimous. The question was whether Congress should be petitioned not to grant leave for private vessels to arm. On the question being put, there were but *four* Gentlemen who voted in the negative, and these immediately declared, that they were as much against arming as those who voted in the affirmative on the question — but that for themselves they wished to rest the issue with Congress. — so that it may be fairly said that every person who voted was in Sentiment, as to the measure itself.

The Town appointed a Committee to draught sign and forward a Petition to Congress expressive of their sentiments as stated in their vote. The Committee therefore that they might not mistake or mistate the sense of the Town have couched the Petition — nearly in a transcript of the vote. The Committee do themselves the honor of addressing the Petition to your care

[19] This letter, and the petition therein mentioned, were the occasion of Otis's published *Letter to General Heath.*

as the immediate *Representative* of *our District*, and request that
you will embrace the earliest moment to present it to Congress,
whether a resolution on the question, has passed, or not, — and
that you will give it such support as it may appear to deserve.
It is also requested that you would communicate the subject to
all the other Gentlemen representing this Commonwealth. But
the Committee request that there may be no delay in present-
ing the Petition. What other towns may say, or do, I cannot
tell, one thing is certain there never was a time in which the
people in general appeared to be more *opposed* to *war* with any
nation under Heaven, than is expressed at this time — and
they look upon arming of private vessels but little short of a
declaration of it. The Gentlemen in trade, or a part of them,
may be in favor of arming. Heaven grant that those who steer
the public Barke, may run for the Haven of Honor, peace, prosperity and happiness of our own Country.

### OTIS TO JONATHAN MASON, JR.[20]

Philadelphia, March 22 [1798]

After reading the President's message you will naturally
conclude that we are forthwith occupied in concerns of the first
magnitude. The case, however, is otherwise. — The opposition
leaders pretend that they cannot act without knowing the contents of the late dispatches; and this excuse which is made only
for want of another, is countenanced by a seeming apathy of the
friends of the Government, arising merely from the scruples of
a few individuals, without whose aid we cannot act; and who
are also chagrined by the suppression of the dispatches. This
state of things cannot continue long. A disclosure of the late
information received by The Executive would probably elec-
trise the whole American people, *or demonstrate such an utter
prostration of national spirit & honor as would shew all hopes of
resistance to be vain*. But if propriety should still forbid the
communication, it is morally certain that facts of a nature not
to be concealed, and indicative of a settled purpose in the
French Government to humble and to ruin us, will follow in

---

[20] From the *Columbian Centinel* of March 31. This is the extract referred to
in Mason's letter of March 30. It is headed: "Highly Important, And from a
Source of the First Respectability."

rapid succession, and produce the same effect that would follow upon publishing the dispatches.

It must be obvious to all who reflect, that the Executive would gladly impart his knowledge of any facts that would so fully justify his conduct, confirm the friends and confound the adversaries of the Government, as it is presumed these dispatches would do. He has accordingly at one period hesitated on this subject, as I am informed, though not officially. — Two principles have hitherto decided him in favor of witholding them: A regard to the *personal safety* of the Commissioners, and an apprehension of the effect of a disclosure upon our future diplomatic intercourse. — The dispatches would probably unfold such a scene of corruption among the present men in power, *discord among the Directory*, and such projects for our humiliation, as would excite *indignation without bounds against the Commissioners*, if they should be at *Paris;* and obstruct those *sources of information* on which they and our future ministers to all countries must occasionally depend. These are very serious considerations. It is however very probable that they will be surmounted, so far, at least as relates to a part of these dispatches if a resolution should prevail, to call for information. Such a motion is to be expected, and many of our friends think it best merely to vote against it without much debate, and permit it to be carried, by means of a few of the federal men who think well of the measure. — The responsibility for any disadvantage resulting from the disclosure of the papers, will fall on the right spot, and the advantage arising from the impression would be common to us all.

### JOHN GARDNER [21] TO OTIS

Boston March 24 1798

\*   \*   \*   \*   \*   \*   \*   \*   \*   \*   \*

At Roxbury & Milton there have been town meetings against *arming the merchantmen*, and the votes proposed by the Demo's were carried by large majorities. Our enlightened *Miltonians* were quite violent upon the occasion. I found it necessary to *spout*, (for the first time in my life) against the

[21] This is probably John Gardner (1770–1825), son of Dr. Samuel Gardner of Milton.

policy of the people's interfering with those measures of defence, wh. government may find it necessary to adopt. But it was without effect. Even Mr. Robbins [22] who has always been so popular with them, was treated with no kind of respect or attention. He made a pretty good speech, and certainly full moderate enough — but was frequently interrupted and told he had better hold his tongue if he could not talk to the purpose!

I see by the papers that you have had a dispute with *Giles*, & think you were very properly severe upon him. I hope you will not be obliged personally to expose yourself, but am convinced you would sooner do this, than give way to him. My opinion of this *Giles* is that he is a *Brag* & a *Bully*, & (though I admit he might be brought to fight) that he is not fonder of it than other people. If he crowds you, it will be in consequence of his knowledge of your happy domestic situation, and your coming from a part of the country where duelling is not in vogue. . . .

### JONATHAN MASON, JR., TO OTIS

Boston March 26 1798

My dear Sir.

. . . We have already had two Town meetings upon the subject of arming with the Roxbury General [23] at the head of them, & God knows whether we shall not have two & twenty — as the fire seems to spread & the wind is tolerably high. I have doubts whether it will be tryed in Boston. We are industriously spreading the news of a postponement of a discussion of the question, which will in a degree damp this poison, & which I pray God may take place. I do not wish to see the character or courage of the Country called in question, but Fabian prudence was never more necessary. We have a singular enemy, extremely powerfull, but extremely diseased & almost all mankind unite in this Opinion, that a great change if not political death must speedily take place. In a revolution, if we shall not have committed ourselves, we certainly have everything to hope, & in the event of a general peace, may reasonably expect, that all our difficulties will subside. If united among ourselves, such have been our

[22] Edward H. Robbins (1758–1829), afterwards Lieutenant Governor of Massachusetts.
[23] William Heath.

injuries from that republic, that we ought to hazard the last shilling to obtain satisfaction, but the infatuated state of our Country, the barefaced conduct & exertions of the faction within us, would paralize every effort of administration & finally end in civil War. If we are now prostrate, we must thank ourselves; for the same conduct by the same faction pursued with respect to any foreign nation who might have the same power & ambition, would bring down the same insult, injury & contempt as we now meet with from France.

Without flattery, your speech & *conduct* in the session are both approved by your friends, & a continuance of steady support, firm but moderate, general & not personal, to the present administration & measures will not only insure you the approbation of your constituents, but I think also their Obligation. For in your present task, must be a great share of bitter, with precious little sweet. It did not become you to court a duel, & I think you did nothing to avoid it, which a Man of courage & honour wd not justify. The debates of all your gentlemen however are by much too personal, & I cannot but think that if each one would try in that particular to reform himself, it would greatly add to his honour & fame, & remove the difficulty. A man may shew to his enemy Great Bravery without mixture of any passion. . . . We are barren of all news. Ames is very sick at Dedham & has been confined for the month past. The public part of your letters I take care to shew the Cabot, Lowell & Higginson *crew* for without their approbation, Where will the *fat* be? [24]

Adieu God bless you, & preserve you from Fire, powder & the Sword

JONA MASON JR.

JONATHAN MASON, JR., TO OTIS

Boston Fire Insurance Office.
March 30th. 1798

My dear sir.

I received your deeds by the last Post, also your letter of the 22d. The contents do not dismay those who are well affected.

[24] A significant reference to the Essex Junto, and their control of political favors.

The expectations of Federalists have long since subsided, as
they respected either compensation or justice from the French
Republic. On the contrary, their Fears only have been, that
they have observed an insidious doubtful kind of conduct,
which would in this country have increased & confirmed the unhappy division among us. The present information in a degree
removes those fears, & as far as I can see has already had a happy
effect with us. Good People do not appear to be frightened far
from it. Timid ones have their doubts removed daily, & the
Jacobin Class will with us be shortly confined to those who will
sell their Country, and are perhaps among the most abandoned
of mankind. We have long since wanted some line of Conduct
from the French, which should be unequivocal & visible to the
most common eye, that should supercede argument, & not be
capable of wearing two faces. We are going to have that same
thing & it will operate like good medicine upon the body politic. It seems on all hands agreed that a short fever is preferable
to a languishing consumption. We wish much for the papers,
if they can with propriety be made public. The Jacobins want
them. And in the name of God let them be gratified; it is not
the first time they have wished for the means of their destruction. Mr Adams has immortalized himself in the Opinion of
Yankeys — he seems to stand alone with the sentiments he set
out with in 1763 & 75 — & they do not appear impaired. With
these sentiments & a vigorous governmt. to support them, we
have nothing to fear from those rascals on the other side of the
Water. But while he promulgates them & the government para-
lizes them, nothing can be expected from the French but insult
& injury, unless you remove him & every other branch & law
that they do not approve. (I was obliged to permit a part of your
letter to be published in to morrow's Centinel. The *praying* part,
Russell said he would be damn'd if he could publish. So in
future you had better lay that aside, as I am not much better
acquainted with it, than his honor) We must reconcile our
minds to a few moments of Warfare. It will not hurt us, & I
am not one those that think, that it will produce either a civil
war, or break down the great business of society in this Country
which at present appears so well founded.

   We have much to expect from the other side of the Water. &
it is not an improbable conjecture, that the period is not far

distant, when this very conduct of the Executive directory towards this Country, shall be brought as a specific charge of complaint against them, by their successors in Office. A revolution in its nature must be at hand.  No thinking Man believes them to be sincere in the projected invasion — much less that they will succeed if they attempt it.  The money sinews of the Country are now strained & forced beyond their bearing to carry it on, & the day of reconing will follow close at its heels.  Under these circumstances, the Opposition in our Country notwithstanding, If Government continue upright, & firm in their politicks, If they will furnish the Means of defence, If they will shew a handsome regard to themselves, & let the World witness, that tho' they are prudent, they are not afraid, that tho' they forbear, they do not mean to flinch, we shall get along & perhaps renovate that character, which your house has this session greatly tarnished . . .

### THOMAS HANDASYD PERKINS TO OTIS

Boston April 21, 1798 Sunday Eve.

\*　\*　\*　\*　\*　\*　\*　\*　\*　\*　\* \*

Knowing how much pleasure you will receive, from a measure now in operation with us, I enclose you the copy of an address, which was opened yesterday & received in a few hours 150 names.  A Committee of 36 persons, such as Jones, Davis, Parsons, Dawes, Higginson &c are to hand it round tomorrow — it seems to unite all parties, except such as we shou'd feel disgraced in having with us even in a good cause.  I think it probable, that after we get the strength of the Town pledged in this way, it will get the finishing stroke by a Town Meeting, when perhaps the *Town* will invite our fellow Citizens in the Country to adopt a similar measure.  It is a melancholy concession to make, that our government has need of this sort of aid, but as we cannot deny the fact it is a duty in us to give it.

You may recollect the Knot of Jacobinism, which was concentrated at Sam. Turells shop in State street, with C. Marshall at the head — these same people have volunteered in signing & forwarding this measure.

I congratulate you most heartily on the very general satisfaction, which your letter to Heath has given — the Chronicle of *tomorrow*, says handsome things about it, which to be sure is rather against it, but we are all open to this vehicle of scandal, & therefore if they do *praise you*, you must bear it with fortitude, & hope, that the public in general will not believe you have given them cause. to be serious, it has meet the united approbation of the Federal party, & done much good with those who were luke warm. You have given the Good man such a dose of the "*oyl* of fool," as has satisfyed his vanity, and I have no doubt secured his good opinion. I sat down to write you three words & I have got almost to the bottom of the third page of my paper therefore must say good night, as I am to see the committee to take measures for the morning.

With much regard  Always your friend
T HANDASYD PERKINS. .

### JONATHAN MASON, JR., TO OTIS

Boston May 3d 1798

. . . With us we have nothing to say new at present. We look to you at Philadelphia for the mode in which the true American Character & Spirit is to display itself to the eyes not only of France but all Europe. Hitherto we have had no reason to be ashamed of it, & I hope the damn'd Cankerworm that now feeds upon our vitals will not blast in our manhood, what we acquired when only in infancy. This dispute is not to end in Smash only. We must have a brush with the gentlemen, unless a new administration when in power will undertake to punish these flagellators of all Europe. I pray God, for a speedy succession, & that the Fact may take place.

Yrs

J MASON JR.

### JONATHAN MASON, JR., TO OTIS

Boston May 28. 1798

. . . In New England we sail full as fast as you do in Philadelphia. It does not take us a month to make an alien bill, or raise a Provisional army. We have a large majority that are inclined to do all those things heartily. War for a time we must have, & our fears to the Northward are, that you will cripple the Executive — that you will rise without a proper *climax*. Our Commissioners are in jeopardy. True but they have already said & done eno' with your assistance to loose not only their liberty but their Heads, if the French Directory thirst after the blood of three poor defenceless citizens. Therefore it is now to be wished, that Congress under those apprehensions, will not leave anything undone that ought to be done, & we pray that decisive orders may be given & that accussed Treaty may be annulled. If we are to fight & cannot run, Custom has made it necessary, that we should season our Conduct, with a proper proportion of Crowing. The time is now passed, when we should fear giving offence. There has been a moment, when we have suspended principles, & even parted with them for the sake of peace, but that Conduct has brought upon us Insult & injury. As to Union among ourselves, I speak of my own State, there never was a greater. Thro' out our Country, the Yeomanry are not only united but spirited — if any thing, forward of the Seaports. There never can be a greater conviction take place, & there is no jacobin now existing, that would not be the selfsame base creature, were the French in possession of the Capital. Our elections for Representatives, tho not the most able, are decidedly federal & the droping of Dr. E[ustis] has laid the party completely prostrate. In private life a manly, clever fellow, but in Politicks, Insane. Harder for him in this situation to do a right thing, than in the other, a wrong one — every opening was tendered to him, every delicate mode made use of, & Interviews solicited, but all to no purpose, & he must either fall, or upon the seat there must be at least a luke warm friend, perhaps an open enemy, & him, a leader. His resolutions & measures were accordingly adopted & effected. The Legislature will forward you a handsome, spirited address & nearly unanimous. As to private news or scandal we have none. To morrow, Increase [25] will be in his robes, & Mr. Bobo, as was once before said, tho' perhaps not upon a more dignified occasion, up to his —— in business. What more will you have? Our bank House is going on swimmingly — if it needs a shove, push it for God's sake, for instead of thirty, it will cost sixty thousand dollars. . . .

[25] Increase Sumner, Governor of Massachusetts.

# CHAPTER VII

## DEFENSE AND REPRISAL

### 1798, ÆT. 32

THE news revealed by the publication of the X. Y. Z. dispatches called for no change in Federalist policy. It simply demonstrated that such measures as Adams and Hamilton and Harper and Otis had been urging for the past year, were absolutely necessary to defend the nation's commerce, and to vindicate its honor. There was no need to declare war on France. The first impulse, indeed, of an ardent Federalist, on reading of the outrageous treatment of our envoys in Paris, and the insolent threats of the "fate of Venice," must have been warlike. We have the authority of Jefferson's *Anas* (his private diary of fugitive political gossip), quoting Otis as one of his sources of information, that the propriety of declaring war was debated in a caucus of Federalist Congressmen, and defeated by a majority of five.[1] Otis was probably one of the minority. Although he deprecated war previous to the month of April,[2] he later

[1] Jefferson, *Works*, IX, 195-96. The *Anas*, on this point, is more trustworthy than usual, since Jefferson's information, though third-hand, came from three different sources, including Otis. The time when the caucus is held is simply indicated as "during the X. Y. Z. Congress"; it may, therefore, have taken place at any time before March, 1799. The Philadelphia *Aurora*, a source even less trustworthy than Jefferson's *Anas*, reported in 1800 that seventeen Federalist Senators held a caucus at the Bingham mansion in the summer of 1798, and agreed that all present should pledge themselves to act firmly upon the measures agreed upon by the majority present. M. Ostrogorski, in *Amer. Hist. Rev.*, v, 259. John Adams refers to "nocturnal caucuses at the pompous Mansion House," in a letter to Otis of April 4, 1823. Cf. *Annals Fifth Cong.*, 2629.

[2] "Whether Great Britain is doomed to yield to the arms & politicks of France, or whether the five Kings will squabble with each other, so that

expressed the opinion that Congress made a mistake in
failing to declare war during its second session.

To initiate a war policy at that time, however, would
have been foolhardy from a political viewpoint, and
useless from a military viewpoint. If war must come,
the tactical advantage of its declaration by France was
obvious. In that event the Republican party could continue its opposition only at the cost of political suicide.
For military purposes a system of home defense and
naval reprisals was sufficient to protect American commerce from French spoliation, and prepare the country
for a possible French invasion. This policy had the merit
of uniting the Federal party: the moderates supported it,
as the only way of avoiding hostilities consistent with
national self-respect; and the war Federalists, who counted
on a declaration of war from France, were satisfied with
its provisions.[3] The French government, moreover, could
reply in but one of two ways, either by declaring war,
or, as actually happened, by showing a disposition to
respect our claims. But for the fatal incubus of Alien
and Sedition Acts that they added to this system, the
men responsible for it would receive our unqualified
admiration as politicians and statesmen.

Spurred on by the voice of the nation, by addresses
from their constituents, and by spirited messages from
the President, Otis and Harper had little difficulty in

'honest men may come to their dues,' are events shrouded from our foresight.
I shall bear either of them with Christian Fortitude, if our own Country
can be permitted to remain at peace." Otis to Mercy Warren, March 15,
1798. Warren MSS.

[3] George Cabot wrote Rufus King, February 16, 1799, referring to the measures of the last session: "Genl Marshall [who returned in June] unfortunately
held the decided opinion that France would DECLARE war when the Dispatches
shou'd appear: & T. Sewell with other good men were so strongly impressed
with the advantage of such a declaration by them that they cou'd not be persuaded to relinquish the belief in it — I was astonished that they should have
attributed to the French such miserable policy." *King*, II, 543.

pushing through Congress a plan of defense and reprisal. Although the root-and-branch Federalists of the Essex Junto still complained of the slow movement of this "twaddling, whiffling Congress," [4] it seemed a different legislature from the timid, vacillating body of the past winter and spring. Dayton and the waverers came back into line, and the party caucus made all Federalists pull together. The Republicans were dismayed. "The opposition in our house appears at present so disconcerted," writes Otis (April 14), "that we proceed in business with less difficulty than formerly." A week later, disheartened at the Federalists' strength, opposition members from Virginia and Kentucky began to slip away from Philadelphia, in order to kindle a back fire of state rights against the Federalist system. Gallatin and Macon still led the opposition, still opposed with a zeal worthy of a better cause, every measure for national defense or retaliation against France. They were, however, no longer dangerous. With a normal Federalist majority during the remainder of the session of ten to fifteen votes, Otis and Harper were given full swing.

Back of Congress and the Executive stood Alexander Hamilton, ruling the Federal party, and through it the nation, from his law office in New York. Almost every act of the session may be traced to his letters.[5] On Otis and Harper fell the task of turning his recommendations into bills, and pushing them through. Jefferson gives us

[4] Gibbs, II, 70.

[5] See especially his *Works*, VI, 270, 295, and B. C. Steiner, *McHenry*, 291–95. The President would submit to the Cabinet a set of questions as to the best policy to follow in a given case, and the Hamiltonian members, Pickering, Wolcott, and McHenry, would procure Hamilton's views and submit them to the President as their own. Through the same channel Hamilton's opinions were probably communicated to Congress. Cf. Harper's resolutions of July 3, 1798 (*Annals of Fifth Congress*, 2084) with Hamilton's "further measures to be taken without delay" of June 5 (*Works*, VI, 295).

in his *Anas* a glimpse of the process during an incipient deal between Otis and Rutledge for measures satisfactory to their respective sections. Rutledge, according to this story, was discussing plans with another member from South Carolina, when Otis came in. "Rutledge addressed Otis. Now, Sir, says he, you must come forward with something liberal for the Southern States, fortify their harbors, and build gallies, in order to obtain their concurrence. Otis said, we insist on convoys for our European trade, and *guarda costas*, on which condition alone we will give them gallies and fortifications."[6] Seeing that ten "gallies," light draught vessels for coast defense, were provided for in an act of this session, we may believe Jefferson's story.

The most essential part of the Federalist defensive programme was to create a navy. Otis, by his oratory and his vote, helped to pass measures authorizing the President to purchase six vessels of thirty-two guns, twelve "twenties," and six "eighteens." A navy department was organized, half a million dollars voted for fortifications, and over a million for arms, ammunition, and matériel.

Far more important than the naval acts, from the political point of view, were the army acts, because they afforded the opposition a powerful lever to operate on popular prejudice. The regular army was increased to a temporary total of thirteen thousand, "for and during the continuance of the present difficulties with France." The President was authorized to accept the services of volunteer troops, paying their own expenses, to be called upon when needed. Gallatin denounced this scheme as class legislation, as an exclusive privilege to young men of wealth. "Does the gentleman suppose that none but

---

[6] Jefferson, *Works*, IX, 192.

the sons of the wealthy will turn out in defence of their country?" replied Otis. Most prominent, however, in the military legislation was the Provisional Army Act, of May 28, 1798.

According to this law the President, in case of a declaration of war against the United States, or of imminent danger of invasion before the next session of Congress, might recruit ten thousand men for three years' service. The officers were to receive their appointments immediately, but to draw no pay until actually called into service. The bill, originating in the Senate, was immediately denounced by Nicholas and Gallatin on its appearance in the House. In their estimation no increase of military force was necessary when militia was available, and further the bill provided an unconstitutional transfer of legislative power to the Executive. The spectre of a standing army, words that still held unpleasant memories for Anglo-Saxons, was conjured up. Otis undertook to answer all these objections. He had, he insisted, a high opinion of our militia, but he was surprised to hear that it would be an efficient defense against the veteran troops of the French Republic. If the Revolution had taught us one military lesson, it was that militia could not be relied upon for steady military operations. He reiterated the arguments contained in his letter to General Heath, concerning the possibility of a French invasion, and pointed out that it would be natural for France to conceive that she had the power of invasion, if we should decline to raise any force to meet her. It was worth a hundred times the expense of raising the provisional army to change foreign opinion of our weakness, and he, for one, wished that provision had been made for fifty thousand instead of for ten thousand men. As for the constitutional objection, Otis considered it "no time for nice constitutional scruples. No army can be raised without giving the President a certain amount of power."

Republican opposition on this ground was simply due to fear of executive power, when wielded by a Federalist President. The Provisional Army Act was, in fact, a close parallel to the Militia Act of 1795, the constitutionality of which was unquestioned, and the imputation that it created a standing army was without foundation. The measure provided for merely a paper army, a skeleton army. As Otis said, in debate, the bill "only declares that if existing circumstances shall make it necessary, then the President shall raise an army not exceeding a certain number of men. It may happen that the necessity may not exist; but the gentleman from Virginia must be able to fathom the intentions of France further than I can pretend to do, if he can say that no such necessity *can* exist. If what was said by the agents of that Government to our Envoys can be relied on, there is a direct threat to ravage our coasts."

Another and more serious charge against the Army Acts of 1798 would scarcely be worth refuting, but for its acceptance by an eminent modern historian.[7] This indictment, that the regular and provisional armies were designed primarily to suppress democracy, and not to protect the country against France, is not supported by the slightest evidence. The motive of the measure clearly lay in the Federalists' fear of a French invasion, as expressed by Otis in his letter to General Heath, — a fear that was groundless, as subsequent events showed, but perfectly genuine. It is true that the threatened rebellion in Virginia and Kentucky in 1799 postponed the reduction of the regular army to a peace footing, and that Hamilton later desired to use the army for purposes of

[7] Henry Adams, *Gallatin*, 199, 211.

conquest and personal glory; but the statement that the
army acts were conceived for dragonnading is entirely
unfounded.[8] The regular army never reached its legal
limit, and the provisional army never passed the skeleton
stage; but both measures acted with salutary effect on
the French government, by showing that America had
both the spirit and the means to defend herself. Politically, however, the army act resulted unfortunately for
Otis and his party. Because no French invasion ever
took place, Republican leaders and editors were able to
convince thousands that the "standing army" of 1798
was designed to enforce the Sedition Act, and to crush
out personal liberty.

In order to meet the necessary increase of expenditure,
a direct tax was levied on houses and slaves. By a somewhat clumsy classification the rate of taxation on houses
was made progressive — increasing from one fifth of one
per cent for a house valued at five hundred dollars to one
per cent for a house valued at thirty thousand dollars.
In the debate on this measure, on June 26, we have the
interesting spectacle of two Democrats in the opposition,
Samuel Smith and Edward Livingston, who insisted that
the progressive principle was too hard on the well-to-do,
while Otis, a large real-estate owner himself and a member of the supposed aristocratic party, defended a progressive increase of rates, on the ground that good houses
are a better criterion of the wealth of their owners than
any other form of property.[9] In the end, most of the
Republicans and all the Federalists voted for the bill.
Although carefully planned to make the burden of taxation fall on those who were best able to bear it, this direct

[8] It is interesting to find that similar charges were made by Fox and Sheri-
dan and the English democratic clubs against William Pitt at this period.
J. Holland Rose, *William Pitt and the Great War*, 284, 510.

[9] *Annals of Fifth Congress*, 2053–57.

tax produced a small insurrection in Pennsylvania, and became in the public mind an engine of Federalist oppression.

The second portion of the Federalist programme was to retaliate in kind against French spoliations. All vessels flying the American flag, whether merchant vessels, privateers, or men-of-war, were authorized by Congress to capture French armed vessels, and to recapture their American prizes. Commercial intercourse with France was suspended, and the Treaty of 1778, which the French had long since ceased to observe, was denounced. Otis, who early in the session expressed himself as opposed to half-way measures, constantly defended these policies in debate, while the opposition protested at every step. By the end of the session, July 16, 1798, Congress had created a state of quasi-naval war, differing only from an actual declared war in that Frenchmen were not proclaimed public enemies, and the capture of unarmed vessels was not permitted. During the two and one half years that elapsed before the Republic came to terms, our infant navy rescued American commerce from the harassing depredations of the French privateers, and worsted many a French national ship in single combat. For this glorious result of his favorite policy, President Adams deserves the much-disputed title of "Father of the American Navy." When he became President, there was no American navy. During his administration, as he boasted in his old age, "I humbled the French Directory as much as all Europe has humbled Bonaparte. . . . I built frigates, manned a navy, and selected officers with great anxiety and care, who perfectly protected our commerce, and gained virgin victories against the French, and who afterwards acquired such laurels in the Mediterranean and who have lately emblazoned themselves and their country with a naval glory, which I tremble to think of." [10] Otis was equally proud of his services, in pushing through Congress, against the violent opposition of the Democracy, this naval policy which made the Stars and Stripes a terror to the Tricolor, and trained the ships and sea-fighters that humbled the Union Jack in 1812.

[10] John Adams, *Works*, x, 152.

# CHAPTER VIII

## A SYSTEM OF TERROR

### 1798, ÆT. 32

THE measures of defense and retaliation, described in the foregoing chapter, are the bright side of the Federalist system of 1798. Prompted by a legitimate and patriotic desire to force French policy into the open, the party admirably succeeded in its purpose, and brought self-respect to the American government and people. On the other side, we have the Alien and Sedition Acts, induced by a spirit of hysteria and political intolerance, which proved fatal to their authors. Under this title are included the Naturalization Act of June 18, 1798, the Act Concerning Aliens of June 25, the Act Respecting Alien Enemies of July 6, and the Act for the Punishment of Certain Crimes (Sedition Act) of July 14. The two Alien Acts were justifiable, though unnecessary, measures of self-defense against French spies and *intrigants*, but the Naturalization and Sedition Laws belong to a different category. Designed primarily not for defense against a foreign power, but for offense against the Democratic party, they were calculated to rob that party of an important element of its vote, and to make political opposition to Federalism a crime. They were the principal cause of the Federalist defeat in 1800. Harrison Gray Otis, who was responsible as much as any man for their passage, always defended the principles of these laws, and must therefore share their obloquy.

First of these measures to reach enactment was the

Naturalization Act, extending from five to nineteen years the period of residence necessary for aliens who wished to become naturalized. The reason for this move on the part of the Federalists was obvious, — the Republican party was absorbing the foreign vote. Originally the Federalists had no objection to speedy naturalization, but after the French Revolution they repented their early liberality. From 1792 on, Europe outside France became an uncomfortable place for French sympathizers and Republicans, and a stream of Irish, Scotch, and German malcontents began to flow into the United States. These classes naturally spurned the party of conservatism and privilege, and, as soon as they became naturalized, joined the party that stood for Gallomania and democracy. By 1798 the alliance between native democracy and the Irish vote, which has endured to this day, was already cemented. The apprehension of his party is reflected in a remark of Otis in a letter to his wife: "If some means are not adopted to prevent the indiscriminate admission of wild Irishmen & others to the right of suffrage, there will soon be an end to liberty & property." [1]

Modern conservative parties have met a similar situation by attempting to outbid their opponents for the foreign vote through flattery and corruption. The

[1] There is a delightful example of this same attitude in a letter of Uriah Tracy of Connecticut, dated August 7, 1800: "In my lengthy journey through this state [Pennsylvania] I have seen many, very many, Irishmen, and with a very few exceptions, they are United Irishmen, Free Masons, and the most God-provoking Democrats on this side of Hell." — Gibbs, II, 399. In 1798, Rufus King, the American minister in London, exerted his influence successfully with the British government to prevent Irish political exiles from being sent to the United States. He distinctly avowed that the Irish were not wanted, "because a large proportion of the emigrants from Ireland, and especially in our middle states, has upon this occasion arranged itself upon the side of the malcontents." The complete correspondence on this incident may be found in C. R. King's *Rufus King*, II, 635–49.

Federal party was more self-respecting and more direct. It determined to strike the evil at its roots, and *destroy the foreign* vote. This purpose was first distinctly avowed by Otis, in the first session of the Fifth Congress. He undertook, on July 1, 1797, to defend a proposed tax of twenty dollars on certificates of naturalization. The opposition immediately charged that the object of this resolve was not to raise revenue, but to restrict immigration. Otis acknowledged the charge, and defended the proposition in a notable speech. After an attack on the French Revolution, he remarked:

> The Amendment will not affect those men who already have lands in this country, nor the deserving part of those who may seek an asylum in it. Persons of that description can easily pay the tax; but it will tend to foreclose the mass of vicious and disorganizing characters who can not live peaceably at home, and who, after unfurling the standard of rebellion in their own countries, may come hither to revolutionize ours. I feel every disposition to respect those honest and industrious people. . . . who have become citizens . . . but I do not wish to invite hordes of wild Irishmen, nor the turbulent and disorderly of all parts of the world, to come here with a view to disturb our tranquillity, after having succeeded in the overthrow of their own Governments.

This effusion, dubbed "Otis's Wild Irish Speech," caused much comment in the party press.[2] Otis, nevertheless, did not secure his object, for the twenty-dollar proposition failed to pass.

When the publication of the X. Y. Z. dispatches, on

---

[2] It even brought forth a piece of political doggerel entitled "An Irish Epistle to H. G. Otis," one stanza of which is not bad:

> "Young man. We would have you remember
> While we in this country can tarry,
> The 'Wild Irish' will choose a new member
> And will ne'er vote again for *young Harry*."

Otis was finally driven to an explanation that by "wild Irishmen" he did not mean the whole Irish nation.

April 5, 1798, gave them the undisputed mastery of the House, the Federalists did not wait long before restricting the enfranchisement of immigrants in a much more direct manner. The first step in the Alien and Sedition system was taken on April 19, by referring the question of amending the old Naturalization Act to a committee, which simply recommended a prolongation of the aliens' term of residence before naturalization. This suggestion failed to satisfy Harper and Otis. The former asserted, "the time is now come when it will be proper to declare, that nothing but birth shall entitle a man to citizenship in this country." Otis proposed to substitute for the committee report, a resolution "that no alien born, who is not at present a citizen of the United States, shall hereafter be capable of holding any office of honor, trust, or profit, under the United States," to which Harper wished to add, "or of voting at the election of any member of the Legislature of the United States, or of any State." These propositions, if adopted as law, would certainly have accomplished their object in destroying the Republicans' foreign vote, and in preventing future Matthew Lyons and Albert Gallatins from exercising their talents in a manner inimical to Federalism. Seldom has so barefaced an attempt to injure a political party been made in Congress. Otis's proposition was much too high-toned for most of his party, one member of which persuaded him to withdraw it, as unconstitutional.[2] But the legislature of his native state stamped his policy with its approval, when three months later it proposed to amend the Constitution by excluding foreign-born citizens from the House and Senate.

*Otis: no alien hold office of honor or trust in U.S.*

[2] *Annals,* 1573. In 1798, no one supposed that Congress had the power to alter the qualifications for membership prescribed in the Constitution. After the Civil War, however, there was no question about this prerogative.

After Otis's resolution was withdrawn, the House returned to the original proposition of restricting naturalization. A bill was finally drawn up, in which fourteen years was adopted as the minimum residence for an alien before making application for citizenship, with five years additional before naturalization. This became on June 18, 1798, the Naturalization Act, which, until its repeal in 1802, deprived the Republican party of its usual accessions of foreign-born voters. Otis, however, never forsook his Native American policy; we shall see his disqualifying proposition reappear in his Report of the Hartford Convention.

The Naturalization Act was a political manœuvre pure and simple, but the two Alien Acts, which form the next steps of the Alien and Sedition system, arose from different motives. Their basis lay in a Federalist notion that the country was filled with dangerous Frenchmen. There was in fact, a considerable body of proscribed Jacobins in the country, and French agents had been caught in the act of stirring up sedition on the Western and Northern frontiers. After the X. Y. Z. dispatches were published, the Federal party wrought itself up into an extreme form of Gallophobia that constantly reminds one of the days of the Popish Plot, or the recent hysteria in England over German waiters. It was commonly supposed that the United States contained over thirty thousand Frenchmen, constantly engaged in intrigues against the government, and ready in case of invasion to rise as one man and murder their hosts. Some would-be Titus Oates was continually coming forward, in 1798 and 1799, with a tale of a deep-laid plot. President Adams, for instance, was informed anonymously that the Frenchmen in Philadelphia were planning on May 9, 1798, the day of national fast, to destroy Philadelphia by fire, and to massacre the inhabitants.[4] Although this Federalist panic reached its height in 1799, it had gone far enough by May, 1798, to warrant the hustling of all Frenchmen out of the country. How far the paroxysm had affected Otis may be judged by a perfervid speech he delivered during the debate on June 16, 1798:

In my humble opinion, there is greater danger from this source than from any other. I believe that it has been owing to this cause that all the Republics in Europe have been laid prostrate in the dust; it is this system which has enabled the French to overleap all natural and artificial obstructions; to subjugate Holland and Italy; to destroy the Helvetic Confederacy, and to force a passage through rocks and mountains, which have been for ages sacred to the defense of liberty; it is this system which has watered the tomb of William Tell with the blood of widows fighting over their slaughtered husbands, and with the tears of orphans who survive to swell the procession of the victors. . . . The European Republics . . . boasted of their patriotism and courage, . . . yet when the hour of trial arrived, it appeared that secret corruptions and foreign influence had completed their work; upon the slightest shock, those Republics crumbled into fragments.

This general state of mind inspired the Alien Acts, rendering every alien in the United States subject to arbitrary arrest and expulsion. So far the responsibility for this legislation has not been fixed upon any one individual or group in the Federal party, but doubtless its passage was suggested by contemporary legislation in Great Britain. There is, in fact, a certain rough parallel at this period between the problems of the governing classes in England and the United States, and in the solutions attempted. In 1798, both England and the United States were threatened by a French invasion. The one country was at war with France, the other on

[4] Adams MSS., "Gen. Cor., J. A., 1797-98," 173, 175.

the brink of it. In both countries existed a large body of French sympathizers, who strengthened the ranks of the opposition, and who, it was believed, were stimulated by French emissaries. William Pitt met these difficulties by coercive legislation, directed both at foreign spies and domestic conspirators.[5] The Act of Congress "Concerning Aliens," in 1798, bears so marked a resemblance to Pitt's Aliens Act of 1793, which had just been renewed, that one is forced to the conclusion that Otis and his colleagues were taking a leaf out of the experience of the great English statesman.[6]

The subject of aliens was taken up by the House of Representatives on May 3, when Otis, attempting to hasten matters with a vigorous speech, insisted the time had come "to take up that crowd of spies and inflammatory agents which overspread the country like the locusts of Egypt." "Something ought to be done which would strike these people with terror," he said — "I do not desire ... to *boggle* about slight forms, nor to pay respect to treaties already abrogated, but to seize these persons, wherever they can be found carrying on their vile purposes." In due time a bill was reported, which, much to Otis's disappointment, was restricted in its operation to time of declared war.[7] The Senate, however, had already supplied the deficiency. In that body a "Bill Concerning Aliens" had been under consideration since April; it was passed on June 8 and sent down to the

[5] Cf. Mr. Rose's chapter on "The British Jacobins," and pp. 282-87, 333, 349-50, of his *Pitt and the Great War*.

[6] The provisions of the British Aliens Act that reappear in the American Alien Act of 1798 are the method of expulsion, the system of licenses, and the requirement that masters of entering vessels must report the names and descriptions of all aliens on board. The British law provided a death penalty for aliens who returned after expulsion.

[7] This bill became the Act Concerning Alien Enemies; a superfluous measure, and never put in force because formal war was never declared before its expiration.

House. It gave federal courts cognizance of all offenses under it. The President was authorized to order out of the United States an alien whom he considered dangerous, after examination by a magistrate. Any alien thus ordered to depart might be given a license to remain, on proving, to the President's satisfaction, his good character and behavior. For failure to comply with an order of expulsion, he must be tried before a federal court, the whole machinery of enforcement being thus safeguarded from state interference. The penalty for an alien's return, after being expelled, was life imprisonment, but this harsh provision was struck out in the House. Otis proposed an amendment, which was adopted, declaring that an expelled alien could take with him his personal property, and that any property left in this country should remain subject to his disposal. This provision was so far in advance of contemporary European legislation that it was widely commented upon, and reflected great credit on its author. One of his friends wrote from Paris: "The clause which you caused to be introduced into the Alien bill . . . has been published here in all the papers, it is spoken of in the highest terms of praise, and has done you much honor & your country important services at this moment." [3] As thus amended, the Senate Alien Bill passed the House by a vote of forty-six to forty, and became law on June 25, 1798.

The Alien Act has received universal abuse from politicians and historians to this day. Impolitic the measure certainly was, in the light of the antagonism it aroused; unnecessary it proved to be, since it was never

[3] Richard Codman to Otis, August 26, 1798. The *Centinel* of October 31, 1798, quotes a paragraph from the Paris *L'Ami des Lois*, 2 Fructidor, An VI, commending Otis's amendment, and adds, "We are well assured that this liberal and judicious provision had a great influence in obtaining a repeal of the Embargo on American vessels."

enforced; but constitutional it certainly was, and a proper measure of precaution in the contemporary state of foreign relations. The leading arguments presented against its constitutionality, both in the House debate, and in the Virginia and Kentucky Resolutions, are as follows: (1) The power to expel alien friends, not being delegated to the United States, is reserved to the state governments. (2) The act was contrary to that article of the Constitution, which states that "the migration and importation of such persons as any of the States now existing shall think proper to admit, shall not be prohibited by the Congress prior to the year 1808." (3) The summary administrative process of expulsion infringed the "due process of law" provision of the Bill of Rights. To these objections Otis and his Federalist colleagues answered: (1) That, since the power to expel aliens resides somewhere in every nation, any common-sense construction of the Constitution must regard it as implied under the treaty-making power of the federal government. To leave the power of expulsion to the states would produce a strange state of affairs. "What will be our situation," said Otis, "if any one of the States may retain a number of men whose residence shall be proveably dangerous to the United States?" (2) The "migration and importation" clause was placed in the Constitution, as every one at the time knew, in order to prevent interference with the slave trade. (3) The Alien Act contemplated a crime, for which "due process of law" was necessary, only if an alien returned after expulsion, in which case a jury trial was provided.[9] As for

---

[9] Argument of William Gordon of New Hampshire, *Annals*, 1984. Cf. W. A Sutherland, *Notes on the Constitution*, 648: "The deportation of Aliens is not a punishment nor is it a deprivation of liberty without due process of law." All these arguments will be found repeated in the various published defenses of the Alien and Sedition Acts.

the expediency of the Act, it proved unnecessary, and was never enforced; but, intended only for use in emergencies, it was a proper method of precaution with war impending. Even before its passage, a large number of Frenchmen hastily left the country, indicating that their consciences, at least, were guilty. That the Alien Act should inflame every one of Democratic tendencies was a matter of course, for it was aimed chiefly at Frenchmen, it extended the power of the Executive, and, in the provision requiring the registration of immigrants, it put on immigration the first restraint known to federal legislation. But latter-day criticism of it as an arbitrary and unconstitutional measure seems a little out of date, since the passage of the Chinese Exclusion Act. The decision of the Supreme Court supporting this recent law simply repeats Otis's old arguments, and completely justifies, from a constitutional standpoint, the alien legislation of 1798.[10]

At the apex of the Alien and Sedition legislation stands the Sedition Act of July 14, 1798. No act of Congress has ever attracted so much well-merited odium, or proved so fatal to its authors, as that unhappy law. It stands out unparalleled in American legislation as a thinly disguised attempt to treat political opposition as a crime, and to stamp criticism of a party as sedition. In his advocacy of it Otis committed, except for his promotion of the Hartford Convention, the worst mistake of his political career.

[10] "The right to exclude or expel all aliens, or any class of aliens, absolutely or upon certain conditions, in war or in peace, being an inherent and inalienable right of every sovereign and independent nation, essential to its safety, its independence, and its welfare, and being a power affecting international relations, is vested in the political departments of the government, and is to be regulated by treaty or by Act of Congress, and to be executed by the executive authority according to the regulations established." 149 U. S. Reports, 698 (Fong Yue Ting v. United States).

As with the Alien Act, it is well-nigh impossible to **fix** individual responsibility for the Sedition Act,[11] but **its** motives clearly lay in Federalist intolerance and fear of criticism, stimulated by the example of the British government. There is no doubt that the authors of the Sedition Act desired to muzzle the opposition press; **and** their provocation was great. The *Aurora* and its imitators were constantly telling their readers that the Federalists had picked a quarrel with France in order to raise a standing army, form a British alliance, and establish a monarchy. General attacks on the Federalist system were varied by gross assaults on individual characters. But William Cobbett's *Porcupine's Gazette* was a more than sufficient antidote to the scurrility of the *Aurora,* and Otis and his friends failed to see that an open and free discussion was the only way to meet attacks on their good faith. They were blind to Lord Bacon's wise maxim: "The punishing of wits enhances their authority, and a forbidden writing is thought to be a certain spark of truth that flies up in the face of them that seek to tread it."

Intolerance, however, was not the sole motive of the Sedition Act. The Federalists wished to strike at an aspect of French policy which seemed to them most dangerous. This was what President Adams called "a disposition to separate the people of the United States from their government," [12] — a sort of propaganda that

---

[11] No hint as to its origin appears in the Otis papers, or in any of the printed or manuscript correspondence that I have examined, excepting in a letter of May 2, 1798, in the Adams MSS., from Dr. Cotton Tufts of Weymouth, Massachusetts, to the President, urging that a Sedition Law be passed.

[12] Message of May 16, 1797. Otis states, in his *Letter to William Heath* (p. 24), "The object, Sir, of the present Directory, is to divide the people from the government, and subdivide the people from each other. You are assured of this by our Envoys; . . . by their envoys uniform and repeated appeals to the

had been a right hand to French policy in Europe, and with which America had been threatened in more than one communication from the Directory. To the ardent Federalist of 1798, every Jacobin squib was a manifestation of this "novel and alarming principle, the art of separating the people of every nation from their government, ... the most important engine of disorganization and anarchy ever invented by the ingenuity of man." [18] On all sides he saw "sedition, privy conspiracy, and rebellion," and consequently reacted toward the good old doctrine, so comfortable to governments, of passive obedience. For examples of precautionary measures it was only necessary to turn to Great Britain. England needed no general Sedition Act, for sedition was cognizable under her common law; but the ministry of Pitt had been marked by drastic proclamations and laws against

people." A Federal grand jury in Virginia, as early as May, 1797, presented "as a real evil, the circular letters of several members of the late Congress, and particularly letters with the signature of Samuel J. Cabell, endeavoring, at a time of real public danger, to disseminate unfounded calumnies against the happy government of the United States, and thereby to separate the people therefrom, and increase or produce a foreign influence, ruinous to the peace, happiness, and independence of the United States" — cited in the *Life of Jefferson*, II, 376, by H. S. Randall, who calls it "the first note of the Sedition Act." The same attitude is shown by Otis, in the debate, May 15, 1798, on the petition of Captain Magnien's Grenadiers, a militia company of Portsmouth, Virginia. The petition, which is an excellent example of the doctrines fundamentally opposed to Federalism, states: "We view with extreme concern the attempts that are evidently making by men high in authority to widen the breach between the United States and the French Republic, by holding up to the good people of these States the late unworthy propositions of certain unauthorized persons at Paris, as the act of the French government, when in reality, the face of the despatches cannot warrant any such conclusions." It goes on to accuse the administration of striving "to involve us in all the calamities of a war with the most powerful Republic on earth; ... and ... an alliance with a nation which is ... under the guidance of the most foul and corrupt government on earth." Otis remarked, "The solvent of sedition has taken possession of the hearts of these addressers, and alienated their affections from their government."

[18] Quoted from the reply of the Massachusetts House of Representatives to Governor Sumner's speech at the opening of the June session, 1798.

seditious writings and meetings, and by judicial decisions
defining the crime so broadly as to cover ordinary party
opposition.[14]

The Sedition Bill was introduced in the Senate, passed
that body on July 5 by a vote of 18 to 6, and was sent
down to the House. Here the language of the bill was
considerably altered. The first section, declaring American adherents of France liable to the death penalty for
treason, was struck out altogether; and two clauses,
mitigating considerably the severity of the Senate bill,
were added.[15] Bayard of Delaware was responsible for a
praiseworthy amendment permitting a defendant to give
as evidence the truth of the alleged libel — a privilege
unknown to the English law, or to that in most of the
states.

One should read the amended Sedition Bill in order
thoroughly to appreciate it. The second section defines
as a crime, to be tried before a federal court, the writing,
printing, or uttering of anything against President or
Congress with intent "to bring them . . . into contempt
or disrepute, or to excite against them . . . the hatred of
the good people of the United States, or to stir up sedi-

[14] J. H. Rose, *Pitt and the Great War*, 24, 285, chap. VII. Lord Justice Clerk
defined the crime of sedition as "endeavoring to create a dissatisfaction in the
country, which nobody can tell where it will end. It will very naturally end in
overt rebellion; and if it has that tendency, though not in the view of the
parties at the time, yet, if they have been guilty of poisoning the minds of the
liege, I apprehend that that will constitute the crime of sedition to all intents
and purposes." *State Trials*, XXIII, 766.

[15] The changes made by the House in the Senate bill, besides those mentioned
above, were not important. Alexander Johnston states otherwise in his article,
"Alien and Sedition Acts," in Lalor's *Cyclopædia*, with regard to the substitution of a new second section, but the words with which he characterizes the
Senate's second section — "whose intentional looseness and vagueness of
expression could have made criminal every form of party opposition to the
federalist party" — apply equally well to the second section of the final Act.
The only essential difference between the two was the lowering of the penalties.
Johnston also erred in saying that the Alien Act aroused more opposition than
the Sedition Act.

tion within the United States," or to excite insurrections or to aid hostile designs of a foreign nation. The punishment for these crimes was to be "a fine not exceeding ten thousand dollars, and imprisonment not exceeding two years." This section made it possible for federal courts to brand ordinary party opposition as a crime. How else can unworthy public servants be exposed, but by bringing them "into contempt or disrepute"?

Otis from the first took a leading part in the debates on the Sedition Bill, and adopted the position of the most advanced Federalists. On July 10 occurred the principal debate: Otis and Harper against Gallatin and Nicholas. Otis delivered one of the best speeches he ever made in Congress, a defense of the jurisdiction of the federal government over seditious libel; a speech distinguished by careful preparation and documentation, and by sound and statesmanlike interpretation of the Constitution. The objections to the constitutionality of the bill, he said, might be reduced to two inquiries: (1) Did the Constitution originally give Congress jurisdiction over the offenses described in the bill? (2) Did the amendment to the Constitution, stating that Congress should make no law abridging the freedom of the press, take its power away? Otis decided the first point emphatically in the affirmative: —

With respect to the first question, it must be allowed that every independent government has a right to preserve and defend itself against injuries and outrages which endanger its existence; for, unless it has this power, it is unworthy of the name of a free government, and must either fall, or be subordinate to some other protection.

He pointed out that Congress had already undertaken to punish crimes against the United States, not specified in the Constitution, such as perjury, bribery, and stealing public records.[16] In answer to the second question, Otis insisted that the bill would not abridge the freedom of the press, but merely bridle its licentiousness. He referred to Blackstone's famous definition of freedom of the press, — freedom from censorship previous to publication, not freedom from prosecution for libel, — and, quoting laws and judicial decisions in states which had freedom of the press clauses in their constitutions, he demonstrated that Blackstone's definition had always prevailed. This argument was illustrated the following year by the condemnation in a state court of Abijah Adams, co-editor of the Boston *Independent Chronicle,* for seditious libel; a case which showed that prosecution under the common law of states could be even more severe than under the Sedition Act, since the truth of the alleged libel could not be offered as a defense.

Otis's speech of July 10 formed the basis of every contemporary justification of the Sedition Act, and his arguments have stood the test of time,[17] while those of the Virginia and Kentucky Resolutions, the most powerful on the other side, have not survived. Like every other argument of the state rights school, the "Resolutions of '98" deny to the federal government the necessary means of perpetuating its existence, when threatened by sedition or rebellion. In like manner, Otis's interpretation of

[16] This is the only weak part of Otis's argument. Gallatin pointed out, in reply, that the statutes mentioned were "necessary and proper" means of carrying out enumerated powers of Congress, — to establish courts, to establish executive departments, — whereas no enumerated power existed which a sedition law could carry into effect.

[17] His main argument is repeated by the Supreme Court in the Legal Tender Cases (1871): "That would appear, then, to be a most unreasonable construction of the Constitution which denies to the government created by it, the right to employ freely every means, not prohibited, necessary for the preservation, and for the fulfillment of its acknowledged duties. . . . It certainly was intended to confer upon the government the power of self-preservation." 12 Wall, 528.

the First Amendment to the Constitution has prevailed:
— Blackstone's definition of freedom of the press "has
been accepted as expressing the views of those who
adopted this amendment"; [18] and many of the great
commentators on American constitutional law have
substantially agreed with Otis's final conclusion, that
the federal government has the power to punish seditious
libel. [19]

Twenty years later, when Otis was in the United
States Senate, the question came up of indemnifying one
of the victims of the Sedition Act. Otis, who was then the
only member in either House of Congress that had voted
for it in 1798, took up the gauntlet of Senator Barbour of
Virginia in defense of his old principles. "With respect
to the constitutional question," he said, "I am content
to declare that my mind has always reposed upon a single
consideration, detached from all others, as sufficient to
uphold the Act. All governments must possess an inherent right to punish all acts, which being morally
wrong, tend directly to endanger their existence or safety.
This power would be implied in the Constitution, even
though no express words had conveyed the authority to
make all laws 'necessary and proper,' to give effect to the

---

[18] T. M. Cooley, *Constitutional Law* (3d ed.), 300. H. W. Biklé, in *Amer. Law Register*, I, 15–16, and Cooley, *op. cit.*, 300 *et seq.*, point out that Blackstone's definition has been applied in several cases, adopted by Chancellor Kent (*Commentaries*, II, 17), and cited in the recent *American and English Encyclopædia of Law*, N. S., VI, 1002. Cooley believes Blackstone's definition to be insufficient, and that the amendment was meant to preserve freedom of public discussion, as well as to exempt the press from censorship in advance of publication.

[19] For example, Biklé, *op. cit.*, and others cited in his note 67; Cooley, *op. cit.*, 305; W. W. Willoughby, *Constitutional Law* (1910), 845. Another objection to constitutionality of the Sedition Act, raised at the time by Gallatin, and brought up since by historians, is based on the principle that federal courts have no jurisdiction over common law offenses. The objection is not well taken, for when the courts were given jurisdiction over seditious libel by Act of Congress, it became a statutory, and not a common law offense.

instrument. Without such a right, no government is competent to the great duty of self protection." [20]

A few days after this speech was delivered, Otis received from an old political enemy a letter that must have given him as much satisfaction as any he ever received in his life. The writer was Judge Story of the Supreme Court, the most eminent of commentators on the Constitution.

Salem Decr 27, 1818

Dear Sir

I have the pleasure to acknowledge the receipt of your package covering the Washington City Gazette. I have read your speech with great interest; & equally admire its manner & matter. Such arguments composed in a tone of manliness, urbanity, & candour do honour to our Country. As a citizen of Massachusetts I feel proud that the redeeming spirit of her eloquence is heard with so much effect in the Senate of the Nation.

At the time when I first turned my thoughts to political subjects in the ardour of very early youth, I well remember that the sedition law was my great aversion. With the impetuosity & desire of independence so common to zealous young men, I believed it to be unconstitutional. I have now grown wiser in this, & I hope in many other respects; & for many years have entertained no more doubt of the constitutional power of Congress to enact that law, than any other in the Statute book. My present opinion has been forced upon me by reflection, by legal analogy, & by calm deliberation. You may smile at my confession, which I hope you will not call, as Mr Randolph on another occasion did, "a precious confession."

The truth is & it ought not to be disguised, that many opinions are taken up & supported at the moment, which at a distance of time, when the passions of the day have subsided, no longer meet our approbation. He who lives a long life & never changes his opinions may value himself upon his consistency; but rarely can be complimented for his wisdom. Experience cures us of many of our theories; & the results of measures often

[20] *Mr. Otis's Speech on the Sedition Law* (see bibliography).

convince us against our will that we have seen them erroneously in the beginning. I hope I shall never have any pride but to do right, & fearlessly to acknowledge my errors when I perceive them.

With my best wishes for your personal happiness & a sincere interest in your public character I beg the honor of subscribing myself most respectfully

Your obedt friend & servt.

JOSEPH STORY.

With all due respect to Judge Story's opinion, there is still one conclusive objection to the constitutionality of the Sedition Act, — the extent of its scope. The second section was broad enough to include not only libels that threatened the life of the state and the peaceful working of its functions, but also those that threatened the supremacy of the Federal party. "It failed to draw the line between such publications as vitally affected the security and vigor of the government, and such as did not." This defect appeared in the enforcement of the law, which was prosecuted vigorously. Under its cover several persons were fined and imprisoned for publications and utterances that were little more than scurrilous criticisms of party policy. From a political point of view, moreover, the measure was suicidal. It revolted the popular sense of personal liberty, and acted like oil on the flames of defamation that it was calculated to quench. There is reason to believe that a portion of the Federal party foresaw this result, since many Federalists present at the time the vote was taken, refused to vote for it.[21] Otis, however, and the Federal party as a whole, were highly pleased with the Alien and Sedition system.

[21] The vote was 44 to 41, the smallest majority of any Federalist measure since the publication of the X. Y. Z. dispatches. Only two members from south of the Potomac voted *Yea*.

"Each factious alien shrinks with dread
And hides his hemp-devoted head;
While Slander's foul seditious crew,
With gnashing teeth retires from view." [22]

The legislatures of Virginia and Kentucky "saw in those untoward measures the racks and thumb-screws of a political inquisition." [23] In their famous Resolutions of November and December, 1798, the latent doctrine of state sovereignty was cast in a definite formula, in order to prove that Congress had no right to adopt such a system as the Alien and Sedition Acts. Otis undoubtedly shared the general opinion of his party, and regarded the "Resolutions of '98" as abominable heresies. The vitality of these declarations, however, was remarkable. Their basis, the assertions "that the Government created by this compact was not made the exclusive or final judge of the extent of the powers delegated to itself," that "each party has an equal right to judge for itself, as well of infractions as of the mode and measure of redress," was laid up in the treasury of state rights for any one to use who would. Otis, himself, was glad to draw upon it in the days of embargo, non-intercourse, and Madison's war.

[22] R. Alsop *et. al.* (the "Hartford Wits"), *Political Greenhouse for 1798*, 8.
[23] J. C. Welling, "Connecticut Federalism" (*Addresses, Lectures, etc.*), 296.

# CHAPTER IX

## THE REPUBLICAN COURT[1]

### 1797–1801, ÆT. 32–36

POLITICS was not Otis's only occupation and amusement during his career as a member of the Fifth and Sixth Congresses. His social importance in Boston and his honorable official position gave him and Mrs. Otis the entrée to the most aristocratic society America has ever seen, the nearest approach to a court that the Republic has ever tolerated.

Philadelphia, at the end of the eighteenth century, had an undisputed leadership among American cities in population, commerce, and literature. In Philadelphian society there were then, as to-day, two distinct elements: the one was composed of old families of Quaker stock, kindly and intellectual, but somewhat rigid in social matters; the other, a liberal and pleasure-loving set, consisted, for the most part, of descendants of colonial government officials, and of English merchants, allied by marriage, in some instances, with the new "stock-jobbing aristocracy" that Jefferson detested. It was a

[1] The main sources for this chapter are Otis's letters to Mrs. Otis, and the manuscript memoirs of a Philadelphian, son of one of the persons mentioned in this chapter, and related to many of them. Born after the events described, he wrote his account of society during the Washington and Adams administrations for the amusement and information of his children, from first-hand testimony of members of that society, and from family traditions. He knew Mr. Otis very well, and was an intimate friend of two of his children. Since the writer was always unwilling that his work should be published, it seems due to him now to suppress his name. The manuscript was placed at my disposal through the kindness of his son. I have also drawn on R. W. Griswold's *Republican Court* (1855), a miscellaneous compilation of fact and gossip.

cultivated and cosmopolitan group. The men were edu-
cated usually in the English universities or the Temple;
the women, after presentations at the court of George III
or of Louis XVI, transplanted into Philadelphian society
the manners of English aristocracy, and the fashions of
Paris. Wealth these men and women possessed through
foreign commerce and finance, and they knew how to use
it to advantage. The selection of Philadelphia as the
temporary capital of the nation, from 1790 to 1800,
added strength and prestige to this society. The federal
government at the time was composed largely of gentlemen; in the Federal party, which possessed the Executive, the Judiciary, and a majority of the Legislature, no
man not a gentleman by birth or education was eligible
to office. Eliminating certain Democratic members of
Congress, the federal government resembled a large club
of well-bred men from all parts of the country. It represented our national aristocracy of education and talents,
which, as John Adams said, will continue to exist "as
long as some men are taller and others shorter, some
wiser and others sillier, some more virtuous and others
more vicious, some richer and others poorer."

The happy combination of a national government, a
Federalist administration, and a diplomatic corps, with
the cultivated native society of Philadelphia, and the
constant influx of distinguished foreign visitors, gave
Philadelphia from 1790 to 1800 all the best characteristics
of a court. It was far more cosmopolitan than the smaller
courts of Europe, and differed from them in that no
distinctions of rank were known among its members.
Even President and Mrs. Washington were merely *primi
inter pares*. But no court could have been more intolerant
of political dissent. Owing to the political bitterness of
the times, Democratic gentlemen and their families, no

SALLY FOSTER OTIS

From a miniature by Malbone.

matter how high their social qualifications, were rigidly ostracized by the best society in Philadelphia.

For persons of undoubted social position and political orthodoxy, like Mr. and Mrs. Harry Otis, this society was decidedly agreeable. During Washington's administrations, the young couple frequently visited the Samuel A. Otises, who had come to Philadelphia with the federal government. Harry Otis, ever witty and convivial, and his wife, whom Griswold describes as "remarkable for beauty and wit, as well as for an intellectual vivacity, tempered always by an indescribable grace," became general favorites at court. Through Mrs. Otis's girlhood friend, Sophia Francis, who married Otis's friend George Harrison,[2] they became intimate with the whole Willing and Bingham connection, which constituted a ruling oligarchy in Philadelphia society. Mrs. Harrison's uncle, Thomas Willing, head of a great mercantile firm and president of the United States Bank, was chief of the clan, which embraced the Francises, Hares, Powels, Byrds, Harrisons, and Binghams.

Mrs. Otis accompanied her husband to the first and third sessions of the Fifth Congress, in May, 1797, and October, 1798; but with the cares of an ever-increasing family she later had to remain in Boston during the greater part of her husband's congressional career. Otis felt severely this separation from his wife and children, and mainly for this reason he refused to be a candidate for reëlection in 1800. While he was away, however, he made the best of things among his friends who never permitted him to be lonely, and to amuse his wife he wrote to her a *chronique scandaleuse* of Philadelphia

[2] George Harrison (1761–1845) was a protégé of Robert Morris. He had to begin life over again after the great financier's bankruptcy in 1798, and finally became one of the most respected merchants of Philadelphia.

society, from which we can glean many interesting details of daily life at the Republican Court.

Otis's letters to his wife begin at the opening of the
dull winter session of 1797–98, when everything in politics hung fire, awaiting news from the mission to France.
Vexed at his forced absence from home, Otis was at first
inclined to be scornful of Philadelphia and its inhabitants.
In this mood was the letter of November 17, 1797:

Hitherto I have seen or heard of nothing approaching to
gaiety or amusement.  The theatre is not yet open.  The assembly not begun, and the Ladies not yet ready to scald the
beau monde with hot tea.  I begin to doubt whether the winter
is to be what they stile a gay one — and I really feel no disposition to take an active part in the bagatelle of the hour.  In
short, I am so tranquil in my little chamber, & so constantly
in it, that if you could peep in & see me, with my feet nailed
to the jamb, & my eyes fixed on my book, you might mistake
me for one of Bowens wax figures — though taking my flannel
night gown into view I think he has nothing *quite* so elegant.

And again on November 20: —

Although I have yet heard but once from my dearest friend,
I am in full expectation of a line by this morning's post.  A complete week has now elapsed since my arrival here, and though
I have long since learnt to realize that my mind can never be
tranquil in your absence, yet I hardly expected to be so discon-
solate an old Bachelor as I have found myself.  The Senators
are so dilatory in arriving, that no business has been yet done;
& the city so dull that I have seen or heard of no thing that
wears the air of pleasure or amusement; so that I have ample
time to devote to my books; & with the exception of a quarter
of an hour each morning, I have kept my chamber from seven
untill three o'clock, & have returned to it again always before
nine.  Whether it be that commercial derangements, or the effects of the yellow fever, (which may be deep though not visible)
have spread a gloom over the city, or whether the very atmosphere is impregnated with Quakerism, & Tom Paine's word

gives a drab colour'd cast to the houses and people, I will not pretend to determine, but certainly there is less appearance of the bustle of business, and of the splendour of fashion than I expected to see at this season. Nor can I but admire the readiness with which the people and especially our friend Sophia invent apologies for the procrastination of the public amusements and of the private parties; and if the winter should pass away without either, many fertile expedients will be found to evade the charge of inhospitality, & if every member of Congress should be obliged to mumble his dinner with none but his Landlady, during the session, you may assign whatever reason you please, but the want of a social temper & courteous manners in the inhabitants. It is not however to be denied with truth, that Quaker and German habits and manners characterise the body of the Citizens. Those who constitute the fashionable world are at best a mere oligarchy, composed of a few natives and as many foreigners. Having none to rival or eclipse them; or contend with them for the right of entertaining strangers, they pursue their own course without interruption. They will tell you that they can give you nothing to eat or drink in summer; because they leave town & reside in the country, & in winter you must wait for their civilities untill the time arrives for commencing the *Parties*, which is sometimes a month or six weeks later than at others, as Mrs. A happens to have finished her new drawing room, or Mrs B. to have gotten up from her last *accouchment*. My experience is yet to inform me wherein consists the pleasure, elegance & taste of these Parties. As the ladies on these occasions vie with each other in dress, I presume the eye at least must be gratified, but I fancy they are often very formal, unenlivened by general conversation and that the food for the mind contains as little nourishment as the cold tea which is applied to the dilution of the grosser part of the system. But it is not just in me to complain. My casual intimacy with a few families places me on a footing of domestic intercourse which is sufficiently agreeable, and having general invitations to two or three houses, I can partake of the pleasures of society in a way most conformable to my taste. I do not wish to enlarge my acquaintance, as I could not cultivate one more extensive with convenience to myself — and while I remain in public life, my main attention, from duty and choice must be directed to business. I have dined once with Cutting at Mrs Grattan's, once at Yznardis,[3] in great stile; & yesterday in the country with Jonathan Williams.[4] I am engaged for *next Christmas* with Mrs Powell, but with nobody for the Christmas *after* next. Rutledge has brought his wife and three Children, they are at lodgings; he has dined *once* with an old friend from *Carolina*, but has not another invitation yet. Mrs Grattan has a project of hiring the Government House, for the purpose of a Subscription Assembly. Mrs. Adams's first drawing room will be on friday; and afterwards once a fortnight. Mrs Liston[5] is not yet in town; & Mrs. La Frery sent her husband[6] to enquire about and after you, & indeed one would think from the numerous enquiries that you would be in great demand if here.

As the New Year approached these complaints of dulness cease in Otis's letters, for he was asked to more parties than he cared to accept. "The Binghams and Willings are civil and attentive. I dine with old Square Toes[7] on tuesday — no common favor this" he writes, — the disrespectful epithet referring to old Thomas Willing.

Another mid-season letter:

My dear Sally will conclude that I am beginning to get into a habit of dissipation or some other bad way by my short letters. It is true — I was last night at Henry Hills with a great concourse of both sexes, who danced and appeared to be happy. I neither danced nor supped, but retired at an early hour. In

---

[3] Joseph M. Yznardi, a Spanish gentleman, son of the United States consul at Cadiz, was a resident of Havana, and frequent visitor to Philadelphia. Otis writes, December 5, 1793, "On friday, Yznardi gave a splendid dinner, at which I was a guest. It is said he has a very lucrative contract, for supplying flour to Havannah, and he certainly discovers every disposition to spend at least *a part* of the profits among his friends."

[4] Jonathan Williams (1750–1815) was a nephew of Benjamin Franklin, and like his uncle distinguished in various activities, diplomatic, military, judicial, political, literary, and scientific.

[5] The wife of the British minister.

[6] The Chevalier Cipriano de Freire, the Portuguese minister.

[7] This was a contemporary nickname for old gentlemen who stuck to the old-fashioned square-toed boots, after pointed boots had become the fashion.

going to these places I experience but little positive enjoyment, but think it my duty to cultivate the acquaintance of fashionable and agreeable people who may contribute to your happiness this spring and next winter. Harry who is a great amateur of the fine arts & fine women, has a famous Statue of the Venus of Medicis, but it being intimated to him that the attitude & native beauties of the fair Goddess would beam too full upon the eye he had her dressed in a green Silk *Lacedemonian* Dress — much like Madame Tallien's — & which giving room to conclude that more was concealed than was really true, only made matters worse. This Evg there is a teaparty at Phillip's. Monday a dance at Liston's, Wednesday a dinner at do., thursday a party at Mrs. Mifflins to all of which I am invited. To some of which I may go. But I can with good conscience sing, "there's little pleasure to be had when my dear Girl's away." . . . The weather grows pleasant, the roads good, and I am impatient to remove all obstacles to your coming to the arms of

Yr affect

H. G. OTIS

Winter seasons in Philadelphia were gay and brilliant. Besides the subscription assemblies and private entertainments, each foreign minister gave a dinner and a ball once a fortnight, and the President and married members of the Cabinet gave private and official dinners and receptions. Color and life were everywhere. The "levelling process of France" had not yet brought the dress of gentlemen to democratic black, and the fair women of the Republican Court dressed like the beautiful subjects of Gainsborough and Sir Joshua. The Duc de la Rochefoucauld Liancourt, who visited Philadelphia at this period, writes: "Le luxe est, comme je l'ai dit, très-grand à Philadelphie, pour la table dans les jours de cérémonie, pour les voitures et pour la parure des dames. J'ai vu des bals, au jour de naissance du Président, où les ornemens de la salle, l'élégance et la variété des parures rappelaient l'Europe; et dans cette comparaison, il faut convenir que la beauté des dames Américaines aurait l'avantage." [8]

The President and his Lady were the official heads of Philadelphia society. General and Mrs. Washington, had been the actual heads also, but President and Mrs. Adams, although experienced in the society of foreign courts, allowed their position to go by default, and were not greatly liked in the society of the Capital. Otis's father, and his aunt Mercy Warren, were close personal friends of the Adamses, who in consequence frequently asked the young Congressman to dine. On one occasion, after a family dinner at the President's, Otis writes his wife, "the retirement of Mrs A. &c gave me the opportunity for a tete a tete with him, which I improved in soliciting for our Friend" — for an appointment, it appears. "I was graciously received but fear the applications are so numerous I shall not prevail." Later: "I was last Evg at the Drawing Room. It was the second evening, but only 16 Ladies were present, perhaps the dullness of the weather was the cause." And on another occasion: "In the morning . . . I went to visit the President. It was nominally grand Levee day, but *really* attended to by a very few persons except the official and diplomatic characters. The weather was bad. Among other Ladies was Madame de Freira who always talks a great deal about you, & who threatens very hard to notice you, when you come next winter."    .

[8] La Rochefoucauld Liancourt, *Voyage dans les Etats-Unis*, VI, 330. Otis sends his wife a few hints on ladies' fashions in December, 1799: "Wigs are *out* here, but the hair is dressed like a wig, with the hair of the back part of the head brought forward forming a sort of bandeau ornamented with little *combs*, some of which I will send you if you have none in Boston. Black Velvet great coats made like an open gown are also the rage. Would not my Velvet suit make you one? If not buy a new one. In short let me know all you want, & indulge me in my only real pleasure that of contributing to your wishes and comfort."

President Adams did not add to his popularity in Philadelphia by refusing to attend the "Birth-night Ball" on February 22, 1798. John Adams always resented playing second fiddle to Washington, whom he considered much his inferior in ability, and he took as a personal insult the public celebration of Washington's birthday instead of his own. The incident gave huge delight to Jefferson and his followers, who, with their usual tendency to magnify trifles, regarded birth-night balls as indications of monarchical designs on the part of the Federalists. "The court is in a prodigious uproar over the event." — "The late birth-night certainly has sewn tares among the exclusive federalists," wrote Gallatin and Jefferson. Otis sympathized with the President. He writes on February 24:

The Birth night ball of last evening was I am told respectably attended, tho by no means equal in splendour & numbers to the last. . . . The President did not attend, & his refusal has given considerable offence, even to some of the federal party. To be sure his apology was rather formal, but I think he acted rightly upon principle. As President, he ought to know of no distinction among private citizens, whatever may be their merit or virtue; & having never received from the Philadelphians, the slightest mark of attention, he was in my mind quite excusable for declining to be the pageant, to do honor to another. Many families who usually increase the flutter of the beau monde were absent. The Morrisites of course. The Binghams who have lately lost a relation, & the Chews on account of a Mrs. Pemberton who died last Sunday; I am told too that the whole house was very damp and believe I have not lost much.

Mrs. William Bingham was the leader of Philadelphia society during Otis's congressional career. Born Anne Willing, the eldest of the three beautiful daughters of Thomas Willing, she married in 1780, at the age of sixteen, William Bingham, a successful merchant of humble extraction, who had amassed a large fortune through privateering and speculating in government warrants. He was elected to the United States Senate in 1795. The Binghams' "Mansion House," as it was always called, was the centre of Philadelphia social life. It occupied with its gardens and stables almost three acres of land, fronting on Third Street at Spruce, and running west to Fourth Street. In style it was a copy of Manchester House in London, but more splendid than the original, and designed primarily for entertaining. On the ground floor were a banqueting-room and library; on the first story the various drawing-rooms, to which one ascended by a broad marble staircase; the entire mansion was furnished in the best taste of that admirable period of domestic art. Here were entertained presidents and cabinet ministers, senators and representatives of the Federal party, and the distinguished *émigrés*, like the Orléans princes, La Rochefoucauld Liancourt, and the sly Talleyrand, who took a temporary refuge in America. Young Louis-Philippe, the future King of the French, courted Mrs. Bingham's sister, but old Mr. Willing refused his consent to the match when that of the dowager Duchesse d'Orléans could not be obtained. At the Bingham mansion were held the "nocturnal caucuses" of the senatorial ring which in 1799 fruitlessly attempted to impose the will of Alexander Hamilton on John Adams.

Mrs. Bingham, young and fascinating, beautiful and wealthy, was the undisputed queen of the Republican Court. Having passed several years with Mr. Bingham in England, where she was greatly fêted and admired, she imported some of the less amiable traits of English society. Like the Duchess of Devonshire and other great ladies of the Court of St. James, she besprinkled her conversation with oaths, and spiced it with facetious anecdotes. In serious contrast to the false prudery that draped the Venus de Medicis, the taste of that time admitted subjects of conversation that to-day seem vulgar, to say the least. The following extracts are fair examples of such intimate conversations in the Bingham set as Otis relates:

Yesterday I dined at Clymers, with the Bingham and Willing Party. Sophia not there. It was the first day of the Bingham's return from the country. . . . Dolly [9] then began to rally Clymer on the subject of his *Stomacher*, . . . and mentioned that one of the British Princes (I think the Duke of York) who had lately married the Princess Wirtemburg has so protuberant a corporation that he was compelled to order a semicircular piece cut out of his dining table, to give him access to his plate. Mrs. Bingham expressed a hint of sympathy for the *Dutchess*, and Clymer told his sister Francis that he should soon be able to retort this *excellent jest* upon her. All this, and much facetious matter of the same kind was received with bursts of applause that would have done credit to the national convention especially by Miss Abby & Miss Ann, who did not disguise their delight nor their bosoms.

And in another letter,

This week, one day I dined at Harrison's, with a family party and Saml Smith & John Brown [10] as Aid de Camps. Old John after rallying Sophia in no very acceptable strain, upon her unfruitfulness, by a natural but not very flattering transition introduced Mrs. Champlin and her want of prolifick qualities as a seasoning for the Canvas Backs. This topic which had a commencement embarrassing to me, whose feelings were excited for our good friends, terminated in a manner most agreeable. Did you never think says Mr. Brown that Mrs Champlin & Mrs. Otis very much resemble each other? Sophia shook

[9] Dolly Francis, Mrs. Bingham's sister.

[10] Samuel Smith (1752–1839), Representative from Baltimore, later Senator. He is the only Democrat mentioned in Otis's letters as being present at a Federalist dining-table. John Brown (1736–1803), of Providence, a prominent merchant, and member of Congress.

her head with dissenting movement. Mr Otis observed that he had not perceived the likeness, & that after the encomiums bestowed on Mrs C. he should hardly venture to make so flattering a comparison, even if he thought it just. Oh the D——l exclaimed S. Smith, there is no comparison at all. Mrs O with all the advantages of the other lady, shows in an instant that she has all her Days been used to Company, her manners are elegant; but this woman with a pretty face, has the air of a country girl.

Mrs. Bingham's imported manners and mannerisms were after all superficial. She was intensely loved by her husband, who died, it is said, of a broken heart not long after her untimely death in 1801. Although for ten years the focus of metropolitan scandal, no whisper against her good name has come down the channels of historical gossip. Her eldest daughter Anne married Alexander Baring, of the celebrated London banking house. As the first Lord Ashburton, his frank and upright negotiation with Daniel Webster over the Maine boundary prevented a war, and furnished a pattern on which all diplomatic negotiations should be modelled. Lady Ashburton had the satisfaction of founding a noble house, but a friend of Mr. Otis, who visited the Ashburtons in England, found her far from happy. "She met with many mortifications," he wrote in his memoirs, "and from nobody so great as from her son's wife, Lady Harriet, and her proud family, that of Earl Sandwich. I am told that at her son's marriage she was not invited to the déjeuner. Certainly Lady Harriet was the most perfect example of insolent ill breeding I ever saw, treated the poor old lady in her own house, at the Grange, with great coolness if not impertinence."

Mrs. Bingham's second daughter, Maria, furnished scandal for the Republican Court from an early age. An old beau, who visited the Binghams with Otis in 1798, predicted that Maria, then aged fourteen, would not "keep" long. About a year later she fulfilled the prophecy, by making a clandestine marriage with the Comte de Tilly, a handsome and profligate Frenchman. To quote again from the memoirs of Otis's nameless friend:

It was a shocking and scandalous affair, and created at the time prodigious sensation in our highest circles. De Tilly was ready, however, to be bought off. He was bribed to furnish evidence against himself, and the divorce was obtained by influence with the Legislature of Pennsylvania, whether by corruption I am not able to say, but in those days Legislatures were supposed to be unassailable in that way.

Otis commented on the situation in a letter to his wife on January 18, 1800:

First then, I just learn that a bill for divorcing Maria Bingham has passed both houses at Lancaster, where Mr Bingham now is. She was however every day walking with her mother while this business was pending and in a dress which you will hardly believe it possible for a lady to wear at least at this season. A muslin robe and her chemise, and no other article of cloathing upon her body. I have been regaled with the sight of her whole legs for five minutes together, and do not know "to what height" the fashion will be carried. The particulars of her dress I have from old Mrs. F—— who assures me that her chemise is fringed to look like a petticoat. However she and the whole family are evidently dejected.

With her divorce scarcely procured, however, Maria, now aged sixteen, had another lover, a young man named Erving, whom Otis thought "conceited, democratical and niggardly." Here is his opinion on this subject expressed more fully:

Thursday evening Miss Peters gave a ball, to which by Erving's special request I procured his admission. Doubtless his principal view was to meet Maria, to whom his attentions were perfectly ridiculous. He scarcely spake to any other Lady, first he danced with her, then sat by her, then followed her up and down when she danced with other persons like a shadow, and in short was so absolutely inattentive to the ladies of the family that I was mortified. It was hinted to me that he has no chance of success, & that Mam'selle is not smitten.

Erving shortly afterwards received his *congé*, and the interesting history of Maria Bingham is continued by our anonymous friend:

Maria B. afterward married Henry Baring,[11] was divorced from him on account of an amour with Captain Webster, the son of Sir Godfrey Webster and the lady, afterwards Lady Holland, who was herself an American of the great Vassall family and was divorced from Sir Godfrey after the birth of her first son by Lord Holland, who could not take his father's title. Mr. Vassall's fortune was enormous and the husband of his daughter was compelled to take the name of Vassall. After Maria Bingham's second divorce, she married a Marquis de Blaizel, a Frenchman in the Austrian army and a Chamberlain of the Emperor. I knew her in Paris, then an old woman but quite an amusing one. She had seen the world in many phases and had plenty of anecdotes which she told pleasantly. She was a very amiable, kind-hearted woman and her faults and frailties were attributable to neglect, in some measure, and the bad company into which she was thrown. Her mother was devoted to fashion and incessantly devoted to company, left her daughter to the instruction of a French governess, who had been an Actress and was probably bought by de Tilly. Henry Baring who had no sense of honor or delicacy, threw her into the most dissipated company, was glaringly unfaithful himself, and it is said, laid a plan for her divorce when he had fallen in love with a young lady who became his second wife. Whether Captain Webster knowingly lent himself to his friend's scheme, I know not. The poor lady was unhappy with her third husband who was a gambler and always in want of money which she could not supply in sufficient sums to satisfy him, for Henry Baring had managed to retain the greater part of her fortune. She lived in rather an equivocal position in Paris. She was received at the Austrian

---

[11] Brother of Alexander Baring who married her sister.

Ambassador's but not at the English Embassy. The public trial in England was a stigma which the most notorious profligacy, not certified in Court, did not affix. I think Louis Phillippe refused her the entrée of the Palais Royal, though this was probably the act of his virtuous wife, otherwise he would not perhaps, have shunned the daughter of the hospitable house where the exiled French princes were so honorably entertained.

The brilliant career of the family in Philadelphia was brief; from Mr. Bingham's return from Europe [in 1789] with his beautiful young wife to her death in [1801]. She took a severe cold in a sleighing party where she exposed herself too soon after the birth of her son, was attacked by lung fever, went almost in a dying state to the Bermudas which she did not live to reach. Her broken-hearted husband went to England where he died in 1804.

Early in 1798, Philadelphia received a shock by the bankruptcy of the great financier of the Revolution, Robert Morris, whose entertainments up to that time had vied with those of the Binghams in splendor. Extensive speculations during a number of years brought the first crash, concerning which Otis wrote in February:

Poor Mr. Morris was yesterday compelled to surrender himself to his bail, and was bro't to his house in town, with a design of going to prison. He was either committed yesterday, or will be today, the Sheriff having kept him in custody. I am told that his family exhibited a dreadful scene of distress, that Mrs M was almost as frantic, and flew upon the Person who was his bail and who bro't him to town and would have committed violence but was prevented. What an example of the folly and vanity of human grandeur. But a few years since he was in wealth and honor, the most considerable man in the United States, & she ruled the world of fashion with unrivalled sway. He will now probably moulder away a few remaining wretched years in prison, and her joys & comforts have probably forever vanished.[12]

[12] Morris was forced to remain in the Prune Street debtors' prison over three years, and came near dying there.

The great man's fall carried many others with him, including the Otises' dear friends, the Harrisons, who were tided over the crisis by the appointment of Mr. Harrison to the office of navy agent for the government. Bankruptcies were not uncommon in the fashionable world of Philadelphia, and Otis writes apropos of another sensational affair of that sort in 1800:

In short everything confirms my opinion that the capital of this country by no means justifies the luxury and style of life affected by so many. Overtrading, & unbounded credit are the mischiefs; bankruptcies & ruin will be the cure, & though I have never thought or called myself rich, I would not exchange my property for that of many who talk of thousands & tens of thousands, as if dollars were needles and pins. Our friends Willing and Francis stand firm; yet am I glad that the notes I hold of theirs fall due from the 9 to the 19 april. They owe me 12500 Dollars, a very serious sum, and such as I will never again suffer to be dependant on any *personal* security whatever.

The most stirring period of Philadelphia's social supremacy immediately followed the X. Y. Z. disclosures of April, 1798. Mr. McMaster gives a vivid description of that time in his history—the patriotic demonstrations at the theatre when the "President's March" was sung to Joseph Hopkinson's new words, the patriotic dinners and toasts, addresses to the President, serenades, and struggles between black cockade and tricolor. Otis, unfortunately for us, was too full of anxiety over a new addition to his family to refer to these scenes in his letters to his wife, which are interrupted early in May, when she joined him at Philadelphia.

The death of Washington, on December 14, 1799, is the subject of Otis's next letter of this series:

My dearest friend,

The sensation of regret excited by the death of Genl. Washington has suspended all public business, and almost excluded private concerns. Congress will be sincerely engaged for some days in paying honor to his memory. In addition to the measures which you will see detailed in the enclosed papers, the Senate have also agreed to wear mourning during the Session, and the walls of their chamber will be entirely hung with black. A joint committee of both houses have also agreed that a funeral eulogium shall be pronounced, and the orator though not named, will *probably* be Genl H. Lee of Virginia. It is contemplated to turn out all the military and to make a grand procession, and it was proposed in the Committee that the Universities of America should send in rotation every four years, an orator to commemorate the event by an oration at the seat of government. This last project however has not yet been adopted; but the affection and regret of the people will seek for any possible mode of demonstrating their sense of this truly great and irreparable loss.

December 26th, from the House of Representatives:

· Before my eyes and in front of the speakers chair lies a coffin covered with a black pall, bearing a military hat & sword. The chair itself & tables shrouded with black. In the background is Washington's portrait. The Members are all provided with black crape for their arms and white scarfs, and in about one hour we shall march attended by the military in grand procession to the German Lutheran Church where funeral obsequies will be performed and an oration delivered by Genl Lee. The day is fine and the streets already so crowded with people that I found it no easy matter to get hither. The concourse will be immense.

At the end of that week comes a long letter, with some interesting comments on Alexander Hamilton and other notables.

I proceed to give my dearest Sally a journal of the last week of my life.

Sunday the 22d. Went to meeting in the morning & heard a young prig of a preacher, who spliced on the end of his discourse a laboured panegyric on Genl Washington which would have been equally suitable to any other sermon. Din'd with Mr.

Francis, old Brown eloquent in favor of the slave trade. Passed an hour in the evening at Breck's [13] A good house on a Sunday evening to see *strange* faces. The parties are truly *select*, being congregated from all quarters of Europe and America. Monday dined with Harrison & Sophia only, went home early and passed the evening with some members of Congress who called in.

Tuesday Dined at Breck's, with Mrs Church,[14] Miss Schuyler, Genl. Hamilton, Champlin [15] &c &c. Mrs. C. the mirror of affectation, but as she affects to be extremely affable and free from ceremony, this foible is rather amusing than offensive. Miss Schuyler a young wild flirt from Albany, full of glee & apparently desirous of matrimony. After Dinner Mrs. C. dropped her shoe bow, Miss S—— picked it up and put it in Hamiltons buttonhole saying "there brother I have made you a Knight." "But of what order" (says Madam C) "he can't be a Knight of the garter in this country." "True sister" replied Miss S—— "but *he would be if you would let him !*" — Mrs Church took me in her coach to make some visits. Nobody at home but the once celebrated Mrs. Craig, whom I was glad of an oppy of seeing & conversing with for a few moments. Went to *see* supper at young A McCalls; the party made for the new married couple, Erskine and Miss Cadwallader; returned home in Bond's coach and narrowly escaped being *stretched at full length with Miss Bond,* by the coachman who was drunk & tried to overset the carriage. Happily this truly amiable and well bred virgin escaped the disaster.

Wednesday Christmas day. — Dined at Aunt Powell's, [16] with the Hares, Francis's & Harrisons. The Dowager is really afflicted at the death of her old friend the General, but she thinks it necessary to appear more so than she is in fact, and that she is called upon in decency to shed tears whenever his name is mentioned. She made out very well at first, but Mr. Hare with a maladroit perseverence would talk of nothing else, so that

[13] Either "Greenbrier," two miles out of Philadelphia, the estate of Samuel Breck (1771–1862, author of some delightful *Recollections*), or the town house of his father of the same name, formerly a merchant of Boston.

[14] *Née* Schuyler, sister of Mrs. Alexander Hamilton.

[15] Christopher G. Champlin (1766–1840), of an old Rhode Island family, a member of Congress from that state.

[16] Mrs. Samuel Powel, *née* Willing, aunt of Mrs. Bingham, of Mrs. George Harrison, and of Charles Willing Hare.

before the cloth was removed, the old Lady's stock of briny
element being fairly exhausted, she could only look piteous and
at length begged a truce of all conversation on the subject,
which being granted she munched her pies with an air of consolation that was truly edifying. I took tea at Bonds, where as
well as at Mr Ross' I was invited to keep christmas. — Thursday attended the procession dined at the Presidents, sat near
Mrs. Wilson, who astonished me by being very sociable. Evening at Read's with the *Church* party, and passed an hour very
agreeably.    Friday dined at the British Minister's — Mrs
Champlin the only Lady. Last week Mrs Church dined at Lis-
tons & Binghams from the same house, yet the Rhode island
beauty was not invited. You may be assured you experienced
*more* attention here, than *any other* lady has met with since Congress sat in this city. Kit took occasion to tell me that Hamilton (who cast some liquorish looks at his cara sposa, the day we
were at Breck's) appears to him very trifling in his conversation with ladies and that his wife said she did not like him at all.
He was evidently *satisfied* with this intimation. Went with Mrs
Liston to the drawing room in the evening and led her in. Both
rooms were crowded and I missed none of my acquaintance
but Mrs Bingham, who burst the gown she had prepared for
the occasion Saturday. I dine with my father, drink tea with
Betsy Francis, and have not a single engagement on hand untill
— tomorrow. I might here add in a note that I have been
every morning before 8 to Schuylkill bridge, and every evening
in bed at ten. I might also indulge in a comparison of these
scenes, or rather of these vicissitudes of eating and drinking,
with the pleasures which I enjoy in your society . . . but I
should grow serious, and my object being to amuse you in some
small degree I forbear, — and will continue to *kill time.* . . .

About the middle of March, 1800, Otis paired off with
an opposition member, and left for Boston. Philadelphia
remained the national capital only a few months longer.
During the summer and autumn of 1800 the federal
government removed to Washington, where the second
and last session of the Sixth Congress opened in November. Washington City, as Mr. and Mrs. Otis saw it on

their approach, was the sharpest possible contrast to civilized Philadelphia. On a hill, in the centre of the potential city, stood the north wing of the Capitol, the only part completed; a mile and a half to the west was the simple and dignified Executive Mansion. All else was desolation: tree stumps, brick kilns, workmen's huts, a few mean frame dwellings, a wilderness of mud, were all that met the eye within the borders of the federal city. Beyond were the forest and the broad sweep of the Potomac. No mansion houses, no shops, no commerce, no people; luxuries unobtainable at any price; even necessities, such as food and fuel, hard to procure: such is the unattractive picture of Washington in 1801, left by contemporaries, who all agreed, however, in admiring the beauty of the site, the noble Potomac, and the wooded background. Comfortable little Georgetown, two miles west of the White House, proved the salvation of transplanted officialdom; without the lodgings it offered, most of the members of the Sixth Congress must have camped out this first winter, or slept in the Capitol. At Georgetown there were a few good taverns, and a small group of well-bred and hospitable people, who did their best to entertain their visitors.

Otis, looking forward to the end of his congressional career and his long period of absence from his family, was cheerful and optimistic on his arrival. He wrote his father-in-law, William Foster, on November 25, 1800:

We arrived here yesterday without any interruption except one days detention at the Susquehannah river, where we consoled ourselves with *canvas backs* for the detention. Sally appears to me in better health than she has enjoyed for a twelve-month; we are better lodged than we expected and much better than the majority of our neighbours. The place too is more pleasant than I had anticipated, tho' there has been a flight of snow that would do credit to a colder clime and higher latitude.

In January, 1801, the Otises made an interesting visit to Mount Vernon, which is described in a letter from Mrs. Otis to her sister, Mrs. Charles Ward Apthorp:

Washington Jany 13 1801 Monday.

I received my dear Marys letter on friday Evening and notwithstanding her long lectures (as she calls them) I must acknowledge myself much gratified by the whole. On Saturday morning we made up our party for Mount Vernon, Mr Mason, Bayard, Francis Mr O. Betsey [17] & myself in two coachees. The roads are bad beyond the utmost stretch of a new england imagination. we got safe to Alexandria which is eight miles from this place on the opposite bank of the potomack no fine cultivated growns to enliven the scene & not one decent house in this immense space but an unenclosed barren heath it appears to me and what the Virginians call Oldfield — here we were overtaken by Söderstrom, Thornton, Morton (Brother to Mrs Quincy) & Govr Howard [18] who were embarked in the same expedition. we knew Mrs Washington to have ten spare beds — but as that was not sufficient for the whole party, we concluded to remain in Alexandria on Saturday, rise early on the next morning and proceed. the last named Gentn went on & we pased a very pleasant day, walked quite over this little City, which is the perfect Miniature of Philadelphia. in the afternoon Mr & Mrs Callender join'd us, they are on a visit *not being able to exist in Georgetown.* the Evening closed as usual with Cards (the only amusement here known among the men) — Sunday commenced the arduous task. nine in the morning departed, the first mile out of the city lost our way and in this error came near *stalling* three times besides the loss of one hour. returned thro the same boggs and set off anew. Mount Vernon is ten miles distant from Alex. The estate is immensely large and inclosed by a high Virginia fence. At the entrance is a gate, after passing which is

[17] The persons mentioned are Otis's friend Jonathan Mason, then Senator from Massachusetts, James A. Bayard, Mr. and Mrs. Thomas Willing Francis of Philadelphia, and Otis himself.

[18] Richard Söderström, consul-general of Sweden; Edward Thornton, British chargé d'affaires; Jacob Morton or his brother Washington, both of whom were well-known New York Federalists; and John Eager Howard, formerly Governor of Maryland, and at this time United States Senator.

a thick wood 4 Miles in length: here we were by intricate wind-
ings twice led astray. you will imagine by this time we were
almost discouraged — a few straggling miserable negroes the
only moving objects, now & then a Mule the one & the other
alike incapable of giving information in this dilemma. Bayard
who is patience *personified* exclaimed "by heaven! this is too
bad." a mute dispair seemed to seize us — when a lad more
decent than those before seen came in view, we enquired. he said,
"you come wrong but you go right" — here we paused; some
ingenuity was required to solve this enigma, finding our capacity
unequal, a second appeal was more successful. we now learned
that we were going to the Mill, but from the Mill was a road to
the House: *true* a very bad one. this revived our drooping spirits
— the safer way however was to secure this guide, which we
accordingly did — and at half past two surmounted all perils by
land & by water and had the satisfaction to see on a beautiful
emminence the Mansion of the great *Washington* and here
description fails me. I can only tell you tis all that we, in our
most romantic moments have imagined of grandeur taste and
beauty. I fancy the soil is not very good but all that taste and
affluence could affect is here attain'd. The House is antique
like the inhabitant: capacious and substantial affording every
comfort & luxury. the wings are more modern, they were added
some years since by the General; in one is a large Hall hung with
the most elegant painting from all parts of europe, (I presume
presents) — himself & favorite horse not the least interesting.
in the other wing is his own particular apartments his chamber
where he died, his study dressing room &c which have nothing
to distinguish them from the chambers of any other house: they
*reminded me of little Cambridge.* Mrs Washington tells me she
has not had resolution to visit these apartments since the death
of the General. she received us with the most gracious cordial-
lity, in her deportment is that mild benevolence that serene
resignation which Characterises the saint — and she speaks of
death as a pleasant Journey which is in contemplation. at the
same time Chearful anxious to perform the most minute
civility and unerring in every duty. the slaves are for the most
part liberated in this instance. she is not so much at her ease
(as the training of a young crop, we all know, is not a small
taske) some few quite old domesticks perferd remaining, these

are almost useless. the Stables are crowded with horses asses and mules, favorites and by the Genls order exempted from labor. the morng of Monday was delightful cold for this climate. I arose with the sun determined to regale myself in these enchanting walks. Mrs Lewis (formaly the beautiful Ellen Custis) & Bet were already prepared. the house lot & gardens included cover ten acres the wall is of brick which incloses it but sunk so that in appearance tis an Open lawn. the walks are irregular & serpentine cover'd by trees of various kinds but what most pleased me was a labyrinth of evergreens where the sun cannot even now penetrate. This must be a little Paradies in summer. I forgot it was not so even now, seeing the spinach & young Cabages growing in the open air — the Kitchen gardens are also beautifully cultivated. on the front of the House is a gradual declivity to the Potowmac & here the scene is indiscribably grand & beautiful. at the distance of a quarter of a mile is seen the Humble tomb of the illustrious Washington known only by the little willows & cypress that wave their melancholy branches over it. I walked down with a solemn and awful sensation to this sacred spot. the housekeeper offerd to run & fetch the key but as the grownd was damp and we perceived Mrs W. walking in the Piazza we declined. she shewd us into the breakfast Room, where was a most sumptious entertainment which we did ample justice to after our long walk. our visit was now made, but I assure you it was very difficult to get away. she urged us in the most flattering manner to remain a few days with her: I sincerely regretted that it was not in my power as I was facinated with every thing about me. we dined again in Alexandria and slept in Washington on Monday night. and now my dear Mary you will not say I have omitted any part of this rout, and any deficiencies that you may name I will endeavor to make good. I have been trying to finish this letter since Monday it is now thursday & I declined going to the georgtown Assembly where Betsy my Hub. & all the beaux are, determined to seal it this night. perhaps you will say better for me when I tell you I was dancing Cotillions till two on Teusday Ngt, and dined at the presidents today with 30 gentlemen and Ladies a select and agreable party — and tomorrow dear Mary we rise at five and depart for Philadelphia from which place I hope to give you an accurate detail of fashion. in the

meantime wear your wig with a wreath of flowers thro — or a
band of crape folded thick with a long end hanging down on
the right side with a silk, or silver, or bead, tassell & two handsome large feathers on the back part, falling forward. a fine
muslin trimmed with a fine lace without starch is very pretty
if you wear a muslin dress. I advise you to harbour no *evil con-
jectures* about your sister who is in better health and as good
spirits as you generally find her. . . .

Otis's letters which followed his wife to Philadelphia
are full of details on the exciting incidents of the last two
months of the Federalist era, — the attempt to renew the
Sedition and the Judiciary Acts, and the choice between
Jefferson and Burr for the presidency.[19] They also show
that the good people of Georgetown were doing their
best to make their guests forget the splendors of Mr.
Breck's dinners and Mrs. Bingham's balls. On February
1, 1801, Otis writes:

Since my last I have dined with Plater and tried my luck once
more at a ball at Lingans. The Col & I went together, and the
evening being pleasant, we ascended the rock on which the house
is situated & returned without danger. Our entertainment
consisted first of tea, served out about 8 oclock. Then the
dancing continued without interruption untill *twelve. After that*
chocolate in cups with dry toast was handed round among the
ladies, and *after that*, the gentlemen were regaled in a back par-
lour with a cold ham, mutton & tongue.

I have concluded to go to no more balls, for though the party
here was on the whole agreeable & genteel yet they have all the
strangest way of assorting people in the world. There was 3
or 4 federal members of Congress, together with *Christie Randolph Dawson Holmes & Van Cortlandt,* and I confess I do not
enjoy myself with these people.

The objectionable gentlemen were prominent Republicans from Maryland, Virginia, and New York. It was
quite natural for one who had been the target of John

[19] See chap. XII.

Randolph's bony finger and callow invective to take exception to his presence at an evening entertainment; but the only objection to the others was the mere fact that they were Democrats. Otis evidently preferred the strictly Federalist society of Philadelphia.

On February 15, 1801, Otis describes similar gatherings:

My dearest friend

If I mistake not I mentioned in my last that I was at Johnsons and at Burrows' balls the last week so that you see the fatigue of electioneering was diversified by other fatigue. At Johnsons the party was made brilliant by the presence of several really fine and fashionable Annapolitans. The supper however was shabby beyond all former precedent. A sideboard with a round of cold beef & a ham which the dear ladies were obliged to eat on their blessed knees, presented the sum total of the appropriation for the craving demands of divers florid and carnivorous animals of both sexes. Still the evening was sufficiently agreeable, and I have since learnt that I made a conquest of a very charming young lady from the Metropolis of Maryland, to whom I was not introduced & did not speak. *What a misfortune to be so irresistible.*

We fared still better chez Burrows. Fine music & an elegant supper were among the consolations for disappointment at the absence of many guests who were prevented by weather. Sally and her mamma acquitted themselves in their most amiable manner. Huger [20] danced on his toes as usual with every flirt in the room, while his sedate and venerable lady bedizzened & bejewelled kept a stedfast and deploring eye upon his eccentric follies, and turned a *deaf* ear to the civilities and sighs of those who surrounded her. Mrs B—— took care to apprise me that this party was originally intended for Betsy Francis & yourself. That the cake was actually made while you were here, but that a series of accidents foreign and domestic, and of interferences & disappointments enough to melt a heart of stone compelled them to defer it untill this moment.

Thus you see I continue to trifle away the residue of my weari-

[20] Benjamin Huger, a member of Congress from South Carolina.

some pilgrimage; I will not say here how much I miss you . . .
A carriage this moment stops to take me to the capitol and I
must close this letter or lose this mail.

The gallant little note of February 23, here reproduced
in facsimile, concludes this series of letters, in which we
can readily perceive that the removal of the federal
government to Washington had caused a serious rift in
the alliance between society and politics. The Democratic revolution of 1800 effectually completed this
break. No Republican Court was possible with the
materials of the Jeffersonian epoch or the setting of the
backwoods village that Washington remained for many
years. Thomas Jefferson, in soiled corduroy breeches and
slippers down at the heel, receiving the British minister
at the White House, is as typical of the new order, as
were Washington's stately levees and Mrs. Bingham's
balls of the old régime. Aristocracy was beheaded by the
peaceful guillotine of the ballot, and the plain people, led
by the apostle of Democracy, reigned in its place.

Washington Feby 23. 1801

My dearest friend,

Your patriotic permission to me to remain here untill the 4th instant, has rendered you so popular with the Federal part of the house that I believe they would gladly make you Speaker in the room of Mr S— but I wish to see you in no chair, untill I see you in an easy chair in your own chamber, when I should take the liberty to taste of your cheek — I have no earthly thing, to add, having already written to Sophia this morning, and am (in a great worry to see you) as always

yr truly affect
HGOtis

FACSIMILE LETTER OF HARRISON GRAY OTIS

# CHAPTER X

In the interval between the second and third sessions of the Fifth Congress, from July to December, 1798, an important change took place in the state of relations with France. The Directory, alarmed at the unexpected spirit of resentment in the United States, promised to receive an American minister in Paris, and removed obstacles to negotiation by ordering the destruction of American commerce to cease. On the question whether France should be taken at her word, or a policy of no treaty with France, and war to the death, should be followed, the Federal party split in two.

After the three envoys in Paris sent off the X. Y. Z. dispatches, in January, 1798, they prolonged the quasi-negotiations with Talleyrand and his agents for three months. By that time, since Talleyrand refused either to call off his commerce destroyers or to receive the envoys, and hinted that Gerry alone of the three would be an acceptable medium of negotiations, Pinckney and Marshall decided to leave France. The only proper thing for Gerry to have done under those circumstances was to leave likewise. Flattered, however, by Talleyrand's intimations that he alone could effect what the three together could not, and fearful of "provoking" France into a declaration of war, he remained in Paris three months longer, patiently enduring the alternate bluffing and bullying of Talleyrand. Finally this treatment became too much for him, and he demanded his passports. At this point, however, news reached France of the rising spirit in America, and of the new system of maritime reprisals enacted by the Fifth Congress. Talleyrand saw at once that he had overreached himself. The French party in America was not so strong, nor public spirit so humble, as he had been led to expect. His idea, as we have seen, was not to make war on the United States, but to force it, if possible, into giving indirect aid to France against Great Britain, and to gain time in order to secure Louisiana from Spain. He now perceived that he must renounce the first in order to gain the second object. Gerry was detained, therefore, in France, long enough to be shown that the Directory intended to mend its manners. Talleyrand substituted whining for bullying in his diplomatic notes; he resigned all demands for an apology or a loan; he promised to receive any envoy whom the United States might see fit to send. He suddenly pretended to have discovered the piratical activities of French agents in the West Indies, about which the American Government had been complaining for two years, and ordered them to cease; and the Directory lifted an embargo which had been laid on American vessels in French ports. This change of tactics was a triumph for the spirited national policy of the Federal party, a complete justification of its leaders' claim that the only way to get justice from France was to retaliate.[1]

Meanwhile, Gerry's conduct in remaining in Paris as Talleyrand's butt after the other envoys had departed, was the object of bitter attack from high Federalists. Gerry had been suspected by them from the first, since his conversion to Federalism was of recent date and

[1] Cf. Codman's letter from Paris at end of this chapter.

incomplete, and his lack of judgment was now ascribed to
"French Influence." John Adams, at first, was as much
mortified as any one at Gerry's conduct, but, when
Pickering threatened to expose "not his pusillanimity
and weakness alone, but his *duplicity* and *treachery*,"
the President rallied to the support of his old friend.[2]
His private conversation began to show so alarming a
tendency to vindicate Gerry at the expense of his colleagues, that the Essex Junto, after consulting among
themselves, sent Otis to Quincy in order to tell the
President "how much his frankness exposes himself and
his friends." [3] This was but one of many instances in
which Otis's superior tact secured him the honor of performing some particularly delicate or disagreeable political mission. That he succeeded in this case is evident
from a temporary cessation of complaints about the
President's garrulity; but it is left to our imagination to
discover by what means young Otis managed to convince
a pompous and irascible old gentleman, twice his age,
that he talked too much.

About a week before Otis's visit to the President took
place (October 28), Gerry himself arrived in Boston.
"He landed at Long Wharf about one," wrote Manasseh
Cutler.[4] "The Federalists, by agreement, took not the
least notice of him as he walked up State Street; not a
hat was moved." Although feigning indifference, the
Federalists were most anxious lest Gerry follow Monroe's
example and vindicate his conduct in France by attacking
the Federalist foreign policy. It was thought best to send
some one to fathom his intentions, and, as usual, Otis
was selected for the task. At the interview, according to
a letter of George Cabot,

        [2] *King*, II, 397; Adams, *Works*, VIII, 596, 616.
      [3] Gibbs, II, 110.                [4] *Life of Manasseh Cutler*, II, 8.

Mr Otis intimated to him the state of public opinion concerning him: that the friends of the government were not satisfied, and that its enemies had calculated upon finding in him a character round which they might rally with new spirit. He replied that he was sensible of the predicament in which he stood, but he thought it an ill compliment to his understanding to suppose he could be made subservient to the designs of the opposition.[8]

Gerry was as good as his word. Although Federalist abuse of him continued, and Jefferson made a wily appeal to his personal vanity to air his grievances, he made no complaint, and even issued a statement indorsing the Federalist policy.

Shortly after performing these political embassies, Otis was reëlected to Congress. His opponent was General William Heath, — to whom his published letter on the arming of merchant vessels had been addressed, — and a far more popular and formidable adversary than James Bowdoin had been in 1796. The usual duel between the *Centinel* and the *Chronicle* took place both before and after the election. General Heath, who at the worst was but a well-meaning old soldier, not blessed with over-much brain, was attacked in the *Centinel* as "the ridiculous, despicable, weak-minded, weak-hearted Jacobin, commonly distinguished by the appellation of the *Hero of Fort Independence*," a good example of the insolence of Federalism in 1798. The *Chronicle* made no personal attack on Otis, but charged upon the Sedition Law and the Direct Tax, which over half the Republicans had voted for, and endeavored to turn to advantage the rural prejudice against lawyers. It was argued that there were too many lawyers in Congress, that the Sedition Act and the "land tax" were adopted by lawyers in order to make more business for themselves. Let the yeomanry go to the polls, and outvote the foreigners and

[8] H. C. Lodge, *Cabot*, 179.

negroes who secured a majority for Ames and Otis in former elections.[6] The popularity of the Federalist foreign policy is shown by the fact that no one ventured to attack that phase of Otis's activity, beyond the statement that his calling Frenchmen "pyrates, rogues, etc.," was a bar to negotiation. General Heath's candidature was even announced in one instance as that of a "Constitutional Federalist."[7]

In the electioneering Otis took no part. Happily for the peace of mind and the pocketbook of a candidate in those days, any active participation in his own campaign was considered highly improper. But that zealous efforts were made on both sides, is indicated by the size of the vote, which was twenty-seven per cent greater than that of 1796, a presidential year. All the increase in Boston went to Otis, but in the rural part of the district General Heath polled more than twice as many votes as his opponent. The *Chronicle's* campaign against lawyers and the "land tax" was evidently effective.

Political intolerance was fast becoming a leading characteristic of the entire Federal party. Otis, during the winter session of Congress, led an attack on Dr. Logan, a Philadelphia Quaker and Democrat who had gone on a secret mission to France in order to prevent war.[8] Luckily for him, the *ex post facto* provision in the Constitution shielded him from punishment, but no mercy was shown to persons who made themselves amenable to the Sedition

---

[6] *Chronicle*, November 1 and 5, 1798.

[7] *Chronicle*, November 5. In Newark, New Jersey, the Democrats announced their own nominations as the "Federal Republican Ticket," and those of the Federalists as the "Federal Aristocratic Ticket." *Chronicle*, October 22. Ten years later the tables were turned, and Federalist tickets were concealed under such names as "American," "True Republican," "Anti-Embargo," etc.

[8] See letter of Joseph Woodward, at end of chapter, for Otis's part in the Logan affair.

Law. Federal judges enforced it rigorously, and stimulated grand juries to present cases. The first victim was Matthew Lyon, "the beast," the hero of the spitting episode in Congress. He was convicted, fined, and imprisoned for charging the President, among other things, with "unbounded thirst for ridiculous pomp, foolish adulation, and selfish avarice." One Baldwin of Newark was fined one hundred dollars for expressing the wish that the wadding of a cannon, discharged in honor of the President while passing through that town, might find lodgment in his posterior. John Lovejoy of Dedham was committed to jail for erecting a liberty pole with the inscription —

> Liberty and Equality!
> The Vice President and the Minority!
> A Speedy Retirement to the President!
> No Sedition Bill! No Alien Bill!
> Downfall to the Tyrants of America![9]

This persecution extended even into the affairs of private life. To quote a contemporary: "Friendships were dissolved, tradesmen dismissed, and custom withdrawn from the Republican party, the heads of which, as objects of the most injurious suspicion, were recommended to be closely watched, and committees of Federalists were appointed for that purpose." [10]

This whole phase of Federalist policy shows the party's fundamental defect, — a disregard of popular ideas and opinions; a policy suicidal to a party that had to depend for its support on the people's suffrage. John Marshall, alone among prominent Federalists, dared publicly to

[9] *Russell's Gazette*, April 1, 1799. Fisher Ames complained of the "tardiness and apathy on the part of the government, in avenging this insult on law. . . . The government must display its power, *in terrorem*, or, if that be neglected or delayed, in earnest." *Works*, I, 247.

[10] Deborah Logan, *Memoir of Dr. George Logan*, 54–55.

express his disapproval of the Sedition Act. For this independence of mind he received the unqualified denunciation of the Eastern party leaders. "Otis . . . condemns him *ore rotundo*," wrote Fisher Ames; "False federalists, or such as act wrong from false fears, should be dealt hardly by, were I Jupiter Tonans." "What does he mean?" inquired another member of the Junto. "I sometimes have been led to think that some of the Virginia Federalists are little better than half-way Jacobins." [11] If dislike of the Sedition Act was to be the test of Jacobinism, then most assuredly a majority of the American people were half-way, if not fully, Jacobins.

Meanwhile, the Federal party was gradually being shifted into two rival factions. Their nuclei had been formed years before, in the personal rivalry and mutual distrust that existed between John Adams and Alexander Hamilton. The President, who always had regarded Hamilton as an impudent upstart, resented the respect accorded his opinion in the Federal party; Hamilton, on the other hand, considered Adams a vain and pompous old man, totally unfit for his high position. During the election of 1796, he publicly announced his desire that Thomas Pinckney should be brought in as president over Adams's head, contrary to the express agreement of the party caucus.

A quarter of a century later, when he was eighty-seven years old, John Adams wrote Otis a number of letters on the events of 1798 and 1799. In the concluding letter of the series he remarked, "the amount of my former letters to you is this; that all the sovereignty then existing in the nation was in the hands of Alexander Hamilton." The old gentleman here describes the exact state of affairs. At no period in the history of the United States has one

[11] H. C. Lodge, *Cabot*, 179.

man possessed so potent an influence over the federal government as Alexander Hamilton exerted during Washington's second administration, and the first half of his successor's. John Adams was susceptible to influence, when skillfully handled and flattered, and he made an initial mistake in taking over Washington's Cabinet, which contained three men, Timothy Pickering, Oliver Wolcott, and James McHenry, devoted to Hamilton and used to taking orders from him. The President's opening address to the Fifth Congress was an unconscious echo of Hamilton's suggestions to the Cabinet. In a similar manner, all important steps in executive policy, during the first two years of Adams's administration, originated in Hamilton's brain. General Washington, the lieutenant-general of the army, deferred to him in all things, and his influence helped to force Hamilton's policies on the President. Said the victim of this system to Otis, after twenty-five years, "I cannot review that tragicomic farce, grave as it was to me, without laughing. I was as President a mere cipher, the government was in the hands of an oligarchy consisting of a triumvirate who governed every one of my five ministers; both houses of Congress were under their absolute direction."

At the beginning of the third session of the Fifth Congress, in December, 1798, Otis's experience and ability were recognized by an appointment to the important position of Chairman of the Committee on Defense. The following letter, which he wrote to Hamilton a few days after this event, shows that he, too, was completely under Hamilton's influence.

Philadelphia, Dec. 21, 1798.

Sir:

I was very solicitous while you were in the city for the indulgence of an interview with you, that would have enabled

me to learn your opinion in relation to such defensive measures
as ought now to be adopted by Congress; and I called upon you
once with that view; but being then disappointed and perceiving afterwards the pressing nature of your immediate avocations, I chose rather to forego the advantage of your sentiments,
than invade the little leisure you appeared able to command.
Being since appointed chairman of a committee to consider the
policy of extending our internal means of defence, the great confidence which I feel in the correctness of your political opinions,
and your permission on a former occasion to avail myself of
them, induce me to request that I may be honoured with your
general ideas upon this subject, if you can without inconvenience devote an hour to my instruction. In particular, is it advisable to augment the present permanent army under all circumstances? If not, would it be eligible to reduce the number
of men in each regiment, with a view to economy, and to an
application of the money saved to the extension of the naval
armament? or are there any prominent defects in the military
establishment which demand a reform?

Will there be any utility in reviving the section of the act
which establishes the provisional army, or the act for providing for the draft of 80,000 militia?

Does good policy demand very liberal grants of money for
fortifications?

Is it expedient to continue the act prohibiting intercourse
with France and her acknowledged dominions? If so, as the
act now stands, may commerce be carried on between the
United States and any part of the French dominions that shall
withdraw from its allegiance to the parent country? or, if this be
doubtful, would it be politic to grant an express commission
to the President to open the trade with any part of the French
dominions, when, in his opinion, the public good would admit
or require it?

Shall the President be authorized to attack, capture, and hold
all or any of the French West India islands as an indemnity for
the spoliations committed on our trade?

If on this, or any other subjects, you see fit to gratify me with
your opinions, they will be cherished and respected by me without a disclosure of the source from which they are derived; and
if, on the other hand, you think this liberty is not warranted

by the duration or intimacy of my personal acquaintance, you will, I hope, excuse and impute it to an habitual and profound respect for your character and talents.

I am, Sir,

Your most obedient servant,

H. G. OTIS.[12]

This <u>unhealthy state of affairs</u> could endure only by the President's ignorance of the fact that he was being led. Down to June, 1798, he was wholly unsuspicious; but that summer arose the complication about major-generals, which opened his eyes. This incident need not detain us here; suffice it to say that Adams wished to give the three major-generals of the new army, Knox, Pinckney, and Hamilton, the priority of rank that they possessed in the Revolutionary army, which would have placed Hamilton at the foot, and that Hamilton and his friends in the Cabinet, who wished him to be virtual commander-in-chief, used all their efforts to have the old order rescinded in his favor. After General Washington had used his influence in this direction, the President sulkily complied, but, as he wrote McHenry, "there has been too much intrigue in this business." From that point began the parting of the ways between the President and the Hamiltonian wing of his party.

During the third session of the Fifth Congress, from December, 1798, to March, 1799, Otis, as Chairman of the Committee on Defense, recommended to Congress the measures that Hamilton desired, and secured the passage of most of them.[13] It was also during this session that the Federal party was given an opportunity to show that it could repel aggression from England as well as from France. In November, 1798, Captain Loring, of the

---

[12] Reprinted from Hamilton, *Works*, VI, 377.

[13] Hamilton's replies to Otis's letter of December 21 are printed in his *Works*, VI, 379, 390.

British frigate *Carnatic*, boarded the American twenty-gun ship *Baltimore*, took off fifty-five of the crew, and impressed five of them. It was a worse outrage than the *Chesapeake* affair of 1807, but it attracted less interest on account of the naval war with France that was going on. In the House of Representatives, on December 31, 1798, Otis proposed a resolve, calling for information concerning the assault, "as we think it necessary to show Great Britain and the world that instances of abuse of this kind excite a lively sensibility, and that we are determined to protect our flag against any country whatever." A vigorous protest was made by the State Department, and the British government apologized.

The most interesting problem, however, of this winter session was the question of how to treat the changed policy of France. It proved to be a rock on which the Federal party split. In his annual address of December 8, 1798, the President indicated that his mind was favorably inclined toward the friendly advances of Talleyrand. This attitude aroused violent indignation in the ranks of the Hamiltonian Junto, for accommodation with France was no part of their system. Hamilton and his friends considered the French overtures as further evidence of duplicity. Stephen Higginson, of the Essex Junto, wanted a headlong plunge into the European political system, a British alliance, and a treaty of guarantee at the end of the war;[14] Hamilton wrote Otis, and other members of Congress, demanding war with France by the summer, a permanent standing army, and an attack on Florida, Louisiana, and South America. He was then coquetting with Francisco de Miranda's gigantic project for the liberation of Spanish America by

[14] *1896 Reports of the American Historical Association*, 1, 817, 819, 821.

an American army and a British fleet, with Louisiana
and Florida a share for the United States in the plunder.

Hamilton's schemes might to-day be regarded respectfully if Napoleon had not seen fit, in 1803, to toss us
Louisiana, "as a sultan throws a purse of gold to a
favorite." Talleyrand's overtures were sincere in that
he wished to avoid war, and was willing to renounce the
hope of a loan or a secret alliance. They were insincere
in that one of his reasons for avoiding war was a desire
to gain time for the peaceful acquisition of Louisiana.
Even Thomas Jefferson could write, when he heard of
the success of this policy in 1802, "The day that France
takes possession of New Orleans, . . . we must marry
ourselves to the British fleet and nation." Yet in 1798
Hamilton's design was impossible to accomplish. The
United States was no field for the Old-World policy of
foreign war to quell domestic discontent. Well might
Adams feel, as he wrote Otis, "this man is stark mad, or
I am. He knows nothing of the character, the principles,
the feelings, the opinions and prejudices of this nation.
If Congress should adopt this system, it would produce
an instantaneous insurrection of the whole nation from
Georgia to New Hampshire." One needs only to read the
Kentucky and Virginia Resolutions of 1798, to perceive
that such a plan as Hamilton's would not have been
supported six months by the people of the United States.

Hamilton and the Cabinet, then, decided to treat
Talleyrand's overtures as insincere, and declare war on
France. They counted as usual on the acquiescence of the
President, for, in spite of his peaceful message of December 8, he permitted Pickering, during the following month,
to issue as a state paper a pungent analysis of the Talley-
rand-Gerry correspondence, the object of which was to
expose the French statesman's insincerity. Shortly after

this, however, there suddenly dawned on John Adams
the extent to which he had been led by Hamilton and
the cabinet cabal. Convinced in his own mind that the
French desired peace, and determined henceforth to be
President in fact as well as in name, he sent to the Senate
on February 18, 1799, a message that sent Hamilton's
dreams of glory to the limbo of shattered ambitions.
This message, which arrived like a projectile out of a
clear sky, was the nomination of a minister plenipoten-
tiary to the French Republic.

The President's policy was undoubtedly right, but his
manner of carrying it out was a typical instance of his
tactlessness. He had taken this radical departure in
foreign policy without consulting a single member of the
Cabinet. No wonder, then, that Hamilton and his powerful following smelt treachery in the act. Words cannot
describe the feelings of mingled rage, astonishment, and
disappointment with which they received it.[15] They
controlled the majority in the Senate, but, conscious that
public opinion would side with the President, they dared
not reject his nomination. A compromise, however, was
effected; the Senate agreed to confirm a peace commission
of three, instead of a single envoy, and the President
promised not to send them to France until the French
government sent unequivocal assurances that they
would be properly received.

The attitude of Otis on this momentous occasion was
wise and moderate. That he deplored as much as any
one the President's action, is evident from his correspondence.[16] Otis was too much under Hamilton's influence

---

[15] The tense feeling at Philadelphia is well illustrated by a graphic description of a dinner at the President's, in a letter he wrote Otis a half-century later.
Printed at end of this chapter.

[16] "And well may you be in affliction," etc., in Mason's letter of February
27, 1799, at end of this chapter.

to view the inception of negotiations with France otherwise than as a calamity. Yet his political commonsense
taught him what Hamilton and his more ardent followers
utterly failed to see, that the only course now open to the
Federal party was to follow where the President led.[17]
Any attempt to thwart him would render the dangerous
rift in the party permanent and irreparable. Most Federalists thought as Otis did,[18] but a real danger to party
harmony lay in the headstrong intolerance of Hamilton
and the Essex Junto.

Otis did his best to preserve harmony and gain adherents to the President's policy by writing a series of
articles addressed to the inflexible anti-gallicans in his
party. They were published anonymously under the
heading "The Envoy" in *Russell's Gazette*, early in
April, 1799. He begins by stating that the most "respectable and patriotic characters," who have followed French
policy in Europe, feel that "Gallic faith affords no basis
for a safe or advantageous treaty," and desire *bellum
usque ad internecionem*. But although their fears may
be well founded, and although "a continued exertion and
display of our energies might invigorate the tone of the
government . . . and increase our importance in the esti-

---

[17] Stephen Higginson wrote Timothy Pickering from Boston, March 24,
1799: "Mr. Ames, Cabot and myself were at Jona Masons, where we had a free
conversation with Otis, Lee of the Maine, and Gordon of N: H: on the subject
of the late mission. Otis professes to think of the measure as we have all done,
he views it, he says, as an unfortunate injudicious One, tending to induce great
Evils, and incapable of effecting any good; but he is evidently disposed to
palliate and soften as much as possible. . . . he will deprecate and oppose anything like a disapprobation of the measure; but has pledged himself not to
approve. he will be for avoiding both, and will pass unnoticed expressions
which may call for attention, a conduct which will be construed into a tacit
approbation, and incur the displeasure of the combined powers, while it divides
the federalists and strengthens the Jacobins." *1896 Report of the American
Historical Association*, I, 832.

[18] All but two Federalist newspapers supported the President. Cf. Steiner,
*McHenry*, 407–08, Wm. Jay, *John Jay*, II, 296; *King*, III, 183.

mation of foreign nations," public sentiment would not for a moment support such a system in the face of the French offers. "In the opinion of many intelligent men," evidently including Otis himself, war should have been declared by Congress during the second session, and, owing to this "fatal and impolitic omission, the popular zeal and enthusiasm" had subsided "for want of impulse." The only way of repairing this error is "by convincing the people that no occasion of preserving peace has been omitted, and by affording to them another instance of the duplicity and perfidy of France," — an argument intended to reach the war Federalists. The light and informal character of the French overtures has been taken, Otis says, as a proof of insincerity, but "we can never treat, if we must be *first* satisfied of the sincerity of *France*." We must "put their sincerity to the touchstone more than once by taking them at their word." Our honor and dignity will not be impaired by the President's policy. The King of England has twice instituted peace negotiations with France during the present war, and with most happy results on public opinion. A comparison on the score of honor and dignity is not disadvantageous to us. "Can we make war with success, if we reject overtures apparently pacific?"

If Hamilton and the Essex Junto had followed this sound advice, the fatal split would have been averted; but they did not listen to it. The orthodoxy of Otis's Federalism had long been suspected, as we have seen, by the inflexible gentlemen who composed the Essex Junto. Timothy Pickering, a few weeks after receiving Higginson's account of Otis's opinions, in the letter just quoted, was told that Otis was talking rather freely of an "oligarchic faction" that intended to control the government

and elect the next President.[19] A groundless rumor, then
in circulation, to the effect that Otis coveted Pickering's
position of Secretary of State[20] must also have reached
his ears. It was wholly natural, then, that Pickering,
tenacious of his office, and ever on the lookout for political defection, should put the worst possible construction
on Otis's course of action, and ascribe his endeavors
for party harmony to the unworthy motive of place-
hunting. In answer to Higginson he wrote on December
23, 1799:

[Otis] has two principal objects in view: to please the President, & *merit his favour;* and *to acquire popularity.* [I urge
you, and all your] intelligent friends, to whom alone it is practicable, to take some measures, which may controul the projects of Mr. Otis. It is possible you may present to his view some
things more alarming than his present pursuits are alluring.
Vain and ambitious, without principles to controul these dangerous passions, he will work, perhaps fatal mischiefs. The remedy should be speedily applied. I have authority for believing
that he is, and for some time has been, the tool of —— [21] and
the father a miserable tale-bearer. The insinuating address of
the former, and the apparent simplicity of the latter, qualify
them for their respective offices.[22]

Among the Adams papers is a document that seems at
first glance to confirm Pickering's unflattering estimate
of Otis's motives for supporting the President's policy.
It is a letter from Otis to the President, dated February
21, 1799 (three days after the nomination of a minister to
France), in which Otis requests for himself the appointment of Secretary of the Legation at Paris, "if it could be

[19] See above, note 17, and below, p. 182.
[20] Gibbs, ii, 315.      [21] Left blank in the manuscript.
[22] Pickering MSS., xii, 371–75. Higginson replied with some further attacks
on Otis's character. Otis, apparently, was unconscious of the enmity Pickering
and Higginson felt toward him.

accompanied with a provisional appointment to succeed
the Minister at the Hague in the event of his being received at Paris." It is clear, then, that Otis expected to
derive personal benefit from the new policy. But this
expectation did not last long, for the President refused
him the desired position; and as he nevertheless remained
faithful to the Adams wing of the party during the election of 1800, he must have acted from principle, and not
from mere hope of personal advancement.

John Adams was only intermittently bold; he was incapable of carrying out his peace policy consistently.
Instead of dismissing the Hamiltonian members of the
Cabinet, and appointing men who would be loyal to him
and his policy, he not only retained them in office, but
left them in charge of the government while he passed
the spring and summer at Quincy. The result of his
indecision was a brief Hamiltonian restoration; and
when, in May, 1799, a definite welcome to the new mission came from Talleyrand, and the President ordered
his Secretary of State to make preparations for its departure, Pickering procrastinated.[22] By October, after
an absence of seven months from the seat of government,
John Adams finally awoke to the situation, hastened to
Philadelphia, reasserted his power with his customary
tactlessness, and sent off the envoys to France without
consulting his Cabinet. Henceforth the breach in the
party was irreparable. Hamilton and Pickering were not
the sort of men to maintain even a nominal loyalty to
a chief who thus spurned their advice and flouted their
policy.

[22] Hamilton and his friends hoped that the success of Archduke Charles and
Suvarov would soon bring Louis XVIII to his own, and avoid all necessity of
negotiating with the Directory. *Correspondence between John Adams and Wm.
Cunningham* (1823), letter XIV; *Virginia Magazine of History and Biography*,
XII, 409.

## LETTERS ON FRENCH RELATIONS AND THE LOGAN AFFAIR

### RICHARD CODMAN [24] TO OTIS

Paris 26 August 1798

My dear Sir

At a crisis like the present I thought it might be agreable to you to receive a letter from an old friend & acquaintance whose principles you know, and who from having resided so long in this country may be supposed capable of giving pretty accurate information on the actual situation of public affairs here, & particularly as regards the present disposition of this Goverment towards that of America. Mr. Gerry will have made you acquainted with the change that had taken place before his departure from Paris viz. The total relinquishment of all demands of a loan, or money in any shape, a desire to put aside all recriminations for injurious speeches on the one part or the other, & an arrêté of the Directory recalling all Commissions granted to Privateers and ordering new ones to be issued under certain restrictions to respect the neutral flag.

By the last note from Mr Talleyrand to Mr Gerry you will also have observed the assurances of the french Goverment to receive the person the American Govern. might chuse to send to settle finally the existing differences. Such was the state of affairs when Mr Gerry left us, the Directory have been induced to make this essential alteration in their conduct from the representations made to them by Dupont, Kosciusko, Volney & others lately from America, Dupont particularly in a memoire he has lately presented to them has so opened their Eyes respecting the horrid depredations made by their Cruisers in the West Indies (of which I believe they were in a great measure before ignorant) that they *really* appear anxious to convince America of their desire to redress her grievances, to show this desire unequivocally they have passed an arrêté which releases all American Sailors detained in Prisons in the interior & in the different Sea-ports. By another arrêté they have raised the Embargo on American vessels, & Mr Skipwith in a note from Mr

[24] Codman was a Boston Federalist, and a classmate of Otis.

Talleyrand is assured that a minister from America to settle
finally the disputes will be received in an amicable manner.
Much has been done to endeavour to persuade the Goverment
to send a Minister to America to treat at Phila, but there seems
to be a fear that from the present temper of the American Govt
he would not be received, they are therefore not inclined to
risque it.

Such as I have above stated is the present situation of affairs
here, the moment is extremely favourable for an accomodation.
I hope most sincerely that our Goverment will see it in the
same light & once more risque sending a minister. It is remarkable that in the same proportion as the measures of the American Govt have been vigorous & decided, in that same proportion has this Govt been better & better disposed, it has been
owing, in some measure, to their having been lately better informed of the wrongs we have suffered, & perhaps more than
all, the Union which has been displayed in America which has
convinced this Goverment that it is not for their interest to
force America thus united into the arms of Great Britain, they
know well that a nation so united would be an encouraging &
useful ally.

I hope to God that on the arrival of the dispatches which Mr
Skipwith sends, by the Vessel that carries this, no declaration
of War will have taken place or alliance made with great Britain,
if not & the desire for Peace still continues with our Goverment
I think they may count on an equal desire on the part of France,
& a reconcilliation yet be brought about, which ought to be
desired by all true friends to both countries.

Doctor Logan of Phila arrived here about 10 days since from
Hamburg, previous to which the french Goverment had come
to the determination of taking the measures I have mentioned
to you, the manner in which he has expressed himself to the
Directory (for he has had an interview with 3 of them) had been
very satisfactory to me, he had endeavoured to impress on
their minds that none but Intriguants & the Enemies of both
Countries will hold out to them an idea that there will be any
party in America in case of a War to aid the plans of France or
assist them in case of invasion, that on the contrary every
American would regard with horror the very idea of it, & be
ready to rally around the standard of Goverment to oppose

all its Enemies and particularly to resist, with force & energy, a foreign invasion. He has fully explained this to Mr Talleyrand & in so doing has in my opinion essentially served his Country.

The measure taken by our Govt to stop all commercial intercourse with this Country and its dependances has had the best effect, it is an arm that may I think be employed to advantage against any nation that may in future insult us. . . .[25]

. I am with much Esteem Your friend & Obt. Servant

RICHD CODMAN

· Copy. Original by Mr Woodward [26]


JOSEPH WOODWARD [27] TO OTIS

Boston, Jany. 25th 1799.

Dear Sir,

In consequence of your letter to our mutual friend Mr Mason, I here state to you all the circumstances relative to Dr Logan's Memorial to the Minister of foreign Relations in France, which I have any Knoledge of.

After Dr L. had been in paris 10 or 12 days had been many

[25] The remainder of the letter has been quoted above, p. 113.

[26] The original was handed by Otis to the President, on October 28, and by him forwarded to Pickering. (Adams to Pickering, October 29, 1798, Adams MSS.) It failed to convince the Secretary of State of the Directory's sincerity.

[27] Joseph Woodward was the Boston merchant associated with Otis in the Copley land deal of 1795. He was in Paris at the time of Dr. Logan's mission, and on his return brought dispatches from the American consul at Paris, which Otis delivered to the President, and also a copy of the memorial alluded to in this letter. It was shown by Woodward to Otis, to the President (Adams, *Works*, VIII, 615), and to other Federalist leaders, and during the Logan debate was read aloud by Harper, with pungent comments, on the floor of Congress (*Annals of Fifth Congress*, 2619–25). It contained several exceptionable statements — one, for instance, urging the French government to be just in order to "leave the true American character to blaze forth in the approaching elections." Dr. Logan then published a statement ( *Annals*, 2703, n.), to the effect that the memorial was not written by him, but by Otis's friend Richard Codman, who had urged him to present it to Talleyrand, which he declined to do. Naturally this statement caused Otis considerable embarrassment. This letter of Woodward is evidently in reply to one from Otis, requesting precise information on the subject. It raises a direct issue of veracity between Woodward and Logan. Codman's remarks on Logan in his letter to Otis indicate that he approved of the memorial, even if he did not write it.

times at Talleyrands & at Merlins, I was told he was advised
by the Minister to profer a Memorial, Stating his opinion, respecting the United States as relating to the french Republick.
The reason that was given for this was, that If the Directory
wish'd to bring forward any proposition to the Councils respecting America, that they might have some document to ground
it upon, as a change of measures was said to be the Intention
of their Goverment.

A day or two after Mr R. Codman showed me draft of a memorial as he said of Dr Logans writing, which the Dr. had requested him to have copied, by his Clerk in a fair hand, both
in french & English. This draft was corrected & added to before
Copying by Mr Barlow at L. request as I understood, then
written off by Mr Codmands Clerk & given to Dr Logan who
Deliverd it to Tallerand. This I understood by Mr. Codman
& I think from the Dr himself. When I was about to leave Paris
I requested Mr Codman to favor me with a Copy of the Memorial that Dr Logan had presented to the Minister of Foreign
Affairs. This Copy I did myself the honor to Deliver to the
President of the U. S. to do with as he might think Proper And
is the same that has been Published in a Philadelphia news
Paper as having been read by Mr Harper in the House of Congress & laid on the Speaker's Table. I am very much surprised
to hear the Turn that has been given to this transaction by the
Docr. for certainly I conversed with him myself conserning
the Memorial & he had not any secrecy about it. I do not re-
colect any thing further on this Subject. Any use you think
proper to make of this Letter is at your Discretion. And believe me to be very truly your friend

And Humbel Servant

JOSEPH WOODWARD

JONATHAN MASON TO OTIS

Boston Feby 27th, 1799

Dr Otis

And well may you be in affliction. If you have any love of
Country, you must feel at so gross a departure from principles,
so gross a deriliction of position, & so gross a desertion of party.[28]

---

[28] He refers to the President's nomination of a minister to France.

From being respectable in Europe, from having convinced
Great Britain, & from having associated with all friends to Order,
Property & Society, we must be content to sacrifice these advantages & once again become soothers & suppliants for Peace,
from a Gang of pityfull robbers, be by them despised & finally
duped, without attaining in any degree the object of these sacrifices. It will be now seen that the Speech at the Opening of
the Session, which carried its own evidence of the soil in which
it grew, was but preparitory to this Step, that it partook of sentiments & policy, which approved & were in unison with those
of Mr Gerry — That this man the P[resident] has been invariably determined to support, & in this measure, has resolved
publickly to sanction his conduct. This appointment declares
to every American — that the French in the P. opinion, are
desirous of making a peace with this Country — that they are
serious in their desires & that there is a fair prospect of its being
accomplished — further, that it will be equitable, solid & lasting — & that it is our interest to make it. Or why appoint him?
Can any rational man either in Europe or America, who has
paid the smallest attention to the Men & Measures of that nation, join with him in this Opinion. Certainly there is not one.
Neither does he think so himself. I have too good an Opinion
of him to suppose, that he would not esteem it a public calamity,
if the French themselves at this moment, in the present state
of things, had made such advances, as would have rendered it
necessary for our Country to have met them. We are not in a
situation to treat — We are not yet Nationally cloathed. Our
Country & Govermt is yet assuming & accustoming themselves to National Features. Time is wanting to give these
Features, stability. Great Britain well disposed, & France prostrate — we could creep along in our Navy, in our Army, in our
Fortifications, in our Commerce — & all our permanent
establishments, all of which would be opposed by the one or
other of these nations, & obstructed with success, were it not
for the present irregular state of things in this Country & Europe. I have ever considered it peculiarly fortunate, that at
this moment of our marine establishment, Gt. Britain was seriously disposed to be liberal & make sacrifices. With her Frown
only, with a critical discussion & attention to quibbles, she
might totally destroy any strength of ours upon that element.

How came then this Appointment? From personal considerations, & deep rooted jealousies. From a conviction in his own Mind that he is not the choice of the Federalists — that he is the man for the moment, & that they are raising another to supercede him. This haunts him day & night, & gives the tone to the smallest measure of his administration. It is the weak side & there are men enough who know & take the advantage of it. It is to be lamented, that he cannot discern, what is as visible as the Meridian sun — that a firm adherance, to his first measures, adopted from reflection & sanctioned by advice, would have secured to him the chair, immortalized his administration & his Fame would have been forgotten only with that of his Predecessor. But such things are, & you are now to witness — A deriliction of the system of Defence — an evaporation of National Spirit — a Loss of National Dignity — the Frowns of our European friends — the tryumph of our Domestic enemies — An increase of Jacobinic influence, & God knows, but there will be a change of Men & Measures. And how is this thing to be avoided? By a remedy scarcely short of the Disease. By a proclamation to the World that our administration are at points — that the French have an advocate in our President — & that with him our senate are at issue upon a subject the most important ever agitated in the Councils of our Country. I hope this thing will be withdrawn, & if not, I hope in God it will be negatived? The Consequences may be disagreeable, but in the end, after perhaps bringing our government once again to the Precipice, it will prove a measure ill timed, personal, damnable, & deservedly kick'd out of company. I have shewn your letter to but few friends, but have been obliged to read parts of it to crouds. Since which my friend in the Country has shewn me one conformable to yours in all its parts, & Jos. Hall has recd one from J P—— still more so.

The Old way which is most commonly the best way — is to jogg on steadily, independantly, & firmly: — I hope your House will not be wanting in this mode.

Yr friend J MASON

Quincy February 19th, 1823.

Dear Sir

I think you cannot have entirely forgotten a conversation at my table; I had invited a small company of ten or a dozen gentlemen who had always professed to be my friends, among whom were yourself, Mr. Bayard of Delaware, and I think Mr. Sedgwick, it is not necessary to recollect any others. It was at the time when I had nominated an ambassador to France, a measure which produced a real anarchy in the government and infinite vexation to me. It was a *sombre diner*, but, unluckily, the subject of the embassy to France was brought upon the tapis, I remember not in what manner, or by whom. Mr. Bayard began to harangue upon the subject, and, with a dismal countenance, a melancholy air, and a Jeremiad tone, began to prophesy ill, as near as I can remember, in these words: "Ah! It is an unfortunate measure. We know not the consequences of it." And he went on in this whining strain, in a long harangue, till at last he said "England would certainly be offended at it, they could not fail to take umbrage and they might declare war upon us."

Upon the maturest reflection, to this hour I am astonished that my patience held out so long. What was it but a direct attack and insult to me personally, before a select collection of persons who ought to have been my cordial friends and supporters. But this I could have borne; my patience would have held out under all that. But I must confess that such is my nature, that sordid meanness, base hypocrisy, and above all political poltroonery in a just and righteous public cause, never failed to produce in me an exclamation of contempt and indignation, that I never could restrain, and Heaven knows, I have had trials enough of it, in the course of my life. I broke out assertingly upon the occasion, and I said, as nearly as I recollect, in these words or others of a similar import: "Mr. Bayard, I am surprised to hear you express yourself in this manner; would you prefer a war with France to a war with England, in the present state of the world; would you wish for an alliance with Great Britain, and a war with France? If you would, your opinions are totally different from mine." Bayard replied, "Great Britain is very powerful, her navy is very terrible." This put me out of all patience; I broke out, "I know the power of Great Britain, I have measured its omnipotence without treasure, without arms, without ammunition, and without soldiers or ships; I have braved and set at defiance all her power. In the negotiation with France we had done no more than we had a perfect right to do; she had no right, or color of right, to take offense at it, and if she did I would not regard it a farthing. For in a just and righteous cause I shall hold all her policy and power in total contempt." I remember that you, Mr. Otis, afterwards said to me you wondered I had been so severe upon Bayard, for Bayard was my friend; I answered you, I knew him to be my friend, and I knew myself to be his friend, but for those very reasons I used the greater freedom with him — certainly too great for the dignity of my station. But from my inmost soul, I cannot repent it to this day.[29]

[29] As this letter was dictated, I have taken liberties with the spelling and punctuation.

# CHAPTER XI

IN the congressional elections which extended from
April, 1798, to April, 1799, the country at large placed its
stamp of approval on Federalist policy, and returned the
largest majority that the party ever enjoyed. It has often
been assumed that the Federal party was a sectional
organization, centred chiefly in New England. Federalism, it is true, held New England as its last stronghold,
but down to 1801 the party was distinctly a national one.
New England furnished no more than a due proportion
of its leaders; the Middle States furnished Hamilton,
Jay, Dayton, and Bayard; and the South, Harper,
Marshall, Rutledge, Davie, and the Pinckneys. In the
elections to the Sixth Congress, the Federal party swept
the far South, as well as New England, and made substantial gains in Virginia and North Carolina. The
Republican party secured but three members east of the
Hudson, and but one member south of North Carolina.[1]
Hamilton, however, was pessimistic on the outcome of
the elections; he believed "no real or desirable change
has been wrought in those States." Two years sufficed
to show the truth of this surmise. The South, in 1798,

---

[1] Matthew Lyon of Vermont; in Massachusetts, General Varnum of the
Middlesex County District, and Phanuel Bishop of the Third Southern District
(to the east of Rhode Island); General Sumter of Camden District, South
Carolina. The Federalists thus gained two seats in New England, and four in
the far South. In North Carolina they gained four seats, and in Virginia, the
same number.

had much to fear from a French invasion, and responded
to the appeal of a spirited foreign policy. When the
French peril was over, that section lapsed back again
into Democracy.[2] Hamilton also perceived that "some
parts of the Union, which, in time past, have been the
soundest, have of late exhibited signs of a gangrene begun
and progressive." Again he was right, for the Republican
party won six new seats between the Potomac and the
Hudson, which were permanent gains.

Otis was present at the opening session of the Sixth
Congress at Philadelphia on December 2, 1799, and wrote
Mrs. Otis on the following day:

> Politically speaking, I believe the Session will be agreeable
> and harmonious. There appears nothing to quarrell about,
> and I think you will find less asperity in debate and more good-
> nature between the opposite parties than usual. Old Sedgwick
> is chosen Speaker, & much delighted with the appointment —
> We were however obliged to manage a little to secure this ob-
> ject.

As Otis suggested in his letter, the character of the debates in the Sixth Congress differed widely from that in
the Fifth. Then the Federalists had been the aggressors,
hammering out a national spirit from a sluggish majority,
and rashly abusing power when won. In the Sixth Congress, little trace was left of that exuberance of Federalism that produced the Sedition Act. Federalist policy
was now defensive, not aggressive; its object was to maintain a system already established. Even the Essex Junto
asked no more than an extension of the judiciary. The
negotiation with France was about to commence, and the
Federal majority took its cue from the President's sen-

---

[2] It will be remembered that the Essex Junto considered the Virginia Federalists "little better than half-way Jacobins." The two Georgia members of
the Sixth Congress, and David Stone of North Carolina, all elected as Federalists, voted steadily with the opposition.

sible advice in his opening address: "however it may terminate, a steady perseverance in a system of national defence commensurate with our resources and the situation of our country is an obvious dictate of wisdom," — in other words, he advised them to stand pat. Otis, as Chairman of the Committee on Defense, indorsed this policy in a report of January 13, 1800. He recommended that the 3400 men already enlisted in the twelve new regiments be retained, since "the national honor and interest, in the present posture of affairs make it prudent and necessary to continue prepared for the worst event." As a concession to considerations of economy, he advised a suspension of the recruiting service until the "approach of danger should compel the Government to resume it."

The Republican policy of 1800 was to vitiate the Federalist system by incessant attack, and to hold it up to popular detestation and ridicule, with an eye on the coming presidential election. The debates were, however, as Otis prophesied, far less acrimonious than those of the Fifth Congress; and much more time was found for internal legislation. Otis was not so active in this Congress as in the last. The novelty of political leadership had worn off, and his letters are full of anticipation of the approaching end to his congressional career. He and Harper as majority leaders were quietly superseded by a man greatly their superior, John Marshall, who brought judicial moderation and statesmanlike qualities of the very highest order to the service of Federalism.

The actual work of the session was postponed practically a month by the death of Washington on December 18, 1799. John Nicholas ushered in the New Year with an opening shot on the Federalist system, — a resolution to repeal the Army Act of July 16, 1798. On January 11, 1800, Otis wrote:

We have had a most busy week, — Mr Nicholas' resolution was intended to produce the long debate which is annually the result of some jacobin proposition; but as the federalists determined to *stick to it*, and dispatch it in a reasonable time, we have continued sitting untill a late hour every afternoon, and have consequently found ourselves fatigued and disposed to rest after escaping from the polluted atmosphere of the Hall. We buried this baby, last evening, and though the debate was long and animated and your prating husband speechified an hour, there was less acrimony and personal allusion; & in short more decency and attention to feelings than I have ever known on a similar occasion. I am glad it is finished, as it is the most important question that will be agitated; and the only pitched battle that will be fought — and such is the expenditure of ammunition & force that none but slight skirmishes will probably ensue.

The debate, which was, indeed, a lengthy one, served as a sort of clearing-house for political principles. On the one side we hear of the danger of invasion, the awful fate of Switzerland, Genoa, etc. (the list had grown appreciably longer since the day of Otis's maiden speech); on the other side, the maintenance of an army is denounced as oppressive, unduly expensive, and insulting to France. The sensation of the debate was furnished by Democracy's latest acquisition from Virginia, John Randolph of Roanoake, with his shrill voice, diminutive head, and legs "proportioned to the body like a pair of tongs," who denounced the American army as "mercenaries" and a "handful of ragamuffins." [1] Nicholas's resolution was finally rejected by the decisive vote of 60 to 39, and Otis's proposal to suspend enlistments adopted.

The only reported speech by Otis during the debate was short, but significant. He remarked:

I confess I have indulged mournful presentiments of the effects to be expected from a new treaty. I foresee that, like other

[1] J. Schouler, *United States*, I, 453.

nations, we may be compelled to realize that the dangers of peace and amity are the most serious dangers. I know that attempts will be made to demolish the whole defensive fabric which we have erected, and to replunge us into that abyss of debility and inaction from which we shall never escape a second time. With these difficulties I have always thought our Government would be doomed to struggle whenever a treaty should be concluded with France, but I did not expect to see at this time the axe laid to the root of our whole system.

His "mournful presentiments" were well justified, since the history of the next eleven years showed that the American people preferred a foreign policy of "debility and inaction" to the Federalist policy of defense and reprisal. The speech was an indiscreet expression of Otis's discontent with the President's policy, which, nevertheless, he was loyally supporting.

If any one is under the delusion that the present congressional practice of frittering away election year by making political capital is a modern invention, let him read the debates of the Sixth Congress. The Republican party in 1800 threw out a net for political martyrs, and made an excellent catch of bogus ones, who served equally well the purpose of convincing ignorant voters that the Federal party was bent on crushing out personal liberty. Thomas Nash (*alias* Jonathan Robbins, and several other names) was the leader of this noble army; the magic of his name secured countless votes for Jefferson. He was an Irishman, accused of murder on a British vessel, who escaped to the United States. His extradition was demanded by the British government, and granted by the President, after a claim that Nash had made to American citizenship had been proved false. Although before his execution in Halifax he confessed his falsehood, Nash's confession was completely ignored by the Democrats, who attempted to censure the President for his

"executive usurpation" and "unwonted act of tyranny."
Concerning this discussion, which consumed much time
and breath, Otis wrote, March 1, 1800:

Our Demos are sick of their attempt to inculpate the Executive for his conduct in reference to the pirate Robbins. They
wish to postpone or rather to evade the enquiry, but we hold
them to it and it will occupy next week. We have begun upon
the "ways & means," & when the bills relating to these are
passed, I shall consider the main business of the session finished,
and hope that three weeks will be sufficient for these objects.

Other details in the course of congressional business
are given in Otis's pleasant letters to his wife:
February 8, 1800:

You will perceive by the papers that I have offered a resolution to the house for adjourning the first monday in april. Some
of my friends propose to amend it by adding "Provided Mrs
Otis dont come here before yt time." The fact is that we can
and ought to adjourn by that time, but I have no idea the resolution will prevail, though it may be carried in *our* house. My
object was to hasten and dispatch business, and it has already
produced that effect. I still persist in my intention to be home
from the first to the 15 april, "although the heathen may rage
and the people imagine vain things."

February 13:

My resolution to adjourn 1st Monday in april, to my surprise
passed our house by a large majority, but it will remain some
time in the Senate. Indeed it would not yet be prudent for the
Senate to adopt it; for the jacobins would not suffer us to do
any important business, if we were once fairly *committed*. It
will however probably produce the effect to hasten the close of
the session. However this may be it is my present design to
leave them the first week in april. Genl Lee says that if Congress get away in all april he shall tell you when he sees you
that you have saved the U. S. thirty thousand dollars at
least.

February 22:

* I believe that but for me, a committee would have reported
a resolution for a day of *annual mourning* throughout the Union;
as if human nature would weep at the word of command upon
fixed days & seasons; as if there were any analogy between political and personal sorrow. I protested that I would resist
it if alone, and thus gained time, till returning reflection convinced the friends to the measure that it would not be advisable.
However this day produces two orations, both of which I must
hear, & from both of which I am willing to be excused. So my
friends laugh at my motion to adjourn, but as it passed the house,
it was no laughing matter. Whether they adjourn in april or
not, Nicholas & myself have agreed to *pair off* between the 1st
and 10th of that month. An event happened yesterday, which
saves a full week at least. The Bankrupt bill passed the house
by a majority of one yesterday *without debate*. I have not leisure now to inform you how this happened, but so it is, and it
will undoubtedly pass the Senate. It is a great important political measure, — I had no idea of its succeeding.[4]

Throughout this session the air was full of rumors
regarding the next Federalist nomination for the presidency. From the moment that John Adams delivered
his blow to Hamilton's policy, the war Federalists decided on his fall. A letter from Theodore Sedgwick to
Timothy Pickering, on December 22, 1799, indicates that
Otis was already cognizant of this plan, and intended to
thwart it:

The representation made by Mr. [Otis] [5] that there is an oli-
garchical faction whose head is Colo. [Pickering] that the combination was intended to controul the President and direct the

---

[4] The Bankruptcy Bill, which was a favorite measure of Otis, had failed at
the last Congress. Sedgwick wrote that it was important "as well in a commercial as in a political view," since it was likely to gain Federalist voters
among the "discontented." *King*, III, 189.

[5] This and other words in brackets are in Pickering's handwriting. The
letter is in the Pickering MSS.

executive administration of the Government. That the President having discovered the views of these men, has disentangled himself from their controul, and thereby incurred their enmity; and that to reinstate themselves again in power they will oppose his reelection. This is the substance of the general representation.

In a mixed company, at Mr. Tilghman's Mr. [H. G. O.] declared that at the next election, whoever might be associated with Mr. Adams, the electors of Massachusetts would not give their votes uniformly, for fear the election of Mr. Adams would, thereby, be endangered. This declaration which a gentleman has since told me he has repeated to him, as far as Mr. [H. G. O.] may be deemed an authority is of the most mischievous kind, and, destroying all means of confidence or concert, will insure, with absolute certainty, the election of the man we dread, to, perhaps, the office of Vice President.

Timothy Pickering was the fanatic of the Federal party. With him, politics and religion seemed one and the same thing, — a struggle between Good which must be defended, and Evil which must be crushed. The social structure of eighteenth-century New England and the principles of Federalism were the Good; French philosophy and Democracy the Evil. Statesmen of this type of mind are absolutely devoid of tolerance, and careless of the means they employ to gain their ends, — witness the career of John Calvin and Robespierre, Pickering's spiritual ancestor and political brother. He recognized no rules of the game in politics, for politics were to him something more than a game; and his zeal to conquer the powers of darkness, embodied in Jefferson, led him to unworthy intrigues, treasonable correspondence, and avowed disunionism, without the least consciousness of his wrongdoing. The following extracts from his letter of December 23, 1799, to Stephen Higginson, part of which we have already quoted, show that he was absolutely unconscious of his part in the intrigues against the President.

After repeating to his correspondent the rumors spread by Otis, he remarks:

All these positions you will know to be false. You know that I have not the talents to lead a party; while you will allow me such a share of common sense as must guard me against the miserable ambition and folly of attempting it. Acting during my life without disguise, and always manifesting, I trust, the humility which I felt; you will not believe that I ever entertained the intention, singly or with others, to control the President, and to direct the executive administration of the Government. Neither will you believe that disappointment in this ambitious project of controul, has excited the *enmity* of me and of those with whom I think & act; and that we shall oppose the re-election of the President, *in order to reinstate ourselves again in power.*

Then, after disclaiming Otis's imputations, Pickering makes a statement completely justifying them:

I will only add, that certainly we shall all be agreed in the great object of securing *federalists* for the two first magistrates of the Union: that all predilections which would thwart this view ought to be laid aside: and if the State of the public mind should require a change of candidates, that Judge Ellsworth & General Pinckney should be the substitutes.[6]

These remarks are sufficient evidence that Otis's fears for the renomination of Adams had good foundation. Hamilton and the Essex Junto were looking about for any candidate to support against him. John Adams was, to be sure, a most uncertain quantity, and temperamentally unfitted for his high position. Though honest, courageous, and well-meaning, though author of a policy that has stood the test of time, he lacked the very essential qualities of firmness, tact, and the ability to handle men. Unsteadiness of policy and violent outbursts of temper marked the latter part of his administration. At

[6] Pickering MSS., xii, 371–75.

the most critical periods in foreign and domestic politics he shirked his duty by long absences at Quincy, four days distant from the seat of government; and he permitted cabinet ministers to remain in office for a full year after discovering their relations with Hamilton. But to refuse Adams the renomination would be to court Federalist defeat. He was the only leader in his party possessing genuine popularity, and his peace policy pleased the mass of Federalist voters. It would be a difficult matter to explain to them why he should be superseded.

In the early months of 1800 there was considerable talk of abandoning Adams and nominating Oliver Ellsworth for President, as Pickering suggested.[7] A compromise was effected, however, at the nominating caucus, composed of the Federalist members of both houses, held at Philadelphia on or about May 3, 1800. It was agreed that each Federalist elector should vote for John Adams and Charles Cotesworth Pinckney, with the understanding that the former should be elected President. But the friends of Hamilton indorsed this arrangement with the mental reservation of electing Pinckney, if possible.[8]

Otis was not present at this nominating caucus. At the end of March he paired off with Nicholas, agreeably to his promise to Mrs. Otis, and returned to Boston. This early departure from Philadelphia enabled him to take care that the Massachusetts Federalists should secure the full benefit of their local majority in the presidential

---

[7] *1896 Report of the American Historical Association*, I, 824–35; *King*, III, 209; Wm. G. Brown, *Oliver Ellsworth*, 311. An anonymous letter of March 11, 1800, to the President (Adams MSS.) states that Hamilton, Pickering, Wolcott, Dayton, Harper, Hillhouse, McHenry, Carroll, and Sedgwick, are all working for the election of Ellsworth.

[8] Harper to Otis, August 26, 1800, at end of this chapter; Sewall to Otis, December 29, 1800, at end of chap. XII; *King*, III, 232, 240; Steiner, *McHenry*, 459–61; Gibbs, II, 398; Hamilton, *Works*, VI, 436–37, 459; *Niles' Register*, XXV, 258. This caucus is confused by most authorities with the Aurora's "Jacobinical Conclave," an entirely different affair.

election. At that period there was no uniformity among
the states in choosing presidential electors. In some they
were chosen by the legislature; in others on a general
ticket by the people (the uniform practice to-day); in
others by the people in districts, as Congressmen are
elected. Virginia, down to the year 1800, employed the
last method, but when the congressional returns of 1799
made it evident that at least five districts in the state
would choose Federalist electors, the Republican majority
in the legislature abolished the district system and provided for a choice by general ticket. It therefore behooved
Federalist states to follow the same plan, in order similarly to exclude the Republican minorities within their
borders from representation in the electoral college. In
Massachusetts, for instance, a continuance of the traditional district method would be sure to give Jefferson
at least two votes. Otis and the other Federalist Congressmen from Massachusetts wrote a significant letter
on that subject on January 31, 1800, addressed to the
Speaker of the Massachusetts House of Representatives
and to the President of the Senate. After describing the
"plan of the opposers of the General Government . . .
to bend their power to democratize the character of the
state legislature," and among other objects to secure an
"antifederal" President, they remark:

In this critical state of things we feel that it is very important
to guard against *one* antifederal vote from Massachusetts; for
one vote may turn the election.

Whether this is to be done by choosing at large thro' the
Committees,[9] or by choosing by the Legislature, or by uniting
two or more districts for choosing, or in some other mode the
wisdom of the Legislature will determine. We presume not to

[9] This is either a mistake for counties, although it would seem impossible
for a mistake to be made in a document signed by fourteen men; or it reveals
an extent of power in political committees hitherto unsuspected.

determine the mode, but only to suggest the danger which we apprehend and which we in this place, and in our present employment, are perhaps better circumstanced to observe than our friends in Massachusetts can be. Excuse us for suggesting these ideas; our anxiety for the event of the election must be our apology.[10]

Legislative action was, however, postponed to the next General Court, to be elected in April and May. Otis did his best to bring out the full Federalist vote, by making a pungent speech in the caucus, on the evening before the election. The result was not reassuring to his party. It secured a strong majority in the General Court, but its candidate for governor, Caleb Strong, was elected by an actual majority of only one hundred. To allow the people to choose presidential electors by a general ticket, under those circumstances, would be to run the risk of total defeat, — as actually happened in 1804. The legislature therefore decided to appoint the electors itself. This was a legal procedure which was then practiced in five other states; but depriving, as it did, the people of Massachusetts of a privilege they had formerly enjoyed, it aroused great opposition and cost the Federalists a part of their waning popularity. A similar move was contemplated in Maryland, but the Federalists of that state did not dare to put it through.[11]

The month of May, 1800, was full of events important in their bearing on the election. The congressional nominating caucus was held, and the Democrats captured the state government of New York, where the legislature chose electors, thus assuring the twelve votes of that state for Jefferson and Burr. At the same time John Adams came to a tardy determination to reorganize his Cabinet. McHenry was forced to resign on May 6, after

[10] *Proc. Mass. Hist. Soc.*, XLIII, 653, collated with original in Robbins MSS.
[11] See Harper's letters at end of this chapter.

a stormy scene with the President. Pickering, who likewise was requested to resign, refused, because he considered that "several matters of importance" made his
continuance necessary for the welfare of the government.
He was then summarily expelled. Pickering disappeared
shortly from view in the wilds of northern Pennsylvania,
where his land was his only means of livelihood. His influence was so missed, however, by the Federal party
in Massachusetts, that a subscription was taken up in
1802 to purchase enough of his land to enable him to return to Massachusetts. This was an unfortunate act, for
Timothy Pickering became the Calhoun of New England,
and the evil genius of the Federal party. Otis's name is
conspicuously absent from the list of subscribers.

  With the breaking-up of the Hamiltonian cabinet cabal,
the adherents of Hamilton and Adams commenced open
hostilities, in which both sides seemed entirely to disregard the fact that their divisions were Jefferson's strength.
Neither side paid the slightest attention to the caucus
agreement. The Hamilton group bent all its energies to
securing the election of Pinckney. It was a miserable
policy, for conscious as its authors were of Adams's popularity, they dared not avow their object, but sought to
attain it by back-stairs intrigue, mainly by tampering
with the state legislatures that chose presidential electors.
Much reliance was placed on the expectation that the
South Carolina legislature, although Democratic, would
cast its vote for Pinckney and Jefferson, as in 1797. But
Pinckney refused to lend his sanction to this shabby
betrayal of his running-mate.[12] Hamilton made a journey
to Boston in the month of June, apparently in order to
persuade the leaders in the legislature to appoint electors
who would "knife" Adams, and stirred things up on the

---

[12] In June. Steiner, *McHenry*, 459–61.

way by his imprudent speeches.[13] In vain the Federalist press attempted to conceal the schism. It is not surprising to find complaints from the leaders that "the public mind is puzzled and fretted. People don't know what to think, of measures or men; they are mad because they are in the dark." — "They know there is something behind the curtain, and they are angry because they are not told the nature and extent of the difficulty."[14] Some even among Hamilton's friends were disgusted. James McHenry considered his party's conduct "tremulous, timid, feeble, deceptive, & cowardly. They write private letters. To whom? To each other. But they do nothing to give a proper direction to the public mind." [15]

Otis was one of the few Federalist leaders who were not concerned in the intrigue against Adams. This much appears from his correspondence; but we look in vain for any indication of the steps taken by him and other Adams men to thwart their opponents. A rumor reached the South to the effect that "lukewarm Federalists and Adams's private friends," including Otis, Samuel Dexter, Judge Cushing of the Supreme Court, and Elbridge Gerry, were using their influence to get New England electors to drop Pinckney, in order to counteract the extra votes he might obtain in South Carolina.[16] This rumor produced a frantic letter from Robert Goodloe Harper to Otis, begging him in the name of party harmony to see that Pinckney and Adams were voted for equally, and assuring him that there would be no desertion of Adams in the South. We can infer from Harper's next letter that Otis, in reply, insisted that no distinct Adams party

[13] *Independent Chronicle*, July 31, 1800; *King*, III, 275.
[14] Gibbs, II, 394, 409.
[15] Steiner, 462.
[16] John Rutledge, Jr., to Hamilton, July 17, 1800 (Steiner, 463), and Harper's letters to Otis at end of this chapter.

existed, and that no intention was entertained of depriving Pinckney of a full vote; but certain expressions of his seemed to Harper the "seeds from which such a party may spring."

President Adams, on his side, threw discretion to the winds, and inveighed against the "British faction" and the Essex Junto, according to Fisher Ames, "like one possessed." [17] The opposition press naturally did all in its power to fan the flames of jealousy that were consuming Federalism, and sedulously cultivated a belief that the President was seeking Democratic support. In August the *Aurora* printed a foolish letter that Adams had written several years before, accusing the Pinckney brothers of susceptibility to British influence. Hamilton then published a severe arraignment of Adams's character, and a defense of the Pinckneys and himself; the President's friends retorted in kind; and the campaign of 1800 closed with the Federal party turned into a Donnybrook Fair, the Republicans as amused onlookers egging it on, while Jefferson and Burr captured the presidential prizes.

Jefferson and Burr each received 73 electoral votes, Adams, 65, and Pinckney, 64. The Hamiltonian manœuvres were thwarted by one Federalist elector throwing away his second vote, and by a second refusal of Charles Cotesworth Pinckney to accept the vote of South Carolina if coupled with that of Jefferson. [18] To find so striking an instance of loyalty and unselfishness amid the intrigues, lies, and petty bickerings of this campaign, is refreshing.

Yet Adams and Pinckney were defeated by no accidental or temporary causes. The same wave that swept Jefferson into office, swept the Federalist majority out of Congress. Had Otis again aspired to be the represen-

[17] *King*, III, 276.
[18] Rev. C. C. Pinckney, *Thomas Pinckney*, 156; Hamilton, *Works*, VI, 483.

In 1798, Fed. Pop. bec. stood for nat'l honor.
In 1800, Fr. peril gone    Sedit. pros., turan.
+ intol. plcy.
charges + desir.
INTRIGUE AND DEFEAT    191    that r.
urfair.
conc.

tative of the First Middle District, he would in all probability have been disappointed, for young Josiah Quincy,
his successor as Federalist nominee, was decisively defeated. It seems difficult at first to account for the rapid
falling-off of the Federalists' popularity since their decisive victory in 1798. The majority in the Sixth Congress
had not abused its power as its predecessor had in the
months immediately following the X. Y. Z. disclosures.
But the source of the Federalists' popularity in 1798 lay
in the fact that they, in marked contrast to the Republicans, stood for national honor and integrity against foreign insult and aggression. By 1800 the French peril had
evaporated,[19] and with it the passions and the enthusiasm of 1798. Meanwhile, the insidious suggestions of
Jefferson and the Democratic editors, to the effect that
no French peril had ever existed, that the whole X. Y. Z.
affair had been concocted by the Federalists with the object of establishing a standing army and a despotism, —
these rumors had spread and secured believers. The fruit-
less and tyrannical sedition prosecutions, the arrogance
and intolerance of triumphant Federalism, and the cost of
a spirited foreign policy, had all sunk into the popular
consciousness. When we consider all these factors, and
the disgraceful bickerings and intrigues within the party
itself, the wonder is not that Thomas Jefferson was elected
President, but that John Adams was so close a second
in the race.

[19] The treaty of Mortefontaine with France was signed September 30, 1800.
Napoleon in all probability hastened its conclusion in order to influence the
American elections, as it undoubtedly did. The very next day the secret treaty
of San Ildefonso, ceding Louisiana from Spain to France, was signed — a
sufficient justification for a maintenance of the Federalist foreign policy.

LETTERS FROM ROBERT GOODLOE HARPER TO OTIS ON
THE PRESIDENTIAL ELECTION

Annapolis [20] June 25th 1800

.   .   .   .   .   .   .   .

The Jacobins here are "erectis animis," but, as usual, on
most insufficient grounds. Your state has struck a heavy &
well directed blow against them. This, in all probability, will
follow it up. In that case their defeat is certain. I have letters
from Jersey & Delaware, which asure me that no danger is to
be apprehended in those states. Stockton, who is one of my
Jersey correspondents, speaks in very positive terms.

I have yet heard very little from South Carolina. One of
my correspondents, however, in a letter of May 26th says, on
the subject of the Election "There is less of Pinckney than you
would imagine. The Mass of sentiment seems to be divided
between Adams & Jefferson." I mention this to shew you, that
the South Carolinians will not be actuated by narrow local
views, but enter honestly into the general system. There is no
doubt that every federal Nerve in the state, will be erected
in support of Mr. Adams, and that no people in the Union
would more decidedly reject any attempt to supersede him.
They will also support Pinckney, upon the general ground of
giving the friends of the gov't two strings to their bow instead
of one. . . .

Baltimore August 28th 1800

My dear Otis

I fear you and your friends in Boston are ruining every
thing. We understand here, that a party in Boston, which is
called Mr. Adams's Party and led by Messrs Dexter Otis Knox
Cushing Jackson[21] & *Gerry*, is making the utmost exertion to
get the vote of that state thrown away from Genl Pinckney, in

[20] Harper moved permanently to Baltimore in 1799, but continued to
represent the Ninety-six District of South Carolina until the close of the
Sixth Congress.
[21] Samuel Dexter, the Secretary of War; Major-General Henry Knox;
Judge William Cushing, of the Supreme Court; Charles Jackson, a Boston
lawyer.

order to favour, exclusively, the election of Mr. Adams. Dexter Otis Knox & — Gerry, in the same line. Creditisne Pisones! This idea does unconscionable mischief. The federalists here, & in South Carolina, are making the fairest & the most zealous exertions in favour of Mr. Adams. They wish to secure the election to him if possible, but knowing that to be doubtful, they think themselves obliged, by every principle of duty to their cause & their Country, to support Genl Pinckney at the same time, in order to avail themselves of his popularity in the southern states, should their other hope fail. But can it be expected that they will continue the same efforts, if they know that this hope also is to be taken from them, through the exclusive attachment of Mr. Adams's friends in Massachusetts, to his interests? They cannot be expected to do it. They will not do it. I know they will not. Reflect on the consequences of an abatement in their exertions.

Do you calculate on the certainty of Mr. Adams's Success, so as to justify men attached to the federal cause, in dividing the other vote? We understand that you do. For God's sake review the calculation & consider it well. Suffer not yourselves to be misled by the warmth of your wishes. On what, I pray you, does that calculation rest? Can you make it more favourable than the one contained in the enclosed paper? From that you will find, and I believe it may be depended on, that Mr. Adams cannot be elected without either getting two votes at least from South Carolina, or seven from North Carolina instead of five, or nine from Maryland instead of seven.

That he will get a vote in South Carolina is extremely doubtful. The most zealous exertions are making, and unless dampt by you, will continue to be made, in his favour by the federalists there, but their success is extremely uncertain. This is the uniform tenour of all my letters from them, several of which are very late. The mode of choice by the legislature occasions this extreme uncertainty, by exposing the choice to the influence of a few artful jacobins, who will attend the Legislature, and may mislead the uninformed though well-meaning men of whom it is composed; although they could produce little or no effect on the people at large.

As to North Carolina, nothing that I have seen or heard, warrants a reliance on more than five votes in that state. More are hoped for by the federal men there, but not counted on. My information is from Grove with whom I correspond, & from Judge Moore [22] of that state, whom I have very lately seen. In those districts whereon we count, there is division & opposition, and the event, of course, like that of all other popular contests, is more or less uncertain.

To come now to Maryland, there is every thing short of moral certainty, that should district elections continue, Mr. Jefferson will get three votes. There is much probability of his getting four. The federalists are labouring to change the mode to a Legislative choice, and there are good hopes of their success. But it is very far from being certain. This measure is now the point of contest in a popular election. The mass of the people is well disposed, at least a very great majority, but they are inconveably [sic] attached to what they call the privilege of voting for the electors in districts. An immense clamour is raised by the antifederalists about what they denominate the attempt to deprive the people of their privileges. It produces an effect which I did not foresee. Even three weeks ago, I did not foresee it. There was much difficulty in persuading the federalists to venture on the ground. When they first took it, the public mind appeared to acquiesce in the plan. Now there are strong appearances of its taking a different turn. So much is said to the people about the privilege of voting, and they express so blind an attachment to it, that I much doubt, very much indeed, whether they will be persuaded to elect any men into the Legislature, but such as will pledge themselves not to vote for depriving them of this privilege. [23]

This opinion is the result of very recent information from several counties of the state, and of conversations with several leading and well-informed federal candidates. I still have hopes of succeeding. Until lately I was very confident. At present I greatly doubt.

I beseach you, my dear Otis, to weigh these circumstances and to test your estimates by these facts. I declare to you in truth

[22] William Barry Grove and Alfred Moore.

[23] Cf. next letter; Harper to Dayton, July 2, 1800, in *Bulletin of the New York Public Library*, IV, 115; Harper's pamphlet entitled *Bystander, or a Series of Letters on the Subject of the Legislative choice of Electors in Maryland*, Baltimore, 1800; and K. M. Rowland, *Charles Carroll of Carrollton*, II, 234.

and sincerity, that I am labouring with all my might to promote the election of Mr. Adams. I further declare that had I not, from the moment of the New York election, considered it doubtful in the extreme, I never would have countenanced, much less have proposed, the scheme of bringing forward Genl. Pinckney & making him pari passu. This declaration I made, in the most pointed terms, at that meeting,[24] the objects of which are supposed by some to have been so much misunderstood by Mr. Adams. I know this to be the sentiment throughout my own state, this state, and North Carolina. At the same time, I declare, with equal frankness, that I prefer Genl. Pinckney to Mr. Adams; not from personal motives, for I am personally on ill-terms with Genl. Pinckney & always have been, while I have every reason to be satisfied, & even pleased, with the Conduct of Mr. Adams towards myself; but because I think the former, in my Conscience, better qualified to conduct the government. This, however, is a private sentiment, which I do not suffer to influence my conduct. I support Mr. Adams as well as Genl. Pinckney, to the utmost of my power & means, because I think that the good of the common cause requires it, and that the cause ought to be preferred to the individual. I know very many federalists, men too of high name & influence, who feel as I do on this subject. They also act in the same manner. They sacrifice their particular preference to a general principle.[25]

But, let me repeat it again, unless they find a similar disposition in the particular friends of Mr. Adams, they will cease thus to act. They know the success, at least, to be uncertain. They know that of Mr. Adams to be much more so. They therefore wish to encrease the chance, by joining Genl. Pinckney in the federal ticket. But if they find that this source of hope is to be cut off, & every thing exposed to the greatest hazard, through exclusive attachment, in some, to Mr. Adams; in short that the man is to be preferred to the cause; it is difficult

[24] The nominating caucus, in Philadelphia.
[25] McHenry writes Wolcott, July 22, "Mr. Harper is very clearly of opinion that General Pinckney ought to be preferred." Gibbs, II, 385. Cabot said in a letter to Hamilton, August 21, "Mr. Harper writes from Baltimore on the 11th inst, that our friends may now count with some certainty, indeed very great, certainty, on an unanimous vote for Mr. Pinckney in Maryland." Hamilton, *Works*, VI, 459.

to foresee to what extent they may be disgusted, and their exertions abated by such a discovery.

This, let me add, is the last hope of the Jacobins. They exultingly declare, that Mr. Adams' friends will drop Pinckney; that a division, or at least a coldness, will thus be produced; that a division of the federal strength will thus take place; and that the result will be the election of Mr. Jefferson. They work against Adams with all their might; & have little doubt of defeating him. At the same time they endeavour to work on the friends of Mr. Adams to defeat Pinckney likewise; thus to get clear of both.

We learn here that Mr. Adams has declared his willingness to be joined in the same ticket with Mr. Jefferson, but we cannot believe it. If we could, it certainly would not encrease our respect for his heart or his understanding. It is made use of, by the friends of Mr. Jefferson, as an argument in his favour, against Mr. Adams himself.

Lay these things, my dear Otis, seriously to heart. I write them through a strong conviction of their importance; utterly uncertain how they may be received. Let your friends weigh them; some of whom I have the happiness of calling my friends also, & hope that they consider me in the same light. We are in no common times, nor threatened by a danger of ordinary magnitude. Our situation admits of no experiments, no hazzards on the mere calculation of Chances; no sporting with any part of our means. Depend upon it, the fair full & united exertion of them all, is imperiously called for by our situation. Should we suffer particular views, personal attachments, or sanguine estimates of the strength of particular candidates, to produce a division of our force, we shall lose an opportunity perhaps never to be regained; & may live to see our country mourn, in blood & ashes, over the consequences of our mistaken policy.

God bless you my dear Otis. Remember me, & believe me

with sincere affection
your friend & Hbl Servt
ROB: G: HARPER

Sept 3d

Yesterday I received a letter from Grove, dated August 24th. He says that we are certain of five in that state & have *hopes* of seven. He & your friend Hill [26] are re-elected, the former by a vast majority.

R. G. H.

Baltimore Octr. 10th 1800

My dear Otis

You have in a very great degree quieted my alarms, but not entirely removed my apprehensions. For though you assure me that no such party as I spoke of, has been actually formed, & that the views of certain gentlemen whom I highly respect, do not extend as far as I had been taught to believe; yet, with the most perfect reliance on your candour and sincerity, which I trust you need not be assured by me that I feel, I cannot but discern, in some expressions of your letter, the seeds from which such a party may spring, and certain openings to the most dangerous extent of those exclusive views, which I so greatly deprecate.

Why, for instance, do you speak of Mr. Pinckney as the *Competitor* of Mr. Adams? I solemnly assure you that I have never heard him so spoken of by those who proposed the policy of bringing him forward.[27] They intend him, solely, as a prudent mariner does a spare yard, which he wishes to have on board, lest that on which he places his chief reliance should fail him in a storm. In this light I know he is viewed here & every where to the Southward, including South Carolina. Is it without cause that I dread the operation of those feelings which lead us to consider and represent him in the light of a *Competitor*.

Neither is it by any means certain that Mr. Pinckney or Mr. Jefferson must be president in case Massachusetts should vote for the former; for recent accounts from South Carolina, give me very strong reason to believe, that all the votes of that state will be for Mr. Adams, as well as for Mr. Pinckney. The general dispositions of the people are most strong in favour of Mr.

---

[26] William H. Hill of North Carolina.

[27] This statement is hard to believe. Harper was in communication with Cabot and McHenry, both of whom considered Pinckney very much the competitor of Adams, and he must have talked with other Hamiltonians in Philadelphia who held the same views.

Adams; so much so that my correspondents assure me, that if the people individually were to vote for President, he would have at least four fifths of the votes. I know that every nerve of the federal interest in that state, including all the friends & connections of the Pinckneys, and the Pinckneys themselves, (the letter to Tenche Coxe notwithstanding,) will be strained to produce a corresponding result in the Legislature. Those who suspect otherwise, do not form a just estimate of the magnanimity and greatness of mind which characterize those two men & their principal friends.

As to this state, I entertain some better hopes than I did when I wrote to you last. Since that time I have attended one of the supreme courts, & passed through several of the counties. I have seen, or heard from, our friends in most of them. The result is a much stronger reliance than I lately had, on the adoption of the Legislative Choice. But it is still far from being certain. The election takes place next Monday, yesterday week. After the result of that is known, we shall be able to form a more decided opinion.

Upon the whole, my dear friend, I shall still hope for the best, and exert all my little strength in promoting the good cause. I shall moreover rely confidently on your assurance, that you will adopt that policy on which, in my judgment, our safety depends, "as soon as you shall" be *well satisfied* that the election will otherwise be put in jeopardy. I cannot, however, but feel some very unpleasant forebodings, when I recollect that you are *yet* to be satisfied of a fact, the evidence of which, to my mind, seems so compleat.

God bless you & keep you, is the prayer of your affectionate friend

Rob: G: Harper

# CHAPTER XII

## JEFFERSON OR BURR?

### 1800-1801, ÆT 35

OTIS's last session in Congress as a Representative from Massachusetts began on November 30, 1800, after the popular verdict on his party's performances had been given. The Federal government was now permanently removed to Washington. No room could be found in the half-finished Capitol for the House of Representatives, which was therefore relegated to a temporary brick building, disrespectfully known as the "Oven," attached to the south wing. It was kept from falling in on the assembled Congressmen only by strong temporary shorings. The third session of the Sixth Congress is of peculiar interest not only for the election of the President by the House, but for the curious spectacle of the Federalists maintaining and even extending their system, in spite of the rebuke administered to it in the recent elections. Nowadays, a due regard for public opinion prevents a defeated party from abusing that strange provision in our Constitution which permits a Congress to sit for half a year subsequent to the election of its successor. But the Federal party always marched straight forward, without paying much attention to the *vox populi*, which it deemed a very different thing from the *vox dei*. "We shall profit of our short-lived majority," writes John Rutledge, Jr., "and do as much good as we can before the end of this session."[1]

[1] Hamilton, *Works*, VII, 511.

The President in his opening address advised Congress
to maintain the navy that he had done so much to create.
This advice was not needed by Federalists, and not heeded
by their Republican successors. Congress also maintained
the army *in statu quo*. Otis in a long speech expressed his
surprise and disapproval of the semi-annual Democratic
proposal to reduce it; he also "hoped his friends would
do nothing that might be construed into a death-bed re-
pentance of a conduct that constituted their glory and
their pride."

The attempt this session to renew the odious Sedition
Act is the most striking instance of the unteachableness of
Federalism. Otis, in a letter to his wife of January 24,
1801, gives a little inside history of this episode:

> We have had a very animated though unexpected debate
> upon the old story of the sedition bill. The resolution to con-
> tinue the law was introduced by the Chairman of a Committee
> who does not often address the house, a Mr Platt. The inten-
> tion was to take the question without debate, expecting to lose
> it, when some Anti, to puzzle Platt called on him to give his
> reasons for renewing the law. For this fortunately he was
> prepared and spake like a man of sense and a gentleman. The
> gauntlet being thrown, a general engagement ensued which
> lasted three days, and in which of course I was compelled to
> take a part. We however carried the question by a majority
> of one. The bill nevertheless I fear will finally be lost.

Otis's letter seems to indicate that the measure was not
intended to be carried, but only to be brought forward
on principle, and that the whole party defended it, in
order to avoid the imputation of a "death-bed repent-
ance." It is hard to conceive what other objects they could
have had in view, for the Sedition Act, if enforced after
March 4, 1801, would have turned the tables on Federalist
scribblers. The measure was finally defeated, although it
received five more votes than the original Sedition Act.

In January, 1801, Otis was appointed chairman of a committee to report on the condition of the Treasury. This was no easy task, since no examination had been made for some years; and was therefore extremely important to the party in view of gross charges of extravagance and peculation preferred against Pickering and Wolcott by the scurrilous Philadelphia *Aurora*. In the course of the investigation there broke out at the Treasury building a fire, which, according to the *Aurora*, was set by Oliver Wolcott himself to cover his misdeeds. Otis wrote regarding this matter on January 29:

' The infamous suggestions to the disadvantage of Wolcot, ought to be punished with any thing but death. They are atrocious and as unfounded as the pretensions of the authors to honor and veracity. Wolcot had done with the office and left it. The examination of the state of the Treasury had been compleated, and in fact no papers are burnt of any consequence except those of Mr Francis and Mr Whelen, in the destruction of which it is palpable Wolcot could have no interest.

The report of our Committee is highly honorable to the Secretary and was *unanimous*, Nicholas, Nicholson & Stone,[2] being *three* of the Committee. This will set all matters right.

By far the most interesting piece of legislation during this session was the Judiciary Act, extending and strengthening the federal judiciary. Although of no practical result, because it was shortly afterwards repealed by a Republican Congress, the act must be looked upon as the last word of the Federalist system. We no longer need vindicate its authors from the charge of passing it simply to create life offices for worthy Federalists.[3] But what their motives actually were has not yet been made clear. Over

[2] John Nicholas of Virginia, Joseph H. Nicholson of Maryland, and David Stone of North Carolina, all Democrats.

[3] Max Farrand: "The Judiciary Act of 1801," in *Amer. Hist. Rev.*, v, 682.

a year previous to the presidential election, certain leaders of the party, perceiving that the federal judiciary was
the strong arm of the Federalist system, and the only
barrier to state interference, proposed its extension.
As Fisher Ames expressed the idea, "The steady men in
Congress will attempt to extend the judicial department.
. . . There is no way to combat the state opposition but
by an efficient and extended organization of judges,
magistrates, and civil officers." [4] In this branch of the
government the Federalists hoped to preserve their car-
dinal principle, federal supremacy over the states, against
the decentralizing doctrines of Jeffersonian Democracy;
and they succeeded.

Otis took very little part in the debate on the Judiciary Bill, which increased the number of judicial districts
from seventeen to twenty-two, and created a new series
of circuit courts. This establishment was unnecessarily
large for the needs of the country, and conservation of
Federalist principles was assured by the appointment
of John Marshall as chief justice, not by any extension of
the system. As soon as the bill was reported, Otis's mail
was flooded with applications for the new circuit judge-
ships. His former patron, Judge Lowell, wished one.
George Richards Minot, known as "The American Sall-
ust" for his history of Shays's Rebellion, modestly proposed to receive the district judgeship left vacant by
Lowell, to retain his present office of Judge of Probate,
and to "devote any leisure he might have, to literary
pursuits particularly in the line of History." — "Such
laudable and liberal views seem to merit encouragement," adds his recommender. Otis himself was as-
piring to the position of Solicitor-General of Massachusetts, a place which went to another, on account of

---

[4] December 29, 1799, Gibbs, II, 316. Cf. *King*, III, 147.

geographical considerations. On February 18 he writes Mrs. Otis:

> The President has this day nomminated me to be attorney for the United States in the district of Massachusetts. This is the same place which was offered to me by Genl Washington and declined for the *honor* of coming to Congress. It is analogous to the offices of Attorney & Solicitor General, but more eligible for me as I shall be stationary in *Boston*. One circumstance *against* it is I shall hold it during the Pleasure of the President, and though his friends say he will not change any officers but the *heads of departments*, yet I presume in the course of a twelvemonth he will *oust them all*.

As Otis predicted, his tenure of office was short, for Jefferson, considering it no doubt a "midnight appointment," removed him before the year was out.[5]

The most important duty of the House of Representatives in the Sixth Congress was to choose a President. Owing to the smooth working of the Republican machine, and the clumsy method of electoral voting then prescribed, Jefferson and Burr were tied for the presidency with 73 votes each. According to the Constitution, the duty of choosing between them fell on the House of

---

[5] Samuel A. Otis wrote Jefferson, March 11, 1801: "Your goodness will excuse my taking this opportunity to mention my son Harrison Gray Otis, atty. for the Massachusetts district; reinstated in the office by Mr. Adams to which he was originally appointed by Gen. Washington. He resigned the office on being elected to Congress and sacrificed a business that would have yielded him 20000 dollars. With a large and increasing family it became imprudent for him longer to continue in Congress. . . . On retiring Mr. Adams reinstated him in his former office, become vacant by Mr. Davis' promotion; and in which should you be pleased to continue him, I am confident he will discharge his duties with honor & fidelity, in doing which you will oblige an affectionate father." Jefferson MSS., 2d ser., LXIV, 16. Naturally this reasoning did not appeal to Jefferson. Samuel Otis, however, retained his post as Secretary of the Senate. The only movement against him came from the Hamiltonians, who tried to persuade him to resign on the ground that the Republicans would surely supersede him. His estimate of H. G. Otis's probable income was greatly exaggerated; ten thousand a year was the highest possible income to be got from the law in 1800. F. Ames, *Works*, I, 301.

Representatives, the members voting by states, each state having one vote, and a majority of votes being necessary for a choice.

This exigency had been contemplated by the Federalists since August, and by January the party was almost unanimous in the decision to use all its strength in the House to promote the election of Aaron Burr over Thomas Jefferson. So great was their dread and detestation of the leader of the Republican party that Aaron Burr seemed by far the lesser evil to those ignorant of his true character.[6] Many, even, who knew the unprincipled nature of the man, favored his election from the unworthy motives of spite, and the expectation that Burr could be kept "right" by corruption. For much the same reason, great business concerns of to-day prefer an easy-going grafter in power to an upright radical who threatens their interests. Among those who shared these opinions were a judge of the Supreme Court of Massachusetts,[7] and Harrison Gray Otis, who wrote Hamilton, December 17, 1800:

Dear Sir:

There exists the strongest probability that the electoral votes are equally divided between Messrs. Jefferson and Burr. We have certain advices from South Carolina and Georgia, and wait only for intelligence from Kentucky and Tennessee to ascertain the fact. The gentlemen of the opposition are of the opinion that this will be the case. The question now is, in what *mode shall* the friends of the federal government take advantage of this casualty? Can any terms be obtained from Mr. Burr favorable to the true interest of the country, and is he a man who will adhere to terms when stipulated? Is it advisable to attempt a negotiation with him — and in what manner and

[6] See Theophilus Parsons's letter, at end of this chapter. The sentiments of almost every Federalist leader are recorded in Hamilton's *Works*, VI. 486 *et seq.*

[7] See Sewall's letter at end of this chapter.

through what channel shall it be conducted? We are inclined to
believe that some advantage may be derived from it, but
few of us have a personal acquaintance with Mr. Burr. It
is *palpable* that to elect him would be to cover the opposition
with *chagrin*, and to sow among them the seeds of a morbid
division. But whether in any event he would act with the
friends to the Constitution, or endeavor to redeem himself with
his own party by the violence of his measures and the overthrow of the Constitution, is a doubt which you may assist us to
resolve. Your local situation and personal acquaintance with
these men and the state of parties, enables you to give an opinion
upon a subject in which all the friends to the country have a
common interest, and if you can venture to repose your confidence in me, I will most solemnly pledge myself that your sentiments shall be reserved within my own breast, or communicated
only to those whom you may designate. Should our expectation be realized, which we shall know in a day or two, is it advisable to send a messenger to New-York to confer with *friends
there*, or attempt to bring Mr. Burr here? What should be the
outlines of an agreement with him, and (alas! it is a difficult
question,) what security can be devised for his adherence to it?

I am anxious to act correctly and judiciously. It would be
distressing to omit or misdirect an effort which might be bene-
ficial to the country, or preserve the Constitution, and I presume that honor and duty will sanction every endeavor to
preserve it, even by an ineligible instrument. The treaty is [8] before the Senate, and I believe will be found another chapter in
the book of humiliation.

All claims for spoliation, it is said, are suspended during the
war, all public ships captured by *each* party are to be surren-
dered, and in the language of the case of Bullum *v.* Boatum,
after paying all costs we are permitted to *begin again de novo*.
It is very *doubtful* in my mind whether the Senate will ratify.[9]

Hamilton's clear view penetrated this sophistry. By
bitter experience he knew, through and through, the
character of the man by whose hand he was destined to
die. He perceived the lasting disgrace that his party

[8] The treaty of Mortefontaine, with France.
[9] Hamilton, *Works*, VI, 490.

would incur by elevating such a man to the presidency. But his wise counsel was not heeded. Just before the election in the House, the Federalist caucus decided to support Burr; only four members, not including Otis, opposed the decision.[10]  It was decided to commence balloting on February 11, immediately after the formal count of the electoral vote, and to continue without adjournment until a decision was reached.

Otis's correspondence throws no new light on the question of Aaron Burr's attitude toward this movement in his behalf, or of whether a bargain was actually concluded between him and the Federalists, as Otis had suggested in his letter to Hamilton. But it gives a conclusive answer to the charge made at the time, and since frequently repeated, that the Federalist Congressmen intended to prevent an election, and to usurp the government by legislative act, if they could not elect Burr. Rumors to that effect were current at the time, and were deemed sufficiently serious by the Republican leaders to warrant plans for a counter-stroke, by force of arms if necessary.[11] There is no doubt that certain hot-heads in the party did justify these apprehensions. Judge Sewall, for instance, wrote Otis, "it is possible that an election at this time . . . may be wholly prevented. This is most desirable." But the Federalist congressmen concerned always denied that

[10] [R. H. and J. A. Bayard, eds.] *Documents Relating to the Presidential Election in the Year 1801*, Philadelphia, 1831, p. 5. This pamphlet (brought out by James A. Bayard's sons, on account of aspersions on the memory of their father in Jefferson's *Anas* being read in the debate on Foot's Resolution), contains the depositions of James A. Bayard relating to the election in the cases of Burr *v.* Cheetham in 1806, and Gillespie *v.* Smith; depositions of Samuel Smith in the same case; and letters from two surviving Congressmen who took part in the election.

[11] H. Adams, *Gallatin*, 248, 254–63. These stories did not, in general, reach the newspapers, but they were circulated on hand-bills (*Independent Chronicle*, March 2, 1801) throughout the country. Cf. Nathaniel Ames's diary, in A. B. Hart, *Contemporaries*, III, 339.

such a project was ever entertained by them.[12] Otis's contemporary letters to his wife, his confidante in political matters, mention no such scheme, and indicate that he expected the election to terminate in the regular way. The following extracts include all that he wrote her regarding the election.

. February 4, 1801:

We are preparing for the 11th of february. I can form no conjecture as to the result that is worthy of being communicated. It is probable we shall have no choice the first time of balloting and if the Federalists are all firm, we shall carry our point.

Congress Hall, Monday Feby 9, 1801

. . . We are at this instant debating the rules of proceeding at the approaching election. They are enclosed for Harrison's perusal, and *I presume* will be adopted in their present form. In this event you see we are to be shut up for God knows how long, though it cannot be longer than the third of march. Our Committee Room must be garnished with beefsteaks, and a few Turkey Carpets to lie upon would not be amiss.

I do not believe however the obstinacy of parties will endure beyond the second day, but I cannot say who will give way. We shall however have the use of pen ink and paper which is more than all prisoners enjoy & which I shall improve.

On February 11, the official count of electoral votes was made, and the tie between Jefferson and Burr officially announced. Immediately afterwards, balloting commenced in the House, and that afternoon Otis wrote:

We are in Conclave and in a Snow Storm. The votes have been counted in Senate & no choice. We have balloted in the house *seven* times. Thus it stands —

[12] See their depositions, in *Documents Relating to the Election*. A contemporary letter of James A. Bayard was published in 1822 (printed in W. E. Dodd, *Nath. Macon*, 164), stating that the New England members expressed a determination during the election to risk civil war rather than permit Jefferson to be chosen. R. G. Harper then declared (Washington *Gazette*, January 16, 1823, and other leading newspapers) that he had never heard of such a plan.

For Jefferson 8 ⎫
For Burr       6 ⎬ States
Divided        2 ⎭

We have agreed not to adjourn, but we have suspended balloting for *one* hour to eat a mouthful. Perhaps we shall continue
here a week. No conjecture can be formed how it will terminate, but if we are true to ourselves *we* shall prevail. Poor Nicholson is in the *Committee* Room abed with a fever. It is a chance
that this kills him. I would not thus expose myself for any
President on Earth, but being in good health & spirits, . . . I
have no objection to staying here all night.

I am one of the Tellers and so constantly employed that I
cannot write to you at large.

February 15:

The last week has fled rapidly, in spite of the disagreeable and
still unfinished business in which we have been engaged, and
my heart beats higher and my impatience increases as the day
of my departure approaches. If the election should be made,
of which I believe there is little doubt, in a day or two, I shall
probably be off by the 1st of march at the farthest. I shall wait
only for two bills to be passed, the one making the annual appropriation for the support of Government and the other relative to the navy and leave them to wind off the end of the skain.
Yes my beloved angel, with you I shall retire from this scene
of anxiety and bustle, to enjoy the rational and I hope permanent comforts which we have the means of commanding, &
remain a silent spectator of the follies and confusion, of the
strife and licentiousness incident to all popular governments,
and to ours in a most eminent degree.

These letters certainly do not suggest that Otis was
conspiring to prolong the choice over March 3, and
place a Federalist usurper in the presidential chair.
On the following day, February 16, Bayard decided
that no more votes could possibly be secured for Burr.
He and a few others, who saw no use in continuing the
struggle further, decided to obtain what they could from

Jefferson before bowing to the inevitable. Samuel Smith of Baltimore was told that Jefferson could be elected if he gave satisfactory assurances in regard to the public debt and the navy, the abolition of which he was supposed to desire, and the non-removal of government officials. Smith told Bayard that Jefferson had already authorized him to make the statement that he "considered the prosperity of our commerce as essential to the interests of the nation," and that the navy should be increased "in progress with the increase of the nation." In regard to the civil service Smith had a special interview with Jefferson, and brought back word that he "did not think that such officers as the collectors of the port at Philadelphia and Wilmington [who had been mentioned as examples] ought to be dismissed on political grounds only, except in cases where they had made improper use of their offices, to force the officers under them to vote contrary to their judgment." These assurances — the last two of which Jefferson did not adhere to — having been given,[18] Bayard announced them to the Federal caucus on the morning of February 17, after the thirty-fifth ballot had also resulted in a tie. Jefferson's assurance satisfied enough Federalists to break the deadlock. On the next ballot Bayard, to whom the credit for this happy issue is chiefly due, handed in a blank. Morris of Vermont and the Maryland Federalists followed the same plan, thus allowing their Republican colleagues to cast the vote of their states; and Thomas Jefferson was elected President of the United States by a majority of two.

[18] These facts were stated under oath by Bayard and Smith in the Cheetham case (*Documents Relating to the Election*, 11–12), testified to as correct by other Federalists, and evidently believed in by Gallatin (H. Adams, *Gallatin*, 250). Jefferson in his *Anas* (*Works*, IX, 209–11) brands them "as absolutely false." The weight of evidence is against him. Cf. J. Q. Adams, *Memoirs*, I, 428.

The peaceful revolution of the new century was completed; the "sun of Federalism had set." Within a short time Otis and his Federalist colleagues had left Washington, never to return as part of a triumphant majority.

The Fourth of March, 1801, ends an epoch in Otis's life, as in that of his party; it marks the suspension of his career, at the age of thirty-five, as a national statesman. The successful lawyer, orator, and man of business had quickly ripened into a legislator. He had turned out a typical Federalist, representing his party at its best and at its worst: on the one hand, its lofty nationalism and creative genius, on the other, its narrow intolerance and distrust of the people. His brilliant oratory and talent for leadership had aided the carrying-out of a policy of spirited resistance to European aggression and insult, that brought France to terms while it kept intact Washington's standard of Isolation. He had done his best to prevent the fatal rupture in his party. On the other side, Otis must take a full share of responsibility for the hysteria and intolerance of 1798, and for that final act of the Federalist régime, the attempt to make Aaron Burr President of the United States. On the whole, we are forced to the conclusion that it was well for the country that the rule of Otis and his colleagues ended in 1801. Their foreign policy was a conspicuous success, and a refreshing contrast to the half-measures and experiments of the Jeffersonian epoch. But their follies and errors in this period were many, and they were not accidents, but inevitable results of the party's fundamental defect, a defect that could not be shaken off while Hamilton, Cabot, Ames, and Pickering were influential in its councils: they arose from the failure of the Federalists to respect the ideals, the jealousies, and the prejudices of a free people. This fundamental weakness must not blind us, however, to the fact that the Federal party laid down principles of government by which the Union has been preserved, by which these United States must be governed while they wish to remain one nation. To quote a contemporary prophecy of Robert Goodloe Harper:

Names may change; the denominations of parties may be altered or forgotten; but the principles on which the federalists have acted must be adopted, their plans must be substantially pursued, or the government must fall in pieces; for those narrow maxims which apply properly to small communities, and on which speculative men sometimes found their theories, will ever prove in practice wholly inadequate to the government of a great nation.[14]

## LETTERS

### SAMUEL SEWALL [15] TO OTIS

Marblehead, 29th Decr. 1800

My dear Sir,

I am pleased that Mr. Hooper succeeds at length in his petition: I observe by the paper that the House have accepted the report of the Com[mitt]ee.

The issue of the election of President is extremely unfortunate: the only consolation is that the federal party acted with so much unanimity notwithstanding the mistaken efforts of Mr. A's most solicitous friends. He must be satisfied that he was not forsaken or sacrificed by the party, and that, if he has not succeeded, it is only to be attributed to the too frequent vibration of popular elections. So. Carolina did precisely as last May and until the meeting of the Electors, I expected they would do. But at our meeting [16] we had so direct intelligence of the

---

[14] Harper's *Select Works*, 326.

[15] Samuel Sewall (1757–1814); a member of the Sixth Congress from the Salem district, who resigned before the second session on account of a promotion to the Supreme Bench in Massachusetts.

[16] He probably refers to the congressional caucus that nominated Adams and Pinckney.

state of their new legislature and such strong assurances of the intentions of the federal party there, as to excite with me the most sanguine hopes of an issue to the election entirely to the wishes of the federal party. I lament the change; but according to present appearances the federal party here are to gain strength from it. All the light troops of the opposition are disappointed and offended; it was not their intention to loose Mr Adams from the chair. We have heard of the votes from all the states excepting Kentucky & Tennessee: and there seems to be no doubt but these will be uniform with the other antifed. states: The two highest candid. will be Jeff. & Burr, & they will have an equal number of votes. What will be the conduct of the federal party in the house? A sentiment on this subject has become very general here, which I see had been anticipated in the Washington Federalist, — it is, that Burr must be voted for by the federalists as being the least of two evils. I think Burr's objectionable qualities will be more dangerous in the station of V. P. than as chief. He will govern without the responsibility which might check his proceedings: and he will intrigue as from a secret but a very advantageous position. On the other hand as chief, if he has less principle and politl. integrity than the other, as some suppose, yet he has less enthusiasm & philosophy, and is wholly free, I am told, from the nonsense of democratic plans, in which the friends of Mr. Jeff. if not himself, are completely involved. Another purpose may be effected by a steady and decided vote of the federal party for Mr. Burr: it is possible that an election at this time and with the materials you will be confined to, may be wholly prevented. This is most desirable: and this will be the event unless some one of the Jacob. states concurs with the feds. If the Feds. make Mr B. presid., they may retain a necessary influence upon the Admin. and the election itself will divide their adversaries. Perhaps I am reckoning, with great solicitude upon suppositions that are not to be realized: and at any rate I shall suggest nothing that can be new to you; but you must indulge a little to the desire of talking upon this interesting subject. . . .

With sincere respect & esteem    Your most obedt. serv.

SAMUEL SEWALL.

THEOPHILUS PARSONS TO OTIS

Boston Jany. 23d, 1801

Dear Sir —

I am much obliged to you for your polite attention to me on the subject of the Judicial department. I do not think the duties would be severe or troublesome, but from the salary must be deducted about $500 expended in the charge of them; the remainder will not support my large and growing family. My professional income is now greater, and altho' the salary is during life, yet I should feel myself compelled to resign whenever I should be unable thro' age or infirmity to fill the office with some reputation — and until that period I may hope to continue in the practice of the law. I have another consideration which perhaps has induced me to examine the question with less attention. If J. Lowell is not appointed, he will certainly believe himself neglected & will resign which would be disagreeable to us all. And may I not ask how long the present system is to last, if it be established this session?

The two political questions which agitate the public mind here are the election of a President & the ratification of the French Treaty. The Federalists seem not to be united in opinion upon these subjects. As to the first, the greater number prefer Burr. He has no political theories repugnant to the form of the constitution or the former administration — His ambition & interest will direct his conduct — and his own state is commercial & largely interested in the funded debt. If he will honorably support the government for which he has undoubted talents, he will have the support of the federalists and of some of the Jacobins whom he may detach — and his election will disorganize and embarrass the party who have given him their votes. If notwithstanding he should be hostile to the government, he will not only be opposed by all the federalists & by some of the southern Jacobins who disappointed by the event will not willingly contribute to increase or confirm his interest or ambition — but his personal embarrassments will also lessen his weight, by creating jealousy of his sinister intentions. Thus *they* argue. Others are fearful of his activity of his talents & his personal courage. They consider Jefferson as a man cautious thro' timidity — that he will fear to go the lengths of his party, & will thereby disgust many of them: and proceeding slowly the chapter of accidents may furnish opportunities of self defence which the vigour of Burr will not admit of. I trust the federalists in Congress will form an impenetrable phalanx & standing on higher ground than we occupy, will decide with wisdom & vigour.

On the second question it is generally agreed that parts of the Treaty are degrading to us as a nation and injurious to our citizens. But shall it be ratified? Some incline that way. However bad it is a worse one may be made by the approaching administration; and no better can be obtained by any administration. It puts the old treaties out of question, and the repeal of the act annulling them will not revive them so as to give them priority — and its defects are so manifest that a consideration of them will have a tendency to impede the propagation of French principles. Others contend — that our real importance in the scale of commerce will command at some future time a better treaty — that no occasion can warrant a sacrifice of national honour — once lost it cannot easily be recovered— that no embarrassments which this treaty will suspend will protect us against as great mischiefs from future negotiation, (which is purposely left open), by a new administration — that the great objects of our dread are french influence & british hostility — and whether the treaty is ratified or not, a new administration can easily expose us to them. All however agree that the ratification if it take place should be modified by a clause similar to the one introduced into the British Treaty, that it should not affect any prior treaties. Thus you see that however these questions are determined, the determination will have advocates among good men. I am glad that I am not called upon to give my voice on either of these questions, the reasons on both sides are so nearly equal, & the consequences of either decision are to be anticipated in some degree by conjecture only. Were I to decide *today* probably I should vote for Burr & for a modified ratification of the Treaty — to-morrow I might vote differently. However doubtful on these questions, I have no hesitation in assuring you that I am very sincerely

your most obedt. & humble Servant<br>THEOP PARSONS.

OTIS TO MRS. OTIS

Washington 4 Feby 1801

"Midst chains and bolts the active soul is free
And flies unfettered Cavendish to thee."

how if Lord Russell's soul could flie out of jail to the embraces of his friends, it is not extraordinary that mine should escape from the hubbub of a debate about the bill for governing this city to my dearest friend, the companion of my life and the partner of all my joys. It is in this situation now I snatch a moment to reassure you of my own welfare, and what is always more material, to enquire after yours. Thus it is I speak a little and write a little and think a little and laugh a little and wish a great deal that . . . my time of penance was over and gone. After closing my last, I received Dawes letter, by which you perceive that my hopes of office [17] are at end and will understand by what coalition of parties from the east and the west I have been defeated. The Governor from a desire to preserve a *local popularity* has abandoned the dictates of his own judgment and discarded the opinion of the whole court; but this is naturally to be expected from poor human nature. I was prepared for it, and care not a pinch of snuff for the result. It only confirms my opinion, that I must depend on my own exertions, without favor or affection places or promotion for my own prosperity & the advancement of my family, and I feel thank God that while my health continues I can provide for the comfort & happiness too of the dear objects which depend on me and constitute all that is dear to me.

I shall now be constantly with you, and be dispensed from seperations of even three and four weeks at a time which become sufficiently tedious.

You have done well to send for Rush, who I hope however will not bleed you, as I am sure that gentle medicine will answer every purpose.[18] . . .

---

[17] The office of Solicitor-General of Massachusetts.

[18] Mrs. Otis was then at Philadelphia, at the Harrisons'. If she escaped being bled by Dr. Rush, she was lucky — bleeding was his favorite remedy for every complaint from a cold in the head to yellow fever.

What can I desire you to tell our friends in reply to their reiterated proofs of affection for both of us. They know all I can say and feel on this subject; therefore say simply to them that I love 'em dearly.

Your affectionate H. G. Otis.

# CHAPTER XIII

## HARRY OTIS, FRIEND AND HOST

HAVING reached the close of what Otis afterwards called "the first act of my political drama," let us abandon for a time the political viewpoint, and glance at his personality and non-political activities, during the middle period of his life. Harry Otis the husband, father, friend, and host; Mr. Otis the brilliant orator and prominent citizen of Boston, is quite as interesting a person as the Honorable Harrison Gray Otis, politician and statesman. Among the citizens of all classes in Federalist Boston no one was so beloved or respected as he — and in that later Whig Boston, even Daniel Webster did not wholly supplant him in the affections of the people. This widespread admiration was due primarily, not to any supreme qualities as a statesman, or an orator, but to his well-rounded, vigorous personality. Josiah Quincy writes: "Men of the stamp of Sullivan and his friend Otis were more conspicuous for what they were, than for what they did. They were predominant men, and gave the community its quality, shaping, as if by divine right, its social and political issues."[1] But Quincy, himself, who knew Otis intimately notwithstanding the difference in their ages, despaired of transmitting his personality by pen and ink. "I wish it were in my power," he wrote in his diary, "to preserve for posterity some traces of the wit, brilliancy, eloquence, and urbanity of Harrison Gray Otis; for when he is gone there is no man who can make good his place in

[1] Josiah Quincy (1802–1882, son of Otis's contemporary of the same name), *Figures of the Past*, 323.

society," a statement which is hardly encouraging for one who knows Otis only through his writings and tradition.

If the reader expects to find Otis a typical member of a Puritanic society, he will look in vain. Perhaps he has suspected as much already, from reading Otis's letters from the "Republican Court." In Otis were comprehended the best and most charming characteristics of the society in which he was born and brought up, the Boston aristocracy; but in that society there were few Puritanic traits. The same claim cannot be made for the New England country gentry or the middle class at this period; among them the seventeenth-century Puritanic tradition was still fresh and vigorous. The country gentry produced the typical New England statesmen of the time, men like Timothy Pickering and John Quincy Adams, both the very quintessence of Puritanism; Pickering having all the harsh, unlovely characteristics of that creed and race, and Adams all the finer and nobler traits. And both men, it is significant to note, disliked Otis with all the intensity of temperamental opposites. But the leaders of Boston society and Boston Federalism inherited the characteristics of that genial, pleasure-loving group to which Otis's grandparents belonged, the court of the colonial governors. In character they resembled more the familiar type of the Virginia or Carolina gentleman than their own country neighbors. When William Wirt, the distinguished Virginia lawyer, visited Boston in 1829, he was astonished to find that his preconceived notions of Yankee society must be cast aside. "Otis has been twice with me, pressing me to dine with him," he wrote; "I have never received such a profusion of attentions anywhere in my life. I think the people of Boston amongst the most agreeable in the United States . . . they are as

warm-hearted, as kind, as frank, as truly hospitable as
the Virginians themselves. In truth, they are Virginian
in all the essentials of character. Would to heaven the
people of Virginia and Massachusetts knew each other
better!"[2]    Harrison Gray Otis was a typical member of
the class that gave Wirt these impressions.

At the prime of life "Harry" Otis, as his friends always
called him, was slightly above the average height; well
proportioned, with black hair, sparkling dark blue eyes,
a thin, Roman nose, and a ruddy complexion. His personal appearance, combined with his gracious charm of
manner, gave him a rare personal distinction, without
the slightest trace of stiffness or pomposity. Contemporaries always described his appearance as "elegant" —
a word now fallen into bad company — by which they
meant to say that he dressed with care and fastidiousness,
at a period when these qualities were by no means universal among men of his class. Chief Justice Parsons, for
instance, who was the conspicuous opposite to Otis in
this respect, was even accused of returning from a week's
circuit wearing one on top of the other the seven shirts
with which his wife had provided him at the start. Of
Otis it is related that he once met on the street a married
couple of his acquaintance, as the lady was arranging
the shirt ruffles of her untidy spouse. "There — look at
Mr. Otis's bosom!" said she, pointing to his immaculate
ruffles. "Madam," said Otis, with one of his best bows,
"If your husband could look within my bosom, he would
die of jealousy."

The secret of Otis's popularity lay in his tact, affabil-
ity, consideration for others, and a natural courtesy that
came from the heart. To enumerate his circle of loyal
friends would take pages. In Boston the most intimate,

[2] J. F. Kennedy, *Life of Wirt*, II, 268-73.

perhaps, were Thomas H. Perkins, William Sullivan, Isaac P. Davis, David Sears, Dr. John C. Warren, Theodore Lyman, Rufus G. Amory, Jonathan and Jeremiah Mason; in Philadelphia, George Harrison, Judge Hopkinson, and Charles Willing Hare; in New York, Rufus King; in Baltimore, Christopher Hughes and Robert Goodloe Harper; and in Charleston, John Rutledge and Thomas Pinckney. The fact that he formed as warm friendships among men of the Southern and Middle States as among his fellow Bostonians was typical of Otis. Consequently it was impossible for him ever to embrace the extreme brand of New England Federalism affected by the Essex Junto and the "River Gods" of Connecticut. No matter how great the provocation, he could never bring himself to a belief that Disunion was preferable to Union.

Enemies Otis had, as any man with a particle of backbone must have had if he took part in the politics of that day; but he looked on mankind in general without a trace of that sour malignity which appears in the writings of his Puritanic colleagues. His correspondence is remarkably free, considering the political bitterness of his day, from illiberal reflections on men and their motives; there is not, to my knowledge, a single harsh comment on the members of the Essex Junto, whose party selfishness and personal dislike of him he must have perceived. Since, like other party men, his particular abomination was political apostasy, he broke openly with Samuel Dexter after his desertion of the Federal party in 1813. Joseph Story he held suspect for many years on account of his early attachment to the Democratic party. Josiah Quincy once expressed to him the sentiment that President Jackson could say unto this learned judge, after the death of Chief Justice Marshall, as Pharaoh did unto

Joseph, "Thou shalt be ruler over my house." "Joseph, indeed! Why, yes, an excellent comparison," snorted Otis. "Pray, was anything said about his coat of many colors?"

It was impossible for Otis, with his sunny, genial nature, to carry on one of those lifelong political feuds which were meat and drink to some of his contemporaries. The nearest approach to one was his relationship with John Quincy Adams. No two men could have been more temperamentally unlike than Otis and Adams; the former frank, genial, and pleasure-loving, the latter cold, tactless, rigidly conscientious, and above all, an Adams. "What a queer family!" Otis wrote of the Adamses in his old age, à propos of Charles Francis Adams's entry into politics. "I think them *all* (beginning with the grandsire) varieties in a peculiar species of our race exhibiting a combination of talent, & good moral character, with passions and prejudices calculated to defeat their own objects & embarrass their friends, that would puzzle La Bruyère to describe & which has no Prototype in Shakespeare or Molière."

John Quincy Adams seems to have been under the delusion that Otis looked upon him as a rival, and a block to his political advancement;³ but there is not the slightest trace in Otis's writings of any such feeling. Moreover, as Adams's diary and writings on several occasions show a belief that Otis was intriguing against him, the jealousy and rivalry would seem to have been all on his side; yet he was capable, as we shall see, of doing full

³ "I know that from a very early date he [Otis] has personally been afflicted with the feelings of a rival towards me, a vague and general feeling of rivalry, for I never stood in the way of his wishes for any particular object. It was so with poor Bayard in a much greater degree, and with less reason." J. Q. A. to John Adams, Oct. 29, 1816. Adams MSS. In his *Reply* of 1829 Adams writes: "How long it has been since he has seen fit to look at me as an adder in his path is best known to himself."

justice to Otis's character and personality. When Adams was read out of the Federal party for voting for Jefferson's Embargo, the first break between the two occurred. Their fathers were old and intimate friends, and Otis had loyally supported the elder Adams in 1800; but during the stormy years that followed, the clans of Otis and Adams ceased personal intercourse. The following letter from Abigail Adams to her son, then minister to Great Britain, describes the characteristic manner in which Otis brought about a reconciliation, at the beginning of the "era of good feelings":

Quincy, Aug. 27, 1816

My dear Son . . .

In this still calm, and political pause, I must entertain you with domestic occurrences, one of which is a Family visit, which we received a fortnight since from Mr W Foster, your old neighbor,[4] (who lost his Lady about two months since,) accompanied by Mrs A Otis [5] and daughter, Mr H G Otis Lady and daughter and son; who all came in a Body to take tea with us. This visit has been long in contemplation: Mrs A Otis was commissioned to inquire, if your Father would like to receive the visit? to which a candid reply was given that he should be pleased to receive it. Whether the Hartford millstone hung so heavy that it could not be thrown off, or for what other reason I cannot say, the visit was never accomplished untill a fortnight since, when we past a very pleasant and social afternoon together. Upon taking leave Mr Otis in his very civil and polite manner, asked it as a favour that I would dine with him the next week? I replied, that I had long declined all invitations to dinner, as well as all public company, upon which he said it should be only a Family party. I then referred him to your Father who promptly accepted his invitation. Accordingly when the day came, we went, and were most kindly and cordially received by all the assembled families. Mr Mason [and] Mr Tudor were considered former appendages to us, and

[4] H. G. O.'s father-in-law.
[5] Mrs. Samuel Allyne Otis, H. G. O.'s stepmother.

were a part of the company. All appeared pleased and mutually gratified.

I know not when I have past a pleasanter day, and I could not but regret the hour of seperation. All this past off very well. I never expected to hear more of it. But you cannot imagine what a sensation it has created in the Capital. A Gentleman from Town yesterday informd me, that it was a subject of speculation in the public offices. Whether the Stocks have risen or fallen in consequences, I do not pretend to say, but the wise ones cannot comprehend the phenomenon. Some whisper it was to obtain a recommendation for a foreign Mission, — now I do not believe in any such motive I ascribe it to the benevolent desire of extinguishing all party spirit, and to a desire of renewing former friendship, and Family intimacy. As such I received it, and in the same spirit returnd it.[6]

Peace was maintained between the two families until 1828, when the feud broke out afresh, because John Quincy Adams accused the old Federalist leaders of having plotted the dissolution of the Union. An acrimonious controversy between Otis and Adams followed.[7] Yet only three years later Otis again came forward with the olive branch, thereby eliciting angry protests from some of his old friends and associates. To one of them he wrote, on May 20, 1833:

I am told you are curious and puzzled for an explanation of my call on J Q A last year. It was the result of reflection and *principle*. In regard to the Bank and other great measures, he had conducted himself with propriety and ability. I knew he wanted to bury the hatchet, because entre nous, he sent me

[6] Abigail Adams to John Quincy Adams, Adams MSS., "Family Letters," ix. John Adams wrote his son on the same event, August 26, 1816 (*Ibid.*, viii): "As you live: your Father and Mother & Louisa dined last Tuesday in Boston with Judge Otis in the neatest Company imaginable; none but Otis's, Lymans, Thorndykes, Minots, Boardmans and Fosters, except Tudor and Mason. I never before knew Mrs. Otis. She has good Understanding. I have seldom if ever passed a more sociable day. Exert all your Witts to draw Inferences from this Phenomenon. Do you ascribe it to the Eclipse of 1806, to the Comet or to the spots in the sun?"

[7] See chapters xv and xxxi.

word to that effect. The state of the nation, makes it desirable to strengthen the hands and encourage the hearts of all who are able and disposed to render services to the Country, on great occasions, though reliance is not to be placed upon their consistency, and as I could have no personal or selfish motive, & he must know it, I gave him a call which he return'd & there the matter drop'd.

It is a pleasure to note that no better text can be found on which to base a description of Otis's social qualities, than a letter of John Quincy Adams to his father, written on receiving his account of the reconciliation of 1816:

Since beginning this Letter I have received yours of 26. August and 5. September, and am highly gratified by your and my Mother's Account of your social party at Judge Otis's. Among the lights and shades of that worthy Senator's character, there is none which shows him in higher colours than his hospitality. In the course of nearly thirty years that I have known him, and throughout the range of experience that I have had in that time, it has not fallen to my lot to meet a man more skilled in the useful art of entertaining his friends than Otis; and among the many admirable talents that he possesses, there is none that I should have been more frequently and more strongly prompted to Envy; if the natural turn of my disposition had been envious. Of those qualities Otis has many — His Person while in Youth, his graceful Deportment, his sportive wit, his quick intelligence, his eloquent fluency, always made a strong impression upon my Mind; while his warm domestic Affections, his active Friendship, and his Generosity, always commanded my esteem . . . Mrs. Otis is and always has been a charming woman; and I am very glad you have seen them both in the place where of all others they appear to the greatest advantage — their own house.[8]

Otis was famous in his day for that "sportive wit" which Adams mentions among his attractive characteristics. We look in vain for it in his political correspond-

[8] J. Q. Adams, to John Adams, October 29, 1816, Adams MSS. "Family Letters," VII.

ence and speeches, for politics of the Federalist era were so intense and seemed so vital that to season them with humor was considered almost blasphemous. But Otis, who in private intercourse was always bubbling over with spontaneous fun and good nature, was the life of every assembly of men or women where he appeared. At public and private dinners he was the favorite toastmaster. A contemporary diary, describing a party in 1809, writes, "All went off with éclat, except the toasts, which were rather flat. The gentlemen were not prepared to be either witty or sentimental, and impromptus suit the genius of the French better than that of the English or their American descendants. Mr. Otis alone was happy on this occasion; his wit is ever ready." [9] Josiah Quincy gives an equally pleasing impression of him at a cattle-show in Worcester in 1829:

The speeches by Otis and Everett were in the happiest vein; and a grand ball concluded the day. No, it did not conclude it, after all; for near midnight some gentlemen from Providence, who had arrived by the newly opened Blackstone Canal, invited a few of us to adjourn to a room they had engaged and taste some of "Roger Williams Spring," which they had brought all the way from the settlement he founded. Now this same spring, as it turned out, ran some remarkably choice Madeira, and this beverage, served with an excellent supper, furnished the material basis for brilliant displays of wit, flashing out upon the background of hearty and genial humor. Mr. Otis fairly surpassed himself. He was wonderful in repartee, and his old-fashioned stories were full of rollicking fun. I well remember the account he gave of the first appearance of champagne in Boston. It was produced at a party given by the French consul, and was mistaken by his guests for some especially mild cider of foreign growth. The scene was beneath the dignity of history, to be sure; but taken as a sort of side-show, it was very enjoyable.

[9] J. Winsor, *Boston*, IV, 18.

The examples that Mr. Quincy gives us of Harry Otis's humor consist, unfortunately, of puns — a form of witticism then prevailing, and now, happily, gone out of fashion. We shall not repeat them. A more convincing example of his ready wit — although to appreciate it requires some knowledge of Massachusetts topography — was told me by Mr. Frank B. Sanborn, who heard it from his friend Wendell Phillips. It seems that one of the colleagues of Otis and the elder Phillips in the State Senate, about the year 1808, rejoiced in the curious name of Salem Town. On one occasion, when the Democratic minority offered a "joker" resolution, drawn up with the express purpose of trapping unwary Federalists into endorsing Democratic principles, Mr. Town, alone of the Federalist majority, swallowed the bait, and voted "Yea" in the roll-call. Otis came up to him, after the vote had been taken, and remarked in a solemn tone, "Mr. Town, your parents were four miles out of the way, more or less, in naming you." "Four miles, Mr. Otis! What do you mean, sir?" — "Instead of *Salem Town*, they should have christened you *Marble Head!*"

Social life in Boston in the first decade of the nineteenth century was already becoming more elaborate, as a natural result of material prosperity. We hear of numerous private balls, and little cotillion parties, of music furnished by a Turkish band, of peaches and melons in November — not bad, for a town of thirty thousand inhabitants. The waltz was not yet introduced, however, — Otis when seeing it for the first time at Washington, in 1818, thought it an "indecorous exhibition" — and the bulk of the evening parties were simply *conversazioni*, with elaborate suppers. Social clubs for the men, with houses of their own, were not founded in

Boston before Otis's old age, but in this first decade of the
nineteenth century, several of the dinner clubs, which
are still a characteristic feature of Boston social life, were
formed among congenial friends. They met weekly or fort-
nightly at the members' houses or at some well-known
coffee-house. Otis, with William Sullivan, Thomas Handasyd Perkins, and other choice spirits, belonged to one
of these coteries known as the "Saturday Fish Club," of
which little more than the name is known. Sullivan,
however, writes Otis on Sunday, January 13, 1822:

> The club dined yesterday at Mr Joy's — *wine* from 20 to
> 45 years old — and no better for being more than 20. Besides
> the members we had Mr. Henderson of N. York — [and] Mr
> K[ing] — Brother Rufus, who complained to Mr J—— that
> the women wear no *pockets* nowadays. . . . Joy broke the
> sober rules of the club, by bringing in oysters from the shell, to
> give a *gout*, and a market, for his wine; — it certainly needed
> no such aid.

The alliance between gentility and government continued in Massachusetts long after it was sundered in the
nation as a whole. Boston society was Federalist to
the core, and supplied practically all the Federalist leaders. As a consequence, it looked with mingled fear and
contempt upon the Democratic party, and consistently
ostracized the few gentlemen like Elbridge Gerry, Perez
Morton, and (after 1808) John Quincy Adams, who belonged to it. Seldom, before the "era of good feelings,"
was a follower of Jefferson invited to pass the portals
of a leading Boston family. Mr. Theophilus Parsons, Jr.,
tells us, in his memoir of his father, that he never saw a
"Jacobin" in his father's house until 1807, when his
Uncle Cross, a Maine Democrat, was invited to dine there
while visiting Boston. The children examined him attentively, as a specimen of a new and strange breed. In the

course of the dinner, the Chief Justice remarked pleasantly, "Mr. Cross, take a glass of wine with me," and
handed him the decanter, when to the consternation of
the company, young Theophilus called out, "Why, he is
not a Jacobin, after all!" — "No, my young friend, I am
not a *Jacobin;* at least, I hope not," — said Uncle Cross.
"Did you think I was?" — " Yes, sir," said young hope-
ful, "but I see you are not, for I have heard father say,
again and again, that nothing on earth would make him
drink wine with a Jacobin!" — at which point the conversation was broken off by young Theophilus being sent
away from the table.

Another amusing instance of Federalism in social life,
is given in the diary of Otis's half sister, Harriet, at the
age of twenty-four. Speaking of a public ball at Washington, she writes:

An introduction to the Messrs W——, printers and demos,
the most remarkable circumstance — felt my pride a little hurt
but checked such rebellious risings as well as I could at the time
and when such things are over they serve only for diversion.

It is a mistake to put this feeling down to snobbishness.
Strange as it may seem, Otis and his friends, who dreaded
democracy in theory, were in many ways more democratic
than those who occupy a similar position to-day. They
lived on terms of friendly intimacy with their servants,
their tradespeople, and their country neighbors. Mr.
Hale tells us how "almost any morning might be seen
Col. Thos. H. Perkins, Harrison Gray Otis, William (Billy)
Gray, Ben. Bussey, Peter C. Brooks, Israel Thorndike
and other wealthy towns folk, trudging homeward for
their eight o'clock breakfast with their market baskets
containing their one o'clock dinner." [10] One of Mr. Par-

[10] J. W. Hale, *Old Boston Town . . . by an 1801-er,* 12.

sons's stories may give us the key to this seeming inconsistency. When a Salem man asked the elder Parsons why the Newburyporters were forever quarreling about religion, he replied, "Because we look upon religion as having a real importance. We think it worth quarreling about; you don't." The situation was the same in politics. Federalists and Republicans alike, at the period of which we speak, took their politics with a grim earnestness that the present generation can hardly comprehend. To a Federalist, a Jacobin was an anarchist, who would pull down the whole political and social structure; Jacobinism was a disease to be avoided and proscribed. Dance with a Jacobin? Drink wine with a Jacobin? Of course not! Would the daughter of Jefferson Davis have danced with Wendell Phillips? Would Pius IX have invited Cavour to dinner?

The rôle in which Otis always appeared to his best advantage was that of host to this Federalist aristocracy. John Quincy Adams, with all his experience in the society of Washington and European capitals, could write that he had never met a man "more skilled in the useful art of entertaining his friends" than Otis. He and his wife were blessed with the means and facilities for indulging their natural hospitality to their heart's desire. Just before returning to Boston in 1801, Otis sold his house on the corner of Cambridge and Lynde Streets, and built a much larger one, now number 85 Mount Vernon Street, on his portion of the old Copley pasture. This in turn he sold in 1807, and built the spacious mansion, now number 45 Beacon Street. Here was his home for the remaining forty-one years of his life. Few private dwellings even of to-day can compare in size and comfort to the old Otis

mansion. It was open in front on the Common, with a
view of the Blue Hills across the Back Bay, then a broad
sheet of water that came within two hundred yards of the
door. On the other three sides it was surrounded by
courtyards and gardens, with an extensive ell, stables,
and outbuildings.[11] Some idea of its size may be gained
from the fact that in the last eighteen years of its owner's
life it sheltered himself, three of his married children,
with their offspring, each family having a private sitting-
room, besides allowing an entire floor for entertaining, and
leaving plenty of room for guests. Such a house might be
thought enough for any man, but in 1809 Otis purchased
a large farm in Watertown, and by extensive improvements to the house and grounds turned it into a beautiful
country estate, which he named "Oakley" — it is now
the Oakley Country Club. A propos of the purchase,
John Rutledge wrote Otis from Charleston, June 6, 1809:

Having settled the affairs of the State, & put Democracy
"in a Hole," as that queer gentleman John Adams quaintly
said, it seems you have bought a Villa, & are going to indulge in
a little rural felicity. This I presume is the *Ton* at Boston, & as
Mrs. Otis & the President[12] are at the head of the fashionables,
getting this Country seat was, I presume, quite "en regle."
But it really seemed to me that having such a House as you
have, with the whole Common of Boston as an Apendage, &
open & improved grounds all around, might have satisfied any
man of ordinary ambition. I will with very great pleasure send
you an assortment of Seeds of Shrubs & Plants which may sub-
sist in your frozen region — but this, my good friend, is not the
season. I have spoken to a Mr. Champneys who is the President
of our Agricultural Society, & has in this neighbourhood a
prodigiously fine garden, & he promises to make an assortment

[11] The site of the two houses to the east of the Otis mansion (now Mr.
Dixey's, and the annex to the Somerset Club) was Otis's garden until 1831. He
then built one of these houses for his daughter Mrs. Ritchie, and sold the remaining lot.
[12] Otis was then President of the State Senate.

of plants for you in the season, which will not [be] before the month of December. He says that altho' you are an Oracle in Politics & in law, that you are in the very horn book of Botany & Gardening in supposing that Plants can be removed at this Season. As Mr. Robert [Rutledge] has determined to make a visit to Boston I shall have the pleasure of seeing you deo volente about the beginning of August. Before that time I shall take the liberty of introducing to your acquaintance one of my sisters, Mrs. Laurens, who in consequence of indisposition of health must travel this summer & will pass a week or two at Boston. Altho I owe you more on the score of friendship than any man living, yet when Mrs. Laurens leaves us, I must add to my Debt by recommending her to the charities of Mrs. Otis & yourself. I pray of you to present me affectionately to Mrs. Otis, Miss Eliza, Sarah & the young folks. I request you would give my affections to Mason & say to him that I shall be in Boston in August — in the meantime God bless you & yours —

J. R——

Oakley was the scene of many a jolly house party, but the Beacon Street mansion was the centre of Otis hospitality. Here in 1817 Otis entertained President Monroe, during his visit to Boston that inaugurated the "era of good feelings"; in fact, he offered the entire house to the Chief Magistrate and his suite, who refused this lavish hospitality. In the spring and summer a constant stream of family friends came for visits from New York, Philadelphia, Virginia, and Charleston. Almost every visitor of distinction in Boston brought a letter of introduction to Mr. Otis and received his hospitality, — "We have kept tavern for John Bull these thirty years," he wrote in 1820. Every Thanksgiving a huge family reunion of the numerous Otis, Foster, Lyman, and Thorndike connections was held around the great dining-table. In the winter season, there were frequently parties of two hundred or more, and little incidents like the following, related in one of Otis's letters, were not uncommon:

Night before last, Sophia undertook to ask Mrs I. P. Davis and Miss Lovell to eat buckwheats, and the party swelled to between twenty & thirty, — all the 2nd & 3d generation of Fosters, my sisters, Thorndikes, Callanders, Holleys, and half a doz Codmans, Grays, Brooks' &c to fill up chinks.

Those old Bostonians thoroughly and sincerely enjoyed the fine art of eating and drinking. While the Otis family were in residence, a blue-and-white Lowestoft punch-bowl, with a capacity of about ten gallons, was placed every afternoon on the landing halfway up to the drawing-room, and kept filled with punch for the benefit of visitors. Otis was famous as a gourmet and a connoisseur of wines, although how he managed to indulge in the good things of this world on the scale that he did through forty gouty years, is hard to imagine. Family tradition is positive that a regular breakfast dish of his, even at the age of eighty, was a moderate-sized terrine of pâté de foie gras. After beginning the day in this fashion, the Otis family would have a hearty lunch at eleven or twelve, followed by dinner at some time between half-past two and half-past four, and a substantial supper at eight or nine in the evening. It is safe to say that the punch-bowl on the stairs prevented the male members of the family from becoming thirsty during the afternoon, and Otis tradition assures us that a special ice-chest, within easy reach, was kept filled with jellies, whips, and syllabubs for whoever might be attacked by hunger between meals. At the dinner-table, there was none of your modern false modesty about looking at food, — the joints and pies were kept on the table, to regale the sight and the nostrils. Variety was not great, but abundance was unstinted. "I wish you could get here by dinner time," Otis once wrote to his wife, while she was at New York, and the older children at Oakley. He then adds a sketch of the dining-

room by way of explanation. Mr. Theodore Lyman is
dining with Mr. Otis, and William and James Otis, aged
fourteen and fifteen, are seated at the sideboard; all are
eating their soup. A large saddle of mutton adorns the
centre of the table, and the four corners are garnished
with a leg of lamb, a Virginia ham, a "pye," and a salmon.
"Brants & chickens for second course," a note informs
us: the vegetables and dessert are left to the imagination.
If this was a simple family meal, the table must have
fairly groaned at a formal dinner. Otis in his later years
loved to relate the answer of his victualer, when pressed
to tell whether he had any customer so good as Mr. Otis.
After scratching his head awhile, the tradesman, a non-
committal Yankee, replied that he guessed he sent about
as much to the Hotel Albion.

The consumption of old Madeira in nineteenth-cen-
tury Boston was likewise enormous. Otis's old friend,
George Harrison, of Philadelphia, was the United States
agent for the famous house of Duff Gordon & Co., and
received the orders of Otis and his Boston friends for that
king of wines. Here is a sample consignment of Madeira
at forty-six pounds sterling the pipe (a double hogshead
containing one hundred and twenty-six gallons):

| Jonn. Mason | 60 Dy St [13] | £ 46 |
| Ditto | "    " | 82.10. |
| Gardiner Green | "    " | 46 |
| Ditto | "    " | 46 |
| I. P. Davis | "    " | 82.10. |
| John Lowell Junr. | "    " | 60 |
| Thomas Perkins | "    " | 46 |
| Lady Temple [14] | "    " | 46 |
| William Phillips | "    " | 46 |

[13] Abbreviation for "Draft at sixty days' sight."
[14] Widow of Sir John Temple, the former British consul-general, and grandmother of Robert C. Winthrop.

| Jeremiah Allen | 60 Dy St | 46 |
|---|---|---|
| Andrew Allen | " " | 46 |
| Benjn. Bussey | " " | 46 |
| Danl Davis | " ". | 46 |
| Commodore Preble | " " | 46 |
| E. H. Derby | " " | 46 |
| John Phillips | " " | 46 |
| P C Brooks | " " | 46 |
| Andrew Seaton | " " | 92 |
| John Philips Junr. | " " | 23.10. |
| Prentess Mellen | " " | 23.10. |
| Saml S Wilde | " " | 23.10. |
| H. G. Otis | " " | 46 |
| | | £ Stg 1077.10. |

In addition to his quota in the above consignment, which arrived in September, 1807, Otis procured another pipe direct. The previous year, he had received "2 pipes choice particular Madeira wine in strong iron-bound casks at £45 Stg. p. pipe, mark'd H G O branded I A G," and "1 Pipe ditto wine"; but in 1809 he evidently considered it necessary to lay in a new stock, for in that year George Harrison writes, "I will order 'H G O — G H' of very superior wine for you, & God grant that I may partake of it when ripe 7 years hence."

A natural consequence of the high living then prevalent was the gout, with which Otis was afflicted during the last forty years of his life. It was an irritating disease, that soured the temper of many an old gentleman; but Otis's temper and constitution were both proof against it. Although he lived to the age of eighty-three, he retained until the last his wit, good nature, and every quality that endeared him to his fellow men.

# CHAPTER XIV

## FAMILY RELATIONS — EXPANSION — LITERATURE — ORATORY — HARVARD COLLEGE

### 1801–1816, ÆT. 36–51

MANY persons who did not know Otis well, and a number of those who did, imagined him consumed with ambition for political preferment. Otis was ambitious, as most politicians and statesmen are, for as John Quincy Adams once wrote: "The selfish and the social passions are intermingled in the conduct of every man acting in a public capacity. It is right that they should be so, and it is no just cause of reproach to any man that in promoting to the utmost of his power the public good, he is desirous at the same time of promoting his own." Otis liked the sense of leadership, the excitement, and the glory, such as there was, in political life; but he liked still more the quiet of private life, and the liberty to employ his time in contributing to the enjoyment of his family and friends. He frequently refused public office, when the acceptance of it meant separation from his family or interference in any way with his domestic happiness. A few extracts from his letters to Mrs. Otis will show that he was essentially a man of domestic tastes.

December 3, 1797.

You think it probable I shall find this path of politics rough with thorns. I agree that it is very probable. But is it not better to make the experiment early and to realize the vanity of these pursuits in season to leave them and follow such as are more consolatory? I always knew that my habits were naturally domestic and that my happiness was to be found only in the

bosom of my family.  Perhaps however I owe something to my
country, and I may as well discharge the debt now, as at a
time when my children will require my more constant and immediate attention.  I must however consider my seperation
from you under any circumstances, as a chasm in my existence,
which no honors can fill up; & which having once passed, I
shall not consent to widen by leaving you again.

February 4, 1800.

Dear Angel; — but a few weeks and I come to you; never
(unless forced by necessity), never again to quit your side
for distant & tedious employments.  It is my firm resolution,
not to serve another Congress, whether I shall resign, before
the next session, depends much on yourself, if health & inclina-
tion should render it eligible for you to accompany me, & suitable accomodations can be procured it is probable that I may
take you to Washington for one season; but I certainly will
never go there without you.

When he refused the Federalist nomination for Representative and returned to Boston, in 1801, it was with the
hope of giving up politics altogether.  But he was soon
forced back into the whirlpool by the pressure of his
friends and by his own sense of duty.  Every year from
1802 to 1817 he served in one branch or another of the
State Legislature, a career with much hard work, and no
compensating glory.  "I have not yet had a chance of living for myself," he writes his Aunt Warren in 1809, "nor
for the pleasures of and advantages of sweet communion
with any particular connections.  I sometimes am so sanguine as to hope that these blessings are not forever
alienated from me even in this world, but the hours fly,
and my white hairs become daily more discernible."

In 1816, every effort was made to make Otis accept the
Federalist nomination for Governor of Massachusetts.
"I have authorized and requested particular persons to
say in the most positive and unequivocal manner that I

*will not* be a Candidate," he wrote his wife, on January 19 of that year; "I wish not to espouse the Commonwealth while you live, nor to take charge of the immense family, untill my own boys are provided for." In spite of his protests, the formal nomination was tendered to him, and promptly declined. A few days later he wrote Mrs. Otis:

> There is great sensation produced by my declining what all the wise and sagacious heads believe to have been the object of my pursuit for years. . . . Nobody can imagine my motives for refusing what was never refused before, because nobody can conceive that the joys of domestic life and the command of ones own society and movements are to be placed in competition with the honor of the office.

The following year (1817) Otis accepted a seat in the United States Senate, a position considered at that time inferior to a governorship, to which he subsequently aspired; but his action was due to special circumstances, namely, his share in the responsibility for incurring the Massachusetts war claim.[1] The fact remains that he refused the highest honor that his party could bestow upon him, simply because he feared that it would conflict with his domestic happiness. According to family tradition, however, Otis during his later life would have welcomed a diplomatic appointment from the federal government. His friends always believed that any post he desired might have been his, had he confessed his political sins and abjured the Hartford Convention. It was well known that he was frequently conducted to a high mountain-top by leaders of the Jeffersonian party, and shown visions of great offices and honors that might be his, if he would become one of them.[2] But Otis was not

[1] See below, chap. XXIX.
[2] J. Quincy, *Figures of the Past*, 317; S. K. Lothrop, *Sermon on H. G. Otis*, 24; Loring, 202. In 1808, after Christopher Gore had been given the Federalist nomination for governor, the opposition press openly hinted that only in the

the man to renounce the truth and right, as he saw it, for worldly advantage, and he always let it be distinctly understood that whoever chose him, chose an unrepentant Hartford Convention Federalist. It is a great pity that the country could not have had the services of such a man as Harrison Gray Otis at the court of St. James or of the Tuileries; his tactful, genial nature, his fine presence and genuine hospitality, his education and gentle blood, his long experience in public life, all fitted him for a high diplomatic position. But it would have required a remarkable degree of political temerity for any President of the United States to honor the leader and defender of the Hartford Convention.

The position that Otis loved, far more than any political honor, was that of chief of his numerous clan of children and grandchildren, nephews, nieces, and cousins.[3] When he settled down in Boston for good in 1801, he already had a family of six; two children had died young;

Democratic party could an Otis hope to receive due recognition of his talents. In 1816 a number of leading Democrats offered to support him for the Democratic nomination for governor, against Samuel Dexter. (Otis to Mrs. Otis, February 11, 1816.)

[3] His children were as follows:

1. *Elizabeth Gray Otis*, 1791–1824, m. George W. Lyman, son of Theodore Lyman. Four children.

2. *Harrison Gray Otis, Jr.*, 1792–1827, a lawyer of some prominence; m. (1817) Eliza Henderson Boardman, the well-known and public-spirited Mrs. Harrison Gray Otis of Civil War times. Five children.

3. *Sally Otis*, 1793–1819, m. Israel Thorndike, Jr. Four children.

4. *Mary Foster Otis*, 1795–96.

5. *Alleyne Otis*, 1796–1806.

6. *George Otis*, 1797–98.

7. *Sophia Harrison Otis*, 1798–1874, m. (1823) Andrew Ritchie, Jr. Three children.

8. *James William Otis*, 1800–69, a merchant, resided in New York, m. (1825) Martha C. Church, of Providence. Seven children.

9. *William Foster Otis*, 1801–58, a prominent lawyer and churchman; m. (1831) Emily Marshall, the celebrated beauty. Three children.

10. *Alleyne Otis*, 1807–73.

11. *George Harrison Otis*, 1810–33.

and three more were afterwards born: in all seven sons and four daughters. In his family life Otis appeared at his very best. It was usual, in the early nineteenth century, for parents to impress their children with the fact that an awful gulf existed between them and their elders. "Honored Papa," and "Honored Mamma," were the proper titles by which to address a parent, and the formalities of a court were exacted in the daily life of the household. With the Otis family it was otherwise. Harrison Gray Otis, without spoiling his children, made himself their friend, and like Squire Bracebridge, made each and every one feel that home was the best place on earth.

Otis was the patron saint of his poor relations, especially of the loyalist Grays in England, who were ever impecunious. Until 1830 Harrison Gray the younger lived a grumbling existence in London, supported by a small pension from the government, and the little American property that his nephew had managed to save from the old Treasurer's estate. The reader may remember Jack Gray, the young loyalist of 1775, who was entrusted to the Otises in Barnstable for safe keeping during the siege of Boston. His capacity for getting into trouble evidently remained his leading characteristic, to judge from the following letter, from Harrison Gray to Otis, describing Uncle Jack's departure for Demerara to seek his fortune:

N44 Rathbone Place June 4th 1804
Dear nephew —
... Your Uncle saild from Falmouth the 3d of April with a fair Wind which continued three Weeks so I am in hopes he has arrived before this time to the place of his destination. ... I hope to God he will do well. the great expectation I have formed of it has in great measure tranquillized my Pillow, his greatest Fault is being too easy and thinks every person is as well disposed as himself, but unfortunately he had reason to Alter his

Opinion before he left Town as the very Evening before he intended to leave Town he was arrested and taken to a Spunging House by a Man he had conceived to be his good Friend, I had to borrow the money the next day to get him liberated the debt was twenty pounds & the Damn infamous Charges £9.5.7 this happened on a Saturday & I wishd him very much to leave London on the Thursday before as I was sensible he was exposed every day he appeared to a Set of Rapacious Creditors who only wanted to find him to distress him, he thought well of them, the next day After he was discharged from this execrable & infamous place, which is a disgrace to the Government, I was determined to get him out of London & the next morning he went & arrived at Portsmouth in the Evening & he wrote me the day After to say the Ship from the Downs had not got round and the next Sunday following as I was at Breakfast a Knock at my door was Announced, and as Usual I said walk in, and to my Utter *Astonishment*, when I turned my head round, I found it was your Uncle, I was surprized to that degree that I was deprived of the power of Utterance for some time & so was he, when I recoverd I said in the Name of God what has happened have you lost your passage, he said no but as he was going to embark he was Arrested for £13.10 by a Hair dresser who he did not owe one farthing to, and who he saw every day before he left Town, the Scoundrel took the Advantage of his situation as he knew all his moments & swore to his debt. Your Uncle was soaked through as he rode all Night outside the Coach, inside being full. I made him comfortable by a change of Cloaths & lined his inside to prevent his taking cold. the day he was Arrested there was no post to London & he did not know a person there & the Convoy waiting only for a fair Wind to depart under all these unpleasant Circumstances. The Sheriffs advised him to step into the Coach for London & return the next day & they made him deposit all his baggage Watch &c &c as a pledge until he returned, & being Sunday I did not know where to apply for the money as all Banks were shut & most all my Friends in the Country. fortunately the Man of the House where I live had twenty pounds by him which I borrowed and added two more as the Charges was £7.15.6 & immediately sent to take his place for that Evening & after I made him eat a Beefsteak & a pint of Wine I accompanied him

to the Coach & saw him off once more After paying £50.11.1
which to a *positive Certainty* woud have been saved, if he had
left Town the day I urged him. as the poor fellow seemed so
much Affected I could not find it in my heart to say any thing
about it, my Mind was on the torture for fear he would lose his
passage, as the Wind changed favorable. I had no peace until
I heard from him which was on Tuesday dated at 3 oClock
on Monday saying he Arrived at 8 oClock very much fatigued
not having his Cloaths off for 48 hours having rode two Nights
& that the infamous Scoundrels did not discharge him until
3 oClock & he was then going on board as the Convoy was
Under Weigh with a fair Wind. you can better judge of my
extreme suffering, & the torture my mind experienced than
I can possibly find Language to convey and I did not know
until Thursday whether he got on board, this is a true Account
so help me God. remember me affectionately to all your dear
family & I sincerely wish your health & happiness may be as
great as your liberality & Kindness has been to your good Uncle
tho unfortunate he received the twenty pounds from Messr
Dickason & he told me he had wrote you. God bless you &
am in great haste your Affectionate Uncle & friend

H Gray

That Scoundrel Bonaparte is made Emperor of the gauls &c
&c & I am afraid he will ultimately be Emperor *of all the World.*

The fever in the West Indies soon put an end to the
troubles of happy-go-lucky Uncle Jack, and on Otis fell
the duty of helping support the two orphan daughters
left entirely destitute. Otis in fact acquired among the
Gray connection a reputation for benevolence far too
great for his comfort. In June, 1812, he received a letter
from a prominent lawyer of New Orleans informing him
of the sudden death the previous October of "Judge
Turner and his lady," the former a Boston man who had
settled on a sugar plantation in Louisiana, the latter a
daughter of Harrison Gray, Jr. After giving a few details
in regard to the property, which seemed likely to be wiped
out by debts, the writer coolly announced:

I proceed to inform you, that I now send you their seven children by the brig Juno, Capt: Arnold, accompanied by an old Negro woman named Dolly . . . to whom the children are extremely attached. . . . You will be satisfied, I presume, Sir, with my addressing these unhappy orphans to you, in preference to any other person of Mr. Turner's family, whose names have come to my knowledge. I know by letters I have found among the papers of the deceased, that he had a Mother & a sister living, but neither of them in a situation to take such a charge upon them. I know too that he had a brother living in Boston. . . . But Sir, having heard on all hands, that your fortune & respectability render you the only person to whom I can with propriety send them, I cannot hesitate at so doing; and I do it in the full confidence that you will receive and act by them, as I am persuaded our poor deceased friend wou'd have done by yours under like circumstances.

The writer goes on to request that Otis see to the maintenance and education of these seven children, without any likelihood of procuring a penny for their support from their father's estate. Otis, as may be supposed, was somewhat taken aback by this extraordinary announcement. He threatened to send the seven unfortunate orphans back to New Orleans, if sufficient funds for their support were not relinquished from the estate by the lawyers. Since they finally produced the money, Otis was relieved from the painful alternative of adding seven children to his own family of eight, or of letting them become objects of charity.

The first decade after Otis's return to Boston was one of economic expansion, and intellectual awakening for his native town. The population of Boston increased from 24,000 in 1800 to 34,000 in 1810; the import and export trade expanded in even greater proportion. Boston vessels were taking the American flag into every port of the globe. The Canton trade, in which Otis's lifelong friend,

Thomas Handasyd Perkins, made a fortune, was already established, and through Boston enterprise trade-routes were opened to Russia and to the Oregon country, whither Captain Gray's *Columbia* had shown the way. Otis never engaged in commerce, but he did his part in the corresponding development of Boston itself. A long head for business was one of his few Puritanic qualities, since it was mainly by wise investments in real estate that his property grew from nothing at all in 1786 to a considerable fortune in 1810. There were, indeed, few forms of local enterprise with which he was not connected. It was due in part to his foresight, as we have seen, that Beacon Hill became a residential district. The laying out of Charles Street in 1804 opened up this property considerably, and before long the old Copley Pasture began to make some return to the Mount Vernon Proprietors on their original investment and on the large sums they found necessary to expend for improvements.

The town was becoming cramped on its narrow peninsula even in 1801, when Otis joined in several enterprises for securing more room by artificial means. He was a member of the Broad Street Association, that extended the shore line near Fort Hill, and of the corporation that filled in the old mill pond near the present North Station. He was largely responsible for the annexation to Boston of Dorchester Neck, now South Boston, for building the first bridge to it from Boston, and for the earliest development of that part of the city.[4]

[4] Otis, Jonathan Mason, Joseph Woodward, William Tudor, and Gardiner Greene purchased the greater part of Dorchester Neck in 1803, and were incorporated as the South Boston Association. There were only ten families then living on the Neck, and communication with Boston was extremely difficult, both on account of the long détour, and the mud flats in the harbor, which prevented the plying of any regular ferry. After much resistance from Dorchester, the annexation of the Neck to Boston was completed in 1804, and the

The outward appearance of the town was much changed in these years. A former Boston loyalist, who returned as a British spy in 1808, wrote, "The great number of new and elegant buildings which have been erected in this Town, within the last ten years, strike the eye with astonishment, and prove the rapid manner in which the people have been acquiring wealth."[5] Another visitor, in the year 1816, noted that Boston could boast of more splendid private dwellings than any city of four times its population he had seen, in America or Europe.[6] Several blocks of four and five-story buildings had been erected, intruding upon the pleasant gardens and open spaces, and the Exchange Coffee-House, built by a corporation of which Otis was president, arose to the dizzy height of seven stories. For the ten years of its existence (it burnt down in 1818) this structure was the largest hotel and office building in the country.

Expansion during this first decade of the nineteenth century in Boston, was not wholly material. The intellectual ferment of the age, penetrating this conservative town, produced a new interest in literature which prepared the way for the great movement of the Thirties, that made Boston the literary centre of America.[7] Little

Association then built the first bridge across the channel. The influence of commercial interests in South Bay prevented the building of the bridge where it should have been, and the growth of South Boston was thereby impeded. Others besides Otis and his associates reaped the profit of its later development. The bridge which never paid a dividend, was sold in 1832, at six per cent of its original cost.

[5] *Amer. Hist. Rev.*, xvii, 78.

[6] E. S. Thomas, *Reminiscences*, i, 18.

[7] It must be kept in mind that Boston did not earn the title of "Athens of America" until the first quarter of the nineteenth century was well past. At this period Philadelphia was the literary centre, if there can be a literary centre, when no literature of permanent value was produced. It was there that Tom Moore met in 1803 the "sacred few," without whom

> Columbia's days were done,
> Rank without ripeness, quickened without sun.

was produced, but much was read. Suspicious Federalism tabooed the romanticism of Jean-Jacques and his countrymen, who were lumped together as "infidel philosophers," but it welcomed the corresponding movement in Great Britain, since the approval of the British public vouched for the fact that no "disorganizing principles" were concealed therein. The well-worn Popes and *Spectators* and Johnsons were laid aside; Walter Scott, Wordsworth, Miss Edgeworth, and Byron were read by every one.

Otis was not literary in his tastes, during this period of his life. Although the first scholar in his class at Harvard, he always loved men so much better than books, that he found little time for reading. A passage in one of his letters of 1820 to Mrs. Otis indicates his taste in literature, and will probably strike a sympathetic chord in most modern readers:

I have employed myself in reading two volumes of the memoirs of the Margravine of Bareith sister of Frederick 2d, which, as far as I have gone, . . . is more interesting than any romance I have ever read. I advise you to enquire for it. It contains nothing which a married lady may not be known to have read. . . . I worried thro' the Abbot, as I began it with Gorham. As illustrating an incident in the life of poor Mary Stuart not generally known (supposing it to be founded on fact,) it is worth reading, but I think little of it as a romance.

Otis was greatly interested, however, in promoting literary activity in his native town, and he aided one important phase of it, the founding of libraries, literary clubs, and magazines. Two Social Law Libraries were founded in 1806, the Theological Library in 1807, and in the same year the Boston Athenæum, of which Otis was one of the earliest trustees. One of his younger friends was William Tudor,[8] the leader in this early literary movement in Boston, and skilled in many other activities as well. Tudor founded, in 1805, the Literary Anthology Club, which published the *Monthly Anthology*, one of the earliest American literary magazines.

In the period of financial distress incident to Jefferson's Embargo and the War of 1812, the new movement was retarded; and the *Monthly Anthology* brought to an untimely end. After the peace of 1815, William Tudor and his friends took up their work with fresh zeal, and founded the *North American Review* on the ruins of the *Anthology*. Otis's interest in this new enterprise is shown by the following letter from him to Robert Goodloe Harper, dated May 31, 1816.

My Dear Sir

I transmit to you a subscription paper for the N American review. The work has hitherto been conducted in a mode quite satisfactory to the subscribers. The Editor William Tudor Esquire is a gentleman of highly respectable talents & principles and it is believed that with the encouragement of a small additional patronage, the work will be found deserving of a distinguished rank in the literary annals of our Country. If without too much trouble you can procure a few names, you will promote the cause of literature.

A letter from William Tudor to Otis, dated September 2, 1815, is interesting in this connection, as showing in its beginning the movement that led to the Boston Museum of Fine Arts, as well as the writer's aspirations for the literary and artistic preëminence of his native city:

---

[8] William Tudor (1779–1830; Harvard, 1796) engaged in commerce; made the grand tour; helped his brother establish the ice trade with India; wrote the *Life of James Otis*, *Letters on the Eastern States*, and many other works; was joint author of the first Boston city charter; and served as State Representative and minister to Brazil.

My Dear Sir,

A few individuals, (Dr. Warren, I. P. Davis, S. Wells, T. Lyman, D. Sears jr. R. Sullivan, C. Codman &c) have met together once or twice to talk over the possibility of getting up an institution, for the Fine Arts, the enclosed is a hasty first sketch of the paper that was drawn up to form the heading of a subscription paper, & enclose it to you for your perusal, and to draw your pen across what you may think too *broad*, or if there [are] any other ideas will you suggest them. If certain men could be induced to put their hands in their pockets, 30,000 Dolls. might be raised without inconvenience. The *interest* of the sum would at once enable us to make a very great *shew* in two years it would give us copies of all the casts in the Louvre, and some paintings. The income arising from such an exhibition would pay for its charges, and we should have after the first two years 2000 $ to give away to artists, this sum would be a sufficient inducement to bring Allston, Morse & one or two other young men here, and would give us the start of New York & Philadelphia, and strange as it may seem, yet so far as my recollection goes we should have a more complete collection, than any *permanent, public* collection that I know of in London.

Some of the inducements mentioned in the paper as you well know cannot weigh with me "*per la mia disgracia.*" but others do. I wish most heartily the prosperity of the town, and the enlargement of polished society in it. I have heard a good deal of talk this summer, from the circumstances of my residence, among southern people & foreigners, and the general opinion of all these people was that Boston does & must decline, that New York, Baltimore, & Philadelphia must run away with our population & capital. This I do not believe but I believe that exertion is at this time very necessary to secure our standing & future increase. They are straining every nerve in Phila. & Balt. in rivalship, so in New York. The object here contemplated, may with a bold effort at first, go at once beyond them, and will produce permanent advantages. If we can make ourselves the capital of the arts & sciences, and we have already so many powerful institutions that we may do it, our town will increase in that sort of society which is principally to be desired. I think the present state of Europe, will drive many to this country. Other events may happen which will keep up the emigration from England of persons who are not mere laborers & mechanics. An object of this kind trifling as it may be in reality will tend more than ten times the sum employed in any other way to give us our share of this increase of population.

Between four and five thousand dollars were raised for the proposed art collection, but the project languished until 1826, when the Athenæum threw open the first art exhibition ever held in Boston, a collection of casts that in after years formed the nucleus of the Boston Museum of Fine Arts.

Otis's eloquence was the most conspicuous of his varied talents; and made him famous in a period of eminent orators. Down to the last half-century, oratory was one of the most potent forces in moulding public opinion and in arousing popular enthusiasm in America. Since then our susceptibility to the power of human speech has gradually declined, and with this loss has come a deterioration in the quality of our oratory. Fisher Ames, drawing tears from Judge Iredell and John Adams by his remarkable speech on Jay's treaty, makes a picture now hard to imagine. Yet that power then existed, and Otis possessed it to the fullest degree. We have already seen what a prodigious sensation was produced by his first public speech of importance, that on Jay's treaty. With the growing years his mastery of the art increased, until he became the favorite spokesman of Boston town meetings, and in Judge Story's opinion, the best popular orator in the country.[9] Not only to the cultured, but to all classes of people, his word was an electric impulse. It used to be said that Otis excited his Faneuil Hall audiences to such a degree that had he called on the people to follow him to burn the town, they would have obeyed.

[9] Francis Bassett, *Reminiscences* (1871), 8.

Contemporaries all speak of his "voice of silvery sweetness," so modulated as to express every emotion, of his fine features and graceful gestures, of his self-possession and tact. The same personality that won him friends, charmed his audiences. The qualities in his speaking which most impressed his hearers were the spontaneity, the lack of effort, the richness of his vocabulary, and the happy choice of his words. Take this sentence as an example, from his speech in Faneuil Hall after Hull's surrender in 1812:

Our political orb has almost completed its revolution; it is about to set in the cold and dreary regions of Canada, where night and chaos will brood over the last of desolated republics.

No sentence could better express the sentiment of gloom, disaster, and of grim foreboding with which the Federal party regarded the second war with England.

Otis had neither the marvelous intellect and force of Webster, nor the keen reasoning powers of Dexter; but he surpassed even the former in the power of felicitous and spontaneous expression. He was once seated on the platform in Faneuil Hall when Webster, speaking in favor of the Maysville Road Bill, remarked, in the course of his speech, "I am in favor, Mr. Chairman, of all roads, except . . . except . . ." Here he stuck fast for a word, until Otis, who sat near, whispered "The road to ruin!" Webster adopted the suggestion, and inserted Otis's happy phrase as if he had merely paused to make it more effective.

Of this same felicity of expression, Mr. Muzzey gives in his *Reminiscences* another example,—one of the best descriptions of Otis's oratory that has come down to us:

Harrison Gray Otis was, in the year 1828, a candidate for the mayoralty of Boston. The election being on Monday, as was the custom a caucus was held on the Sunday evening previous. Hon. Josiah Quincy was the opposing candidate. Two men of such ability drew a crowded audience. I regarded it as a feast to listen to both of them on the same occasion. Mr. Otis speaks first. His personal appearance is most striking: a large frame, tall, and well proportioned, with a bearing dignified and courteous, a true "gentleman of the old school," — his complexion florid, with bright eyes, and a pleasing and gracious expression, he prepossesses general favor as he rises from his seat. This effect is enhanced by a voice mellow, flexible, and admirably modulated. His gesticulation is graceful, his whole manner persuasive. He is, in fine, of the Ciceronian school, that of the consummate orator.

As he unfolds the policy he shall pursue, if elected, it is evident that he strikes the right key for success. He is applauded at frequent intervals, and resumes his seat amid deafening cheers. It is a trying moment for Mr. Quincy; there are few men who could follow such an effort entirely at their ease. Mr. Quincy, — a manly and noble figure, . . . on almost any other occasion would at once have borne the palm over the ablest competitor. But, with a constitutional hesitancy of speech, he feels, it is manifest, an unusual embarassment. Mr. Otis, seeing clearly what he is attempting to utter, rises, and in a few flowing periods, gives an eloquent expression to the thought of his rival. The effect is electric. His noble magnanimity brings out cheer upon cheer; and it is followed by a speech from Mr. Quincy, comprehensive, logical, worthy of the man and of the occasion.

The most famous of Otis's formal orations was his eulogy on Alexander Hamilton, pronounced at King's Chapel, Boston, on July 26, 1804. Although the only one of his speeches to be published in a collection of American orations, it is far from being his most effective utterance. It opens with a turgid apostrophe to "insatiable death," but the remainder, a somewhat dry outline of Hamilton's career, errs rather on the side of simplicity. To a Democrat, Otis seemed "the least objectionable of these eulogists, because the least false and fulsome;"[10] in the opinion of many Federalists, he did not do his subject justice. Otis was never at his best in formal orations. His peculiar power was extemporaneous; the swift give and take of the Bar and the public forum. Almost any one of his speeches in Congress, even in the imperfect record of the *Annals*, is "good reading."

The literary productions of Otis likewise show this difference. His *Letters in Defence of the Hartford Convention*, the most careful of his works, are dull, and bombastic in manner, but his published *Letter to William Heath*, his "Envoy" letters of 1799, and the off-hand productions of his later years, are lucid and to the point. Of the style of his letters, which are all unstudied productions, the reader has already had ample opportunity to judge. It is unpretentious, sometimes careless, but always clear, easy, and without the slightest trace of pose or cant, — in a word, an admirable expression of his genial and lovable character. In writing, as in speaking, he excelled when unconscious of making any effort.

When over seventy years of age, long after he had retired from active practice of the law, Otis once argued a case of his own, involving the title to his Beacon Hill property. The argument of their aged colleague was a revelation to the young lawyers present, one of whom describes it as follows:

It was something unlike in kind to anything else I ever heard. The winning music of his voice made the hearer reluctant to lose a word; the flow of his language, which was as charmingly constructed and cadenced as if it had all been carefully written by a practiced writer; and the persuasive logic, which led you along almost unconsciously until you stood in the very position

[10] "Anthony Pasquin," *The Hamiltoniad* (Boston, 1804), 20.

in which he would place you, — in each and all of these he was unrivalled. And to all these was added their strongest charm, perhaps, in the apparent spontaneity of it all. There was no effort, no appearance of saying or doing anything in any way which did not come of itself. And I believed then, and I believe now, that this was not apparent only, but real. He had, if ever man had, the *gift* of eloquence. And all, — grace of delivery, sweetness of tone, beauty of illustration, perfect taste in words, and rapidity and clearness of thought, — all blended into one, flowed on like a river, and the hearer was borne along upon the rapid stream, not conscious of its power, and not resisting it.

This may seem, and may be, the extravagant picture of a *laudator temporis acti*. Let me state, however, that by my side there sat a gentleman who had not reached his own foremost place in our profession without knowing as well as any one what were the elements of successful speech, — I hope I do not offend against social courtesies when I name Judge Fletcher, — and he turned to me, as Mr. Otis closed, with the whispered remark: "There is nothing like this now." [11]

The life of Harrison Gray Otis cannot be told without a word concerning his long and intimate relations with his Alma Mater. As President of the Senate of Massachusetts, he was partly responsible — chiefly responsible, some have said — for the Act of 1810, altering the composition of the Board of Overseers, membership in which had formerly been an *ex officio* right of certain state officials and local churches. It was thought desirable by the alumni to make the board both elective and secular, and they brought about this change through the Act of 1810, reducing the number of *ex officio* seats from over fifty to six, and providing for the election by the alumni of fifteen laymen and fifteen Congregational ministers. Otis was chosen a member of the first board elected under this act. Since the law was a Federalist measure, and the newly elected board was composed almost entirely of

[11] T. Parsons, *Parsons*, 183.

Federalist politicians, it was made a point of attack by the Democratic party, and repealed during the second administration of Governor Gerry, in 1812, but reënacted when the Federalists returned to power in 1814. Otis, to whom the degree of Doctor of Laws was given that year, served as Overseer until 1825, and was also a Fellow of the Corporation from 1823 to 1825. But his relations to the University were not merely official. He acted as a father to numerous Harvard students coming from a distance, who were recommended to his care by his friends in the Southern and Middle States. John Rutledge, for example, writes him from Charleston on January 19, 1808:

My dear friend,

I enclose you a draft on Robt Lenox for the use of my Son. That he may learn to keep his own accounts, & have no excuse for incurring any Debts, I wish my good friend that you would pay him monthly Fifty Dollars, or, if it would be more agreeable to him, one hundred & fifty once in three months. With a due regard to economy (which I hope he will observe) Six hundred Dollars a year will be a sufficient allowance during his residence at Cambridge.

March 26, 1809:

I enclose a Bill of Exchange for the use of my Boys. Pray my dr friend, discourage as much as possible their visiting Boston, frequenting Taverns, driving carriages &c &c. It is using a great freedom I know to draw upon your Charities in this way — I also know it is not "Othelo's occupation" to be lecturing & ordering Boys. I know how much, & how well, "he serves the state"; but my friend unless you have the goodness & humility to condescend to advise these fellows, &, by your parental attentions, give some correction to their aberations, I fear that the objects of their residence at Cambridge will not be realized. John writes to me of the brilliance of Mrs Apthorpes Ball, Mrs Otis's Parties, &c. This is all wrong, & these Boys must not be permitted to have any engagements but with their Books.

The undergraduates of Harvard during the early part of the nineteenth century were wont to express their disapproval of existing conditions by the modern methods of strike, boycott, and sabotage. In 1805 occurred the famous "Bread and Butter Rebellion." As a protest against the quality of food provided by the College, the student body refused for ten successive days to attend Commons. The college authorities then suspended regular exercises, and threatened a general lockout; but Otis and Samuel Dexter interposed, and succeeded in restoring peace through arbitration.

Otis's son William was a ringleader in another student uprising of 1818, the so-called "Great Rebellion," which was caused by an attempt of the faculty to enforce discipline, after all the college crockery had been broken during a glorious battle in Commons between freshmen and sophomores. Young Otis, together with George Washington Adams and Josiah Quincy, Jr., stimulated perhaps by the historic names they bore, then rallied the sophomore class around the Rebellion Tree in front of Hollis, as a protest against the faculty's tyranny. President Kirkland summoned them into his presence, and warned them against returning to the tree—which they promptly did. Finally, writes Josiah Quincy, Jr., this "burlesque of patriots struggling with tyrants" played itself out, and ended with several rustications and suspensions. Harrison Gray Otis was absent in Washington at the time, but his son was saved from serious punishment by the interposition of his elder brother Harry, of the class of 1811. Their father wrote their mother on November 22, 1818:

I presume order is restored at Harvard. Old Mr Adams mistakes the genius of the age, to tell of whipping and to practice scolding. The principles of Government in States & Families are changed. The understanding and the heart must be addressed by persuasion and reason, & the bayonet and rod reserved for the last emergency. A boy of 18 for all the purposes of *Government,* is as much a man as he ever will be. He needs advice constantly, and sometimes must be punished by privations of the objects of his desire or pursuit.

After another student insurrection in 1823, when Otis was both Fellow and Overseer, it became evident that something serious was the matter. Harvard College had, in fact, fallen into a rut, and was standing still while the world of learning advanced. It had become a paradise for loafers and for the type of young men then called "bloods," now known as "sports." Instruction was a matter of going through the motions, the curriculum had been unchanged for years, and no encouragement was given to the serious or the advanced student. Professor George Ticknor, fresh from study at the great universities of Germany, perceived these defects, and prescribed remedies which, with the coöperation of the Fellows and Overseers, but against strong opposition from the faculty and conservative alumni, were partially carried out in the year 1825.[12] Their adoption was one of the most important of those steps by which Harvard emerged from an inefficient provincial high school, and became a university in the true sense of the word.

When Harvard celebrated her second centennial, on September 8, 1836, Harrison Gray Otis was elected President of the Day by the alumni, but was prevented from exercising this high function by the sudden death of Mrs. Otis. His life and character were made the subject

[12] *Life, etc., of George Ticknor,* i, chap. xviii. The changes effected were, in brief, the establishment of a tribunal of three for cases of discipline, the abolition of the long winter vacation in favor of one in the summer (the period at which most of the "insurrections" had taken place), greater strictness in examinations, greater supervision over teachers, and an entering wedge of the lecture and elective systems.

of a centennial oration by William Howard Gardiner, of
the class of 1816. Mr. Gardiner ended his eulogy of the
distinguished old graduate with the following toast, than
which none was drunk more heartily on that great day:

Harrison Gray Otis: the *first* scholar of the *first* class of a
*new* nation; the career of his life has been according to the
promise of his youth; he has touched nothing which he has not
adorned; he has been rewarded with no office, nor honor, nor
emolument, to which he was not richly entitled; and, in the
dignified retirement of declining years, he must always possess,
not the least enviable, perhaps, of the blessings which may accompany old age, — one which will dwell with him through
life, and follow him beyond the grave, — the kind remembrance
and most respectful consideration of the Alumni of Harvard.

# CHAPTER XV

## CALM, CONSPIRACY, AND THE CHESAPEAKE AFFAIR

### 1801-1807, ÆT. 36-42

AFTER the election of Jefferson came a brief breathing space in American politics. The European truce suspended the grave questions of foreign policy which had convulsed the country for the past seven years, and removed the principal cause for dissension between Federalists and Republicans. Jefferson governed with a moderation that vexed many of his old friends, and made new friends in the ranks of his former enemies. Federalist leaders in vain sounded the note of alarm at the infiltration of "disorganizing principles." The people were tired of politics; they approved Jefferson's policy of retrenchment; they saw no reason for change.

Harrison Gray Otis began the second and most characteristic portion of his political career at the beginning of this period, in 1802, when he accepted an election to the "Boston Seat" in the Massachusetts House of Representatives. For the next fifteen years he was a member of one branch or the other of the General Court, and during six of them was either Speaker of the House or President of the Senate.[1] Throughout these years Otis was the most popular, though not the most powerful, leader of the Federal party in Massachusetts. The Essex Junto, distrusting him on account of his refusal to take part in the

[1] From 1802 to 1805 in the House of Representatives, and Speaker the last two years; from 1805 to 1813 in the Senate, and its President, 1805-06 and 1808-11; again in the House, 1813-14, and once more in the Senate, 1814-17. The political year began on the last Wednesday in May.

intrigue of 1800 against Adams, never, it seems, admitted him to their secret councils; but he frequently acted in concert with them, and always led in whatever branch of the Legislature he happened to be.

In the political revolution of 1800, Massachusetts almost slipped through the fingers of the Federal party. Their candidate for governor, Caleb Strong, was elected by a narrow majority in 1800, and Boston went Democratic in that and the following year. Once the crisis passed, however, the Federal party slowly regained control. Governor Strong was annually reëlected by an ever-increasing majority, and Boston never again deserted the Federal party as long as it existed. This recovery in 1802 should not be interpreted as a reaction against Jeffersonianism, but as a popular approval of a moderate and efficient administration. Caleb Strong, an honest and unspectacular governor, was tolerant in his Federalism, and exercised a calming influence on party politics. He made a laudable effort to exclude national issues from state politics by frequently reminding the General Court that the national government alone possessed authority over foreign affairs.

Under Strong's guidance, the General Court turned its attention chiefly to internal reforms and to projects of commercial development. In 1802, the year that Otis reëntered state politics, the penitentiary system was instituted, and the application of capital punishment restricted. The principal reforms between 1803 and 1805 related to the judiciary — a department much in need of reorganization. Even with far more courts and judges than were necessary, the division of labor between them was so unequal, the circuits so clumsily arranged, the procedure so complicated, that the delay and the cost of justice had become serious burdens. The first reforming impulse came from the bench itself, which seems to have had a most creditable conception of its functions, and of the proper relations between judiciary and people. Judge Theodore Sedgwick, of the Supreme Judicial Court, writes Otis, February 7, 1803:

> The absolute and uncontrouled independence, of any branch of the judiciary, tends to the establishment of a judicial despotism; and if there has hitherto been no appearance of it, in this state, we are more than indebted to the peculiar *mildness* of temper, and *politeness* of manners of the gentlemen who composed the courts, than to the wisdom of the system.

In another letter to Otis, he calls the Massachusetts judiciary "the most barbarous and absurd that was ever endured by a enlightened people." Evidently the judges of that day were under no illusions as to the inviolability of their privileges and functions.[2]

Although the Massachusetts Bar as a whole opposed any change in a system so profitable to it, Otis gave the exponents of reform all possible aid. The existing correspondence between him and Judge Sedgwick suggests that they two were in a large degree responsible for whatever was effected in that direction. A beginning was made in 1803, by depriving the county courts of session, composed of justices of the peace, of criminal jurisdiction. The ideas of Otis and the judges themselves were then substantially adopted in two acts, of February 29, 1804, and of March 15, 1805, in which *nisi prius* sessions of one or more judges of the Supreme Court were established, in

---

[2] Theophilus Parsons, Jr., wrote of his father, the Chief Justice: "I believe there was nothing which my father more desired than that the people should cultivate in themselves a kind and respectful, but watchful jealousy of the judicial department; and should feel a deep and sincere, and yet a rational respect for it, founded upon a just understanding of the vast importance of its functions." *Life of Parsons*, 199.

addition to the regular sessions of three or more. One judge alone could exercise jurisdiction over all questions "whereof the Supreme Judicial Court hath hitherto had cognizance," excepting capital offenses, divorce, and alimony. Regular circuits were rearranged, in order to expedite matters; the Supreme Judicial Court was reduced from six to five members, and the judges for the first time were given a fixed compensation instead of annual grants. Theophilus Parsons, who was appointed to the vacant chief-justiceship in 1806, proved most efficient in enforcing the spirit of reform.

Legislative action was necessary, also, to improve the banking facilities of Boston, which the expansion of commerce, in these years of peace, had rendered inadequate. John Quincy Adams records in his diary a project of special interest to Otis, the Boston Bank, which he desired to get through the Senate as quietly as possible. The bill provided that no one could own more than fifty shares of stock, except the original proprietors, "about twenty gentlemen," including Otis, who could own up to two thousand shares apiece. Otis did not wish to have the subscription paper made public, and to have his name "bandied about" the legislature. John Quincy Adams, who already looked on Otis with the suspicion of one temperamentally his opposite, had heard rumors that certain shares were set aside for the purpose of corrupting the legislature, and refused to give the bill his support. It finally passed, without the neat provision for keeping the control in the hands of the original proprietors, and with a considerable part of its capital subscribed for by the Commonwealth. Several other banking schemes became issues in local politics at this time; and throughout the period of Federalist rule in Massachusetts the connection between the banking interests and the Federal party was close.[3] Otis' name frequently appeared on boards of directors.

"The federalists must entrench themselves in the State governments, and endeavour to make State justice and State power a shelter of the wise, and good, and rich, from the wild destroying rage of the southern Jacobins." So wrote Fisher Ames, of Massachusetts, in the year 1802,[4] only three years after he and his party had denounced as unconstitutional the attempt of the Virginia and Kentucky Democrats similarly to protect themselves against the Sedition Act. In these words Ames struck the keynote of the policy followed for the next twelve years by his native state.

The Louisiana Purchase of 1803 gave the signal for a renewal of the old party bitterness, and caused the "wise, and good, and rich" of Massachusetts to take their first definite step away from nationalism. News of the cession of Louisiana reached America late in June, 1803. By the Republican newspapers of New England it was received as "glorious intelligence"; by the Federalist press, coldly and without comment. Although nothing emanating from a Jeffersonian administration could expect Federalist praise until subjected to the most rigid and critical scrutiny, still there must have been some difficulty at first in finding fault with an act which thwarted the steady policy of France from 1793 to 1802, and which carried out to its logical conclusion the Federalist policy of 1797.

[3] This is a subject that merits a thorough investigation. One frequently finds complaints in Democratic newspapers that Democrats were discriminated against by the Boston banks. In 1795, Otis's election to the General Court was advocated in the *Centinel* on the ground that he was a friend to the Union Bank. In 1803, the advocates for a new banking scheme founded a party of their own, called the "Middling Interest," which was courted by both Federalists and Republicans.

[4] *Works*, I, 310.

Jefferson had acquired peacefully what Hamilton and Otis had dreamt of securing through war with France and alliance with England. There were, however, just grounds for criticism of the Louisiana Purchase. It was by no means certain that we had not paid fifteen million dollars for a revocable permission from Bonaparte to hold Louisiana against all comers, if we had the strength. The colony had been ceded by Spain to France in 1800, but the transfer had not yet taken place. France had never paid for the territory, and its cession was contrary both to the treaty obligations and to the constitution of France. The boundaries on the east and on the west were indefinite. The position, then, that we had been cheated at the bargain was far from untenable in 1804.

The real cause of Federalist opposition to the Louisiana Purchase lay far deeper than flaws in the title; it was based on the realization that the acquisition of this vast territory threatened the economic and political interests of the Federal party. It would lower the value of Eastern lands, in which Otis and many other Federalist leaders were interested.[5] It would bolster up Jeffersonian Democracy to the westward, and keep Federalism in a perpetual minority. The Eastern leaders[6] were already conscious of the lack of expansive force in their party, which by 1804 existed only as a sickly exotic in the West. Ohio, in spite of the fact that a considerable element of her population was from New England, had just entered the Union with a constitution embodying the most advanced

[5] "The men naturally destined to populate the District of Maine, the vacant lands of New Hampshire, and Vermont will be enticed to the new paradise of Louisiana . . ." — *A Defense of the Legislature of Massachusetts, or the Rights of Newengland Vindicated* (1804), p. 13.

[6] Southern, as well as New England Federalists were strongly opposed to the Louisiana Purchase, but, not having control of their state legislatures, they were not able to express their objections so effectively. See John Rutledge's letter of October 1, 1803, at end of chapter.

ideas of Democracy, and looked to Virginia, not to Massachusetts, for leadership. It was practically certain that the new states to be formed from Louisiana would manifest the same spirit. "Virginia will soon become the Austria of America," wrote a Federalist pamphleteer.[7]

Future prospects for the New England Federalists, with their peculiar economic interests, were rendered the more alarming by the expectation that the new trans-Mississippi states would be slave-holding, and send Representatives to Washington according to the federal ratio. The constitutional provision by which Representatives and presidential electors were allotted to the states in proportion to the free population *plus* three fifths of "all other persons," had long been a rankling sore to New England Federalists. It gave Virginia, a state with a free population slightly less than that of Massachusetts, five more Representatives and electoral votes; it alone secured the election of Jefferson in 1800. Hence arose the proposition to abolish by constitutional amendment the slave representation. An amendment to this effect was introduced in the Massachusetts House of Representatives by William Ely of Springfield, and passed June 20, 1804, by a strict party vote. Otis was then Speaker of the House, and no doubt gave the amendment his full approval. The resolution, commenting upon the unjust and injurious provision in the Constitution by which "a planter with fifty slaves has thirty votes," states that the purchase of Louisiana makes these provisions more injurious, and "will contribute . . . to destroy the real influence of the Eastern states in the National Government," and whereas, a Union of the States cannot harmoniously exist, for a long period, unless it be

---

[7] *Defense of the Legislature of Mass.*, 14. Cf. H. C. Hockett, "Federalism and the West" (*Turner Essays*, no. v.).

founded in principles which shall secure to all Free Citizens, equal political rights and privileges in the government, so that a minority of Free Citizens may not govern a majority, an event which, on the principles of representation now established has already happened, and may always happen. Therefore, to preserve *the Union of the States* upon sound and just principles, and to establish a foundation for general harmony, and confidence among all the citizens of the United States, by securing to them now, and at all future periods, equal political rights and privileges,

*Resolved*, that representatives and direct taxes be henceforth apportioned on the basis of free population only.

With this language of menace to the Union, suggestive of the tone in which the South, at a later period, was accustomed to demand extensions of slavery, Massachusetts entered the road of sectionalism that she followed for the next ten years. Striking, as it did, at one of the "sacred compromises" of the Constitution, Ely's amendment was about as reasonable as would have been a proposition of Virginia to deprive the smaller states of their equality in the Senate. Massachusetts was very properly rebuked by the rejection of the amendment by every state in the Union, with the exception of Connecticut and Delaware, which took no action; but her leaders, not abandoning all hope, revived a similar proposition in the Report of the Hartford Convention.

While the legislature of Massachusetts was contemplating this initial step in sectionalism, the extremist leaders of the Federal party, boldly spanning the successive stages of state rights, were secretly planning for New England the final resort of oppressed sectional minorities — secession from the Union. The conspiracy [8] originated

[8] The sources for this episode are the correspondence in the Pickering MSS. (printed, together with the pamphlets of the later Otis-Adams controversy, in Henry Adams, *Documents relating to New England Federalism*); extracts from letters and memoranda of William Plumer in his *Life*, by William Plumer, Jr.,

with the extreme New England Federalists in Congress, of whom Timothy Pickering, Uriah Tracy, and Roger Griswold were the leaders. These — and the same might be said of the Essex Junto, of Gouverneur Morris, of the leading Connecticut Federalists — were men of one idea and one object: to suppress democracy. Their political theories were founded on the fallacy that the masses in America had the same passions as the Paris mob. Democracy to them meant atheism, destruction of property, and mob rule. "The principles of democracy are everywhere what they have been in France," wrote Fisher Ames in 1803. "The fire of revolution . . . when once kindled, would burrow deep into the soil, search out and consume the roots, and leave, after one crop, a *caput mortuum*, black and barren, for ages. . . . Our country is too big for union, too sordid for patriotism, too democratic for liberty." Looking on current events from this standpoint, radical Federalists saw in Jefferson's attacks on the judiciary, his removals in the civil service, the adoption of the Twelfth Amendment to the Constitution, and the annexation of Louisiana, a prelude to universal chaos. "My life is not worth much," wrote Pickering, "but if it must be offered up, let it be in the hope of obtaining a more stable government, under which my children, at least, may enjoy freedom with security."

The South, they observed, and to a certain extent the Middle States, were already violated by democracy; New England was yet chaste — but every day Pickering and men of like mind saw new barriers to her virtue prostrated. "And must we with folded hands wait the result? . . . The principles of our Revolution point to the remedy

chap. vii; and correspondence of Rufus King in *King*, iii, chap. xxii. Henry Adams's description of the plot in his *United States*, ii, chap. viii, is a masterpiece of historical writing.

— a separation." In their minds arose the picture of
"a new confederacy, exempt from the corrupt and corrupting influence and oppression of the aristocratic Democrats of the South," a confederacy with New England as
its nucleus, the British provinces as free willing adherents,
and New York, to be brought in by the influence of Aaron
Burr, as a western barrier against Virginia, the source of
corruption. Much as her leaders wished the South to
secede in 1861, in order to exclude the poison of abolition,
Pickering and his friends wished New England to secede
in 1804, in order to exclude the poison of democracy —
each assuming that a frontier line could stop a world
force.

This wild and visionary scheme was cautiously broached
by its authors to the Essex Junto in Massachusetts, and
to the Federalist leaders in Connecticut and New York.
Ames, Cabot, Parsons, and Higginson all replied that
secession, although desirable, was impossible — there was
no public sentiment to support it. The people were altogether too contented and prosperous; only the "wise and
good" could perceive danger to society and property in
the annexation of Louisiana. "We should be put in the
background," wrote Higginson, "were we to make that
question the subject of free conversation." In Connecticut, the leaders of Church and State regarded the scheme
more favorably, and in New York the plot found a leader
in the person of "The Catiline of America," Aaron Burr.
His candidacy for the governorship of New York was supported by Griswold and Pickering, with the understanding that if he won, he should lead the new secession movement. Burr's defeat at the polls ended all chance of even
setting the plot in motion. Hamilton had·already expressed his disapproval of the conspiracy, and done his
best to effect Burr's defeat. The latter's demand for an

explanation, Hamilton's defiance, and the fatal duel followed in swift succession. On July 11, 1804, Alexander Hamilton paid the penalty, on the duelling-grounds of Weehawken, for having stood between Aaron Burr and the presidency of a Northern Confederacy.

With this dramatic ending, the disunion conspiracy of 1804, the first serious plot against the integrity of the Union,[9] dissolved. It never had the remotest chance of success, and the fact that Pickering, Tracy, and Griswold could seriously desire it and seriously believe it practicable, and above all intrigue with Aaron Burr to carry it out, shows how thoroughly devoid they were of political morality, how completely out of touch with public opinion, how absolutely incompetent to govern the United States.

Our chief concern in this affair is to find out whether Harrison Gray Otis had any part in it. Otis, as Speaker of the House of Representatives of the leading state of New England, was the first leader outside the Essex Junto to whom the conspirators would naturally turn. John Quincy Adams believed that they had enlisted him. In the course of the presidential campaign of 1828, in which

[9] As all students of United States history know, secession, even in 1804, was no new and unheard-of remedy for oppressed sectional minorities. It was seriously urged by Rufus King in 1794, by Connecticut leaders in 1796, if Jefferson were elected; by John Taylor of Caroline in 1798. It was constantly threatened in the West, from 1784 to 1803, if the federal government should not prevent the closure of the Mississippi; frequently threatened in the South, between 1795 and 1799, in the event of a war with France. So far both parties, and all sections had been equal offenders, and were likewise in the period 1804–1860, as Mr. H. V. Ames's admirable collection of *State Documents on Federal Relations* testifies. Most political thinkers of the first half-century of constitutional government had very little faith in the duration of the Union, and the statement, that such-and-such a measure would "inevitably produce a dissolution of the Union," was a familiar figure of speech in politics. The conspiracy of 1804 was, so far as is known, the first actual attempt to carry secession into effect; but it may well be that others fully as serious previously existed, but have never seen the light.

he was a candidate, Adams published a statement to the effect that the object of the Federalist leaders "was [in 1808], and had been for several years, a dissolution of the Union." He was promptly called to account by Harrison Gray Otis and twelve other survivors of the Federal party. They challenged him to publish the evidence of such a design, and to name the leaders. Adams replied shortly, citing the main facts of the 1804 disunion scheme correctly, but refusing to give any names. This was the first time that the plot had been made public. Otis and his twelve "compurgators," as Adams called them, then published an "Appeal to the citizens of the United States," — composed in all probability by Otis, — in which they "solemnly disavow all knowledge of such a project, and all remembrance of the mention of it, or of any plan analogous to it, at that or any subsequent period." They further stated their belief that no such plan existed.

Otis, then, clearly and unequivocally stated in 1829 that he had not so much as heard of the 1804 plot until 1828. His statement was undoubtedly correct.[10] Adams himself, in the lengthy reply which he prepared to the "Appeal," acknowledges that the 1804 project was "in its nature secret," and admits "Mr. Otis is not one of those whom I ever heard or believed to have been engaged in the project of 1804." Pickering's correspondence shows that the plan was never communicated to any one in Massachusetts outside the exclusive circle of the Junto —

[10] Mr. McMaster assumes, I think without foundation, that the Ely amendment was a corollary to the disunion scheme. (*United States*, III, 47.) He points out (p. 51) three toasts at the Christopher Gore dinner of April 27, 1804, as indicating a general knowledge of the plot among Federalists. Of these the only one which seems to contain a disunion sentiment was "May the dominion of Virginia be limited by the Constitution, or at least by the Delaware," and these words may have been intended simply to express a wish that the Federal party should retain control of the state governments in that region. There is no doubt, however, that secession sentiment existed in Federalist circles that were ignorant of any settled plan with that end in view.

Adams only learned of it by accident. To Otis and his twelve fellow signers, in 1828, the announcement that such a plot existed was a complete surprise, and their disbelief in the story, under the circumstances, was natural.[11]

Harrison Gray Otis, then, had no connection with the 1804 project of a Northern Confederacy. But one question remains to be answered. Was this plot of 1804 an isolated affair, ending with the defeat of Burr and the death of Hamilton, or was it, as John Quincy Adams believed, the alpha to a carefully laid scheme of disunion, to which the Hartford Convention was intended to be the omega? The mere existence, he considered, of a disunion plot in 1804 was sufficient evidence that disunion was the object of the sectional movements in New England from 1808 to 1815.[12] That reasoning does not commend itself to the interests of historical accuracy. The secession movement of 1804 was a select conspiracy, confined to a handful of extremist leaders; the movements of 1808 and 1814 were entered into by the entire Federal party in New

[11] William Plumer, one of the conspirators of 1804, and later an apostate to Federalism, supported Adams's statement in a letter which was published early in 1829. (*Life of William Plumer*, 290.) The truth of his statements was impugned by a number of the 1804 Connecticut members of Congress, who had not been let into the secret (*N.E. Federalism*, no. IX), and Otis therefore considered them false. See his letter of March 5, 1829, to Judge Hopkinson, in appendix to chapter XXXI. Timothy Pickering, the other surviving conspirator, kept a complete silence during the controversy. The existence of the 1804 plot was not established beyond the possibility of doubt until 1857, when part of William Plumer's correspondence of 1804 was published in his *Life*, by William Plumer, Jr.

[12] Mr. Henry Adams assumes (*United States*, VIII, 225), that a New England convention, similar to that of 1814, formed part of the plans of 1804. But William Plumer distinctly states that the plot was to be carried out by individual secessions of states, beginning with Massachusetts. (*Life of Plumer*, 291, 295–96.) In none of the correspondence of that year is there any mention of an interstate convention. Definite measures were to have been decided upon at a meeting of leaders in Boston, which, owing to Hamilton's death, never took place.

England, and their object was not disunion, but, in the one case, relief from the embargo, and in the other, peace and protection to New England interests. Pickering, indeed, attempted to steer the Hartford Convention into a disunion course, but failed. The conspiracy of 1804 was an isolated affair, the real significance of which is personal — the example it offers of the manner in which political jesuits throw aside every scruple to attain their ends.

The subsequent course of events in Massachusetts showed how visionary was the idea of stirring up disloyalty to the Union in that state. The Federal party made the iniquity of the Louisiana Purchase its leading issue in the elections of 1804, but the people were obstinate enough to regard it as a national triumph in which they shared. The Democratic vote for governor increased seventy-five per cent; not quite sufficient, however, to eat away the heavy Federalist majorities of 1803. When the presidential election approached, the General Court dared not repeat its unpopular strategy of 1800, and retain the choice of presidential electors in its own hands. Trusting, however, that the slight Federalist majority in the spring elections would still remain, it did the next best thing, and provided for the choice of electors by a general ticket. This "squeamishness," as the *Centinel* called it, resulted, to the Federalists' profound astonishment, in the victory of the Jeffersonian ticket by a substantial majority. For the first and the last time Massachusetts voted for a President opposed to the Federal party. Connecticut and Delaware alone remained faithful to Federalism; Jefferson was reëlected President by 162 votes out of 176. The Democrats had good reason to believe that Federalism was in its death-throes. According to *The Hamiltoniad*, —

Boston, that royal hot-bed of the States,
Now sinks in grief — now menaces the Fates:
Ot-s, mellifluous Ot-s, cannot please:
His silver accents only charm the Breeze.

During the next two years, a progressive increase in violence was evident in the Massachusetts state elections. The Federalists fought to retain their power with all the desperation of a dying cause, and the Democrats were stimulated to attain a goal that each election seemed to bring nearer, but to keep just out of reach. Torrents of pamphlets rained from party headquarters, and the past records of both gubernatorial candidates were raked with a fine comb to discover incidents to their discredit. In 1806, the Democrats finally secured a majority in the General Court. Otis wrote on May 20, in a tone of bitter jocularity, to his old friend Robert Goodloe Harper:

I believe at length c'est une affaire finie with Massachusetts. The old Governor is elected, but a systematic plan has been adopted by the democratic towns to fill the legislature with their complement of members. Our H. of R. will therefore literally be a council of 500, and you may expect to see us disgraced by a fulsome address to the weakest of possible administrations. If Bonaparte had time to examine our affairs with minute attention, he would think we were making too much haste; we shall be ready for him before he has leisure to take us under his protection. Would your Baltimorians vote for Prince Jerome? I think however we cannot expect to share the honors of the *first line* of Princes. There is not enough of them to distribute among the fallen & falling powers of Europe. A few years will produce a new mongrel breed from the German and Italian alliances, either of wives or mistresses and a few years may probably fit America for the sway of any abortion which it may be convenient to transport. Till when God bless you.[13]

Otis, who was defeated for the presidency of the Senate that year by a majority of one, was, however, instrumental

[13] Harper MSS.

in preserving the governorship for his party. Returns for
governor were exceedingly close. Caleb Strong had, according to Federalist calculations, only 176 votes over a
bare majority of the total vote, which at that time was
necessary for a choice. The opportunity to defeat him by
manipulating the returns was too good to be lost. The
returns were referred for an official count to a joint committee of the General Court, composed of five Democrats
and two Federalists, which proceeded to apply a set of
rules to fit the object in view. It was found that Governor Strong's name was misspelled in the returns of
two towns, that of Sullivan in thirty-one. The committee
adopted the rule that where the spelling conformed to the
sound of the name, the votes should stand, but not otherwise. As the two Strong towns spelt his name *Stron* and
*Srong*, they were thrown out, while most of the Sullivan
votes were spelled *Sulivan* or *Sullivon*, and were therefore
retained. All rejected votes were counted into the total, in
order to keep the legal majority, which Strong must sur-
pass, as high as possible. After deciding every disputed
point in Sullivan's favor, the committee reported that
Strong lacked 14 votes of a majority. The Democrats,
however, did not dare to pull through so barefaced a political steal. A minority report of the Senate, signed by
Otis and his eighteen Federalist colleagues, punctured the
committee's report through and through, and gave the
cue to public opinion, which forced the Democrats to re-
cede. The House was enabled to back down with grace
through the "discovery" of a new technicality in the returns of a Democratic town, which being rejected, gave
Caleb Strong a majority of 40 votes. He was then declared elected.[14]

[14] These facts are taken from Edward Stanwood, "The Mass. Election in
1806," (*Proc. Mass. Hist. Soc.*, 2d ser., xx, 12), and the Senate minority protest, a manuscript copy of which in the Otis MSS. suggests Otis's authorship.

In the following year, 1807, the Democrats finally secured control of every branch of the state government. All signs pointed to the coming disappearance of the Federal party. Vermont succumbed the same year; New Hampshire and Rhode Island had already yielded; in all the United States only hide-bound Connecticut resisted the advance of Jeffersonian Democracy. Had the European peace endured, or had Thomas Jefferson been able to cope successfully with a condition of European war, the Federal party would in all probability have died out for want of an issue, and the " era of good feelings " been anticipated by ten years. But the gods willed it that no permanent peace could be made between England and France, or between Federalists and Republicans in America, until Napoleon should conquer the British Isles, or be driven into exile.

In 1804, Europe resolved itself for the third time into two great coalitions around England and France as nuclei, and Federalists and Republicans resumed their old positions on the outer edges of the warring circles. All questions not relating to foreign affairs again sink out of sight, and as Harper wrote Otis, " The affairs of our own country make a sort of underplot, which engages the attention only because it is near, and in which the miserable actors, . . . excite no other emotions than those of pity and contempt."[15] Throughout the long struggle that ended with Waterloo, the Federalists continued to regard England as the "advanced guard of our country," the exponent of rational liberty and well-ordered government; but the Republican party consistently defended the cause of Napoleon, while he crushed out republicanism and liberty in one country after another.

Nine months after Jefferson's second inauguration,

[15] Letters at end of this chapter.

England, through Trafalgar, became mistress of the seas
and Napoleon, through Austerlitz, master of the Continent. A deadlock was closed between the two belligerents, from which either could escape only by prostrating
the commerce and exhausting the resources of the other.
As in the first half of the European struggle, each belligerent conceived it necessary, in carrying out this starvation
policy, to prevent neutral commerce from trading with
the other nation; and the era of spoliations, captures, and
judicial confiscation of American vessels recommenced.
The situation was difficult for Jefferson to meet. Washington and Adams had been confronted by a similar problem, but generally in relation to one nation at a time.
But from 1807 on, both England and Napoleon seemed to
vie with one another in visiting destruction on American
commerce and insult on the American people. With the
American public irrevocably divided in favor of England
and France, the situation was one from which only an
opportunist statesman of the very highest order, a Crom-
well or a Cavour, could have drawn success — and Jefferson was not an opportunist, but a theorist.

During the first two years of the war, the aggressions
on America came almost exclusively from Great Britain.
In 1804, the British navy renewed its practice of impressing British subjects from American merchant vessels,
even within the harbor of New York. The following year,
Sir William Scott, in the case of the American vessel *Essex*,
handed down a decision in which he announced the principle of "continuous voyages" — that the carrying of a
cargo from the French West Indies to the United States,
there transshipping it and proceeding to France, was in
effect a continuous voyage between the French colonies
and France, and as such, contrary to the Rule of 1756.
This decision cut deep into a lucrative branch of the

American carrying trade. The wise and good of the Essex Junto, whose interests were deeply affected, were nevertheless willing to acquiesce, preferring to swallow humbly such crumbs of trade as England might graciously permit to fall from her table, rather than embarrass her in her struggle with Bonaparte, or give Jefferson the least cause for interference. But the Federal party as a whole was not yet ready to accept this attitude, and in Boston, as in other seaport cities, a meeting of Federalist merchants drew up a strong memorial to the President, denouncing the principles of the *Essex* decision as "unsound in principle, offensive in practice, and nugatory in effect," and praying for measures to "assert our rights, and support the dignity of the United States."

Jefferson responded by following the best Federalist precedents, and sending William Pinkney as envoy extraordinary to England, to join Monroe, the minister resident, in an effort to persuade the British government to abandon the practice of impressment, and renounce Sir William Scott's new theory of neutral trade. They procured a treaty, containing terms so humiliating that Jefferson refused even to submit it to the Senate for consideration.

Unfortunately three of Jefferson's measures the previous year had already convinced such moderate Federalists as were inclined to trust his sincerity, of his subservience to Napoleon. These were the swift passage of the bill appropriating two million dollars for foreign intercourse; the act prohibiting trade with insurrectory San Domingo, in obedience to peremptory orders from the French Government, and the act forbidding the importation of British goods. Jefferson's summary rejection of the Monroe-Pinkney treaty was, therefore, considered evidence of a desire to provoke a breach with Great Britain.

Three months later occurred an incident that for a few brief weeks obliterated party lines in the United States and brought forth the only united expression of American patriotism between the X.Y.Z. disclosures and the battle of New Orleans. On June 22, 1807, off Hampton Roads, the commander of the British line-of-battle ship *Leopard* held up the American frigate *Chesapeake*, and demanded that certain deserters from the British navy, said to be on board, be given up. On being refused, he opened fire, killed and wounded twenty-one of the *Chesapeake's* crew, and forcibly impressed three American citizens and one British subject.

News of this outrage on the American flag reached Boston June 30, and fast on its heels came copies of the spirited resolutions of the citizens of Norfolk, Virginia, and of other towns between there and Boston. The proceedings that followed are of great interest, as indicating a struggle between the Essex Junto, which wished to condone the outrage if not defend the *Leopard*, and the patriotic element of the party, led by John Quincy Adams and Otis.

For a time the news produced the same effect in Boston as elsewhere. All six newspapers, including the *Palladium* and the *Repertory*, organs of the Essex Junto, united in reprobating the British government, but the principal Federalists of the town refused to call a town meeting, probably because they wished to await further information.[16] The Republicans then took out of their hands the opportunity of leading public sentiment, and called a public meeting for July 10. The announcement was made in the *Chronicle* of the 9th, together with a statement that it

[16] In 1811, the Federalists took no action on the Non-Intercourse Act of March 3, which was considered as a prelude to war, until the 31st; in 1809, no meeting on the Force Act, which passed January 9, was held until the 24th.

would be highly improper to admit to the meeting "those whom we have reason to suppose have been the principal cause of our difficulties"—namely, the "Federal leaders," whom the paper accused of indirect responsibility for the *Leopard's* action by their "display of disaffection," which "encouraged the British to try the experiment." This unjust and tactless statement was justly resented by the Federalists, and served only to revive party hatred at a time when all party recriminations should have been suppressed. John Quincy Adams was the only prominent Federalist to attend. The Federalists then called a regular town meeting for July 16, but the Essex Junto, true to the British bias of their minds, were already defending the British side of the case through the columns of the *Repertory*, and refused to assist. The great body of citizens did go, however, since some two thousand persons were present as opposed to two hundred at the Democratic meeting. Harrison Gray Otis, the most prominent speaker, delivered a spirited denunciation of the British outrage. He also served on a committee, composed chiefly of Federalists, that drew up a set of resolutions promising the government their support.[17]

This town meeting of July 16, 1807, separated Otis, Adams, and the body of Federalists from the Essex Junto, and made apparent the willingness of the latter to go to all lengths to defend England and to embarrass Jefferson's administration. To Otis's credit let it be said that he was willing to forget party lines in this period of party bitterness. Unfortunately it was the last time he could be so impartial, for the administration soon embarked in a

[17] *N. E. Federalism*, 183; *Repertory*, July 10, 1807; *Boston Town Records, 1796–1813*, p. 222; J. Q. Adams, *Memoirs*, I, 469. Adams states that Otis proposed another resolution, calling on the government for the protection of a naval force, but withdrew it by request of Adams and Jarvis, because it would imply a censure on the administration.

policy that made it impossible for a Massachusetts man to support Jefferson, and at the same time be loyal to his state.

## LETTERS

After Otis returned to Boston, in 1801, he corresponded frequently with the two South Carolina friends he made at Philadelphia: John Rutledge, who continued in Congress until 1803, and Robert Goodloe Harper, who by this time had changed his residence to Baltimore. The former's views, it will be observed, differed in no way from those of the average New England Federalist, except on the *Chesapeake* incident. I have added a letter from Otis's loyalist uncle, Harrison Gray, giving his view of that affair.

### JOHN RUTLEDGE TO OTIS

Weathersfield July 17th 1803

My dear friend,

Altho' I had a wet ride home, yet it was preferrable to the dusty one I had in going, and the weather considered a pleasant one. Thursday night at 10 o'Clock I arrived in the dark and rain at Pomfret, where I heard a chattering of french, and upon entering the Inn found Gou[verneu]re Morris with two french Valêts — a french travelling companion, and his hair buckled up in about one hundred Papilliottes. His wooden leg, papilliottes, french attendants, and french conversation made his Host, Hostess, their daughters, & grand Daughters, with the whole family, including the Hostler & Betty the Cook maid, stare most prodigiously; and gave me some idea how the natives looked when poor Cooke made his Entrée at the friendly Isles. When I arrived at a village where I the next day dined the Landlord, who proved to be a federalist, told me Govr Clinton from New York had passed by the day before in a coach by himself, & his son in law Mr Genet in company in another coach, & together they had three french servants; and he added, with a most sapient look, that Mr Ben Austin had that morning passed by in a Coach from Hartford, and he could swear these

fellows were not going to Boston for anything good, they were
*three devils*. It was impossible to hear this denunciation without
laughing, and I told him that his Govr Clinton was Govre
Morris, he made many apologies was very eloquent in his
eulogies upon Morris, & expressed very strongly his regrets
that he had not stopped & given him an opportunity of conversing with the great Man who had made such great speeches
in Congress. . . .

### JOHN RUTLEDGE TO OTIS

Weathersfield October 1st 1803

My dear friend —

* * * * * * * * * *

The elections which were held last week were quite as favorable as the friends of national liberty expected, & from what I
hear & see I really believe the fever of democracy has had its
crisis & that things will now be growing better & better. There
is a great sterility of domestic politics, but the meeting of the
*National Assembly* will soon engage public attention. Our *Master* will have mighty fine tales to amuse his *Mountain* & their
mob with — we shall have the prosperous condition of the
Republic eulogized, & hear much of the great advantages which
will obtain to us by the purchase of a trackless world. A Country which when worth the holding will I have no doubt rival &
oppose the atlantic States. I do not mean New Orleans which
was absolutely necessary for us to get, and which in *substance*
is all we have got for our fifteen Millions. This seems to me a
miserably calamitous business — indeed I think it must result
in the disunion of these States — and yet such is the force of
prejudice & popular delusion that the measure cannot yet be
even brought to the bar of argument. I have a letter of a pretty
recent date from London saying Great Britain had captured
four millions sterling value of property from the french &
dutch, and that John Bull was in high Spirits, full of confidence
in his preparations & strength, & not fearful on the score of
invasion. I wait with impatience to hear the fate of these inva-
ders who are I think destined to fatten the fish between the
coasts of france & england. Am I, do you think, to give up all
hope of getting my renegado Peter? If money can tempt your

Constables you may offer & give 300$ for his apprehension.
Pray present my affectionate Comps to your dear Mrs Otis to
whom Mrs R desires to be remembered most respectfully.
That both of you & all of your little tribe may enjoy health
happiness & every kind of comfort is the fervent prayer of

Your sincere friend

John Rutledge

ROBERT GOODLOE HARPER TO OTIS

Baltimore May 27th 1806

My dear Otis

&ast; &ast; &ast; &ast; &ast; &ast; &ast; &ast; &ast; &ast;

I am sorry to find that one of the last of our great federal
posts indeed the last but one, is about to be at length reduced.[18]
You have sustained a long siege, and done the duty of a brave
and faithful garrison; but no works, however defended, can
hold out finally, against the united operation of sap and blockade. It has long been my settled opinion that the delusions of
democracy, like other delusions of the human mind, cannot be
resisted by reason and truth alone. These delusions must wear
out of themselves, be dissipated by suffering, or counter-acted
by other delusions and passions, to which circumstances may
give birth or activity. . . .

In the Drama now acting, or perhaps only rehersing, on the
theatre of our world, my favourite hero is Alexander; whose
character, however, is not yet fully ascertained, and perhaps
not fully formed. Prince Charles comes next, who has at length
arrived at that station in his own country, which alone can
enable a man to display, with effect, great talents and great
qualities. But his talents as a statesman, without which his
military talents though the first of the age must be unavailing,
are yet to be proved. The character & principles of Buonoparte
I detest, while I admire his capacity and his vigour, and am free
to confess that he acts a most important part in the piece. The
parts next in interest are cast in England; but we do not know
much of the actors yet, and what we do know is not much to
their advantage. My feelings and affections, however, are with
them, and I hope that they will worthily sustain their parts.

[18] A reference to the state elections in Massachusetts.

The affairs of our own country make a sort of under-plot, which engages the attention only because it is near, and in which the miserable actors, incapable of "rising to the dignity of being hated," excite no other emotions than those of pity and contempt; or if detested, are detested only as odious reptiles which crawl about our feet, and by their filthiness and deformity fill us with disgust, or excite apprehension by their venomous qualities. Ohe jam satis!

God bless you; ardently wishes, my dear Otis,

Your affectionate friend

ROB: G: HARPER

### JOHN RUTLEDGE TO OTIS

Charleston July 29th 1806

My dear friend

\*   \*   \*   \*   \*   \*   \*   \*   \*   \*

Although I have enjoyed great good health since I saw you, yet I am growing old, my friend; & so grey, that if Mrs O, in any prospect of an increase to your family hereafter, should take a fancy to pluck three black hairs out of my head, as Mrs Pickle longed to out of Commodore Trunnions, she would still be more embarrassed to find them. Assure her however, that she will find me upon that, & upon every other occasion as gentle as a Lamb, & always ready to prove how much I respect, esteem & venerate her. I beg leave with all due humility to kiss Miss Eliza's hand — there is not a fairer one in all Charleston. I beg to be remember'd to my friend Harry affectionately, & to all my young friends of your Nursery.

The friends of good government in this section of the Union, have been filled with gloom by the cloud which hangs over 'the head Quarters of good Principles.' I will not importune you by an enquiry respecting the causes which combined to produce this degraded state, but do most sincerely pray, & hope, that fortune may soon play your wonderfully lucky fools a trick, & make their fall in proportion to their elevation. You are so commercial a people, that I had believed your Politics would have been chastened by the non importation law which is to take place as to certain articles after November; & by the governments acquiescence in Mirandas expedition. We are surely a

set of bungling Politicians — we affront all the powers of Europe
at one time — it would be curious, if they were to act as two
hostile parties do in one of Shakespears plays, agree to suspend
their difficulties untill they had punished us. We have a party,
who know nothing of & care nothing for commerce, & numbers
who, because we are not to be conquered, seem to forget that
we, upon the Coast, at least, may at any time be ruined. By
our last accounts from England the state of Europe seems un-
settled & gloomy. The humiliation of the ancient house of
Austria is deplorable. The king of Naples must yield every
thing, I think, to the superior force, & ascendancy of Bonaparte.
Prussia plays a part which nobody seems to understand — but
England will forever hold out — their sinking fund will enable
them to borrow as much as they please, & their trade is greater
than ever. I have long considered england as but the advanced
guard of our Country, & it is to be lamented, that the conduct of
that government should be such towards a portion of our Countrymen, as to prevent any one american from wishing that their
resistance may be successful. If they fall we do — Bonaparte
neither loves nor values any thing, but the agrandizement of
the Nation, & the extension of his own military fame. To
Messrs. Cabot Ames Perkins Mason Davis &c &c &c pray
make my Comps. acceptable. Adieu my dr Otis & believe me
to be with encreased attachment

Your sincere & faithful friend

J: RUTLEDGE

### OTIS TO ROBERT GOODLOE HARPER

*From the Harper Manuscripts*

Boston 19 April 1807.

My dear friend,

It would give me great pleasure to be instrumental in the
promotion of your wishes to raise a sum of money by loan; but
am unable to give you any encouragement of my being able to
effect it. Indeed I am so little in this way of dealing that I can
only promise you to employ some intelligent broker and ascertain through that medium the practicability of your plan, and
to add to your offers my own assurances of the reliance which I
know may always be placed upon your word and your resources.

It is true that we abound in monied men, but I may add that *opus* nummi crescit quantum crescit pecunia ipsa, and our capitalists here find it easy to invest their superfluous dollars on more advantageous terms than you offer, and the *proximity* of security is a circumstance that will always give a preference to proposals from men on the spot. I presume that the course and relations of business are much the same here as in your city. The minds of men teem with projects, & because everything has hitherto succeeded owing to the unprecedented circumstances of our Country, the conclusion is that nothing can miscarry. Hence bridges, turnpikes, canals, houselots and every species of property are under some aspect or another objects of speculation, and I hope we may never see the ruin as broad as the enterprise. It is the principal misfortune of our country that all avenues to great and liberal and patriotic objects are shut against the noble and highminded; and that the ardour and genius which were naturally to sway the affairs of state, are forced into a competition with mercantile and landjobbing projectors. Hence money is the object here with all ranks and degrees, and though a great deal is accumulated, yet as Paddy would say, still more is distributed, and every reservoir has many aqueducts. . . . You will see Mason on his return and see whether he confirms these ideas, and I will cheerfully cooperate with him, or endeavour without him to obtain the requisite information, which is all I can engage.

I shall in a few days give to a Mr Story[19] from this place a line of introduction to you, at his particular request, and will thank you to pay him such attentions as may be consistent with your convenience and leisure. He is a young man of talents, who commenced Democrat a few years since and was much fondled by his party. He discovered however too much sentiment and honour to go *all lengths*, & acted on several occasions with a very salutary spirit of independence & in fact did so much *good*, that his party have denounced him, and a little attention from the right sort of people will be very useful to him & to us. . . .

I am with great esteem my dr Sr yr. respectful friend

H. G. Otis

[19] Joseph Story.

### JOHN RUTLEDGE TO OTIS

Charleston August 3d 1807.

\*   \*   \*   \*   \*   \*   \*   \*   \*   \*   \*

You are so cool & dispassionate a people in Boston that you seem to have escaped the passion which enflames us, in consequence of the outrage on one of our frigates. Altho' I deprecate war quite as much as any of my friends can, yet, I think, a War (even with Great Britain) would prove more honourable prosperous & safe, & less costly, than a state of Peace in which a foreign Nation is to exercise the right of searching our National Ships. The general business of impressing American seamen was to be sure not worth mooting — where G. Britain has in her service one of our sailors we have twenty of hers on board our Merchantmen, & this is so well known in that section of the Union where Mariners & navigation belong (New England) that complaints have ceased. The complainings come from Virginia, where there are neither sailors nor ships, & where this is contrived to aliment & concentrate the angry passions floating through our Country against G. Britain, Altho' this disgraceful Spirit has brought upon us our present deplorable condition, & this miserable state is chargeable to the Errors & Vices of those Empirics who administer our government, still my friend we must support this government. With our Commerce so extended as it is, & our Keels fretting every sea, we must have a navy; & that will be impossible if our Ships of War are to be searched — we must kick against this & fight against it, & fight as we should pro Aris & focis. Had I more paper I should scribble much more on this topic. Pray remember me affectionately to Mrs Otis & the young folks.

### HARRISON GRAY TO OTIS

N 18 Clipstone St Fitzroy Square [London] Augt 10th [1807]

My Dear Nephew

\*   \*   \*   \*   \*   \*   \*   \*   \*   \*

I hope to God the Unhappy differences between this Country & yours will be amicably settled as a War (which I pray God to *avert*) would be ruinous to both, the Goverment here seem disposed to yield to everything in reason, and the Merchants say, that your Country is grasping at too much, that if you give them an Inch, they want an *Ell*, and that they are never *satisfied* — when both Goverment are disposed for Peace, it is a melancholy consideration that the indiscretion of Hot headed Admirals & Needy Captains & a misguided *Mob*, shoud bring on hostilities between Countries that wish to be at peace, Your Government has not yet sent any Official dispatches of the unpleasant business the President Speech is thought in general to be moderate. It would have been much more so, if he had permitted the fleet that was in distress to have had supplies for *that time* & then not to expect any more hereafter. It would have been but *liberal* to have done it.

Stocks rose yesterday 27 [?] P Cent upon the prospect of Peace upon the Continent as the 13th Article in the Treaty of Peace with Russia & France the Emperor offers his mediation for Peace & the Tyrant accepts — I refer you to the papers for all particulars. With my best love & regards to Mrs Otis and all your dear Flock & may you all live long & be happy is the Wish of your Affectionate Uncle & Faithful Friend

H. Gray.

# CHAPTER XVI

## THE FEDERALIST MACHINE [1]

### 1800-1823, ÆT. 35-58

THE disastrous election of 1800 demonstrated to Federalist leaders the need of solidarity and organization in their party. Two courses were open to them. They might have popularized their party, as the Republicans had done in the Middle States, by adopting the convention of delegates as a method of nomination. But so democratic an institution was contrary to all Federalist faith and precedent, especially in New England. The "Land of Steady Habits" was suspicious of extra-legal machinery. The very word "convention" had an unpleasant Jacobin connotation to its ears.[2] What the Federalist leaders

---

[1] No one has yet described, or even, it seems, suspected, the existence of the Federalist machine in Massachusetts. Even Dr. G. D. Luetscher makes no mention of it in his *Early Political Machinery in the United States* (Philadelphia, 1903), to which, however, I am greatly indebted for its description of other contemporary party organizations. But this is not surprising, for no party machine courts publicity, and the Federalist machine had particular reasons for wishing to remain secret. The Otis MSS. revealed its existence.

[2] The following is a typical Federalist comment upon one of the first county nominating conventions held in New England:

Middlesex Jacobin Club.

"The caucus, *alias* County Convention, *alias* Jacobin Club, ... actually met yesterday at *Noah Brooks'* tavern in *Lincoln*. There was, it is true, much *skulking* and crossing *lots*, before the club got together; but after meeting, they proceeded to *organize*, as they were pleased to call it, pretty much in the manner that the *County Conventions* did in *Shays'* times; and the *Jacobin Clubs*, did under the reign of ROBESPIERRE in *France*. As the Conventioners were all men *picked* by the authors of the meeting, from 24 out of 42 towns, and chosen the Lord only knows how, or whom by; — and as Squire DANA, had the Resolutions already *cut and dried*, at hand, there was a wonderful *unanimity*." (*Centinel*, October 27, 1804.)

needed was a *machine*, that would register the will of the "wise and good" as to nominations, and at the same time reach out to the ordinary voter, on whom (most unfortunately, from the Federalist viewpoint) their power depended in the last resort. And we find that in Massachusetts by 1804[2] there was established a party organization differing absolutely from the usual American type, in that it was thoroughly centralized, made no concessions, even in theory, to popular rights, and was frankly based upon the right of the leaders to rule the party, and through it the body politic. Whatever the origin of this organization, it is safe to say that Harrison Gray Otis had a hand in it. He was a member of the state legislature when it was established, and his correspondence shows him to have been most active in its management.

The starting-point of the Federalist machine in Massachusetts was the adoption of the legislative caucus, consisting of the Federalist members of both branches of the General Court, as the nominating organ for governor and lieutenant-governor. This step probably took place in

The Federal party in New England, between 1808 and 1815, frequently held county conventions to pass resolutions censuring national policy, but never, so far as I know, made nominations by this method before 1817, and after that only exceptionally.

[2] I have reached the conclusion that the Federalist organization in Massachusetts, as we find it between 1804 and 1823, was introduced between 1800 and 1804, since (1) the legislative caucus was only established in 1800 (see next note); (2) various allusions in the *Independent Chronicle* of 1804 (e.g., October 22), indicate that this organization had just been discovered by the Democrats; and (3) William Plumer organized the New Hampshire Federalists in a similar manner in 1804: "Associating with himself five other persons, one from each county, he organized them into a self-constituted State Committee. Under this committee, of which he was chairman, county committees were formed, and under these, town and school district committees, whose duty it was to bring every Federal voter to the polls, and secure, as far as possible, the wavering and doubtful to their ranks." — *Life of Plumer*, 313. Similar organizations were adopted by the New Jersey Federalists between 1801 and 1808 (Luetscher, 88, 92–93); and a letter from James B. Mason, of Providence, to Otis, dated July 11, 1808, shows that the Rhode Island Federalists had by that time gone through the same process.

1800.[4] The method had been in vogue in Maryland since 1788, and, as we have seen, had already been adopted by both parties in Congress, for nominating presidential candidates. For Massachusetts it was a great advance, since previously the nominations for governor had simply been announced in the Boston newspapers — probably at the dictation of the Essex Junto — and had not always attracted the entire party vote. Yet the party leaders responsible for the caucus assumed an apologetic attitude, on account of New England's prejudice against extra-legal machinery; and nominations made by it were generally announced without any indication of their source, or in ambiguous language. This diffidence was particularly apparent in 1808 and 1812, when the Federal party was denouncing as despotic and unconstitutional the nomination of Madison by a congressional caucus.

We are fortunate to have preserved, in a contemporary letter,[5] a vivid picture of the Federalist legislative caucus in session, in the year 1816 when it was necessary to find a successor to Governor Strong. The letter first states that Otis was offered the nomination, but refused it.

Lieut: Governor Phillips was then waited upon by a Committee and the offer of the first place given him and received rather in dudgeon because as he believed the offer had elsewhere been made, he wrote as answer that he would neither accept the first nor second place, and now there was trouble in the camp and various candidates proposed. The President of the Senate [John Phillips] and Speaker [Timothy Bigelow] were both of the Caucus Committee; the latter succeeded in a nomination[6] from the Committee to the grand body. All were surprised,

[4] T. C. Amory, *James Sullivan*, II, 65.

[5] Edward H. Robbins, ex-lieutenant-governor, to Samuel Howe, February 7, 1816. Communicated to me through the kindness of their descendant, Archibald M. Howe, Esq.

[6] Of John Brooks, for governor. The remainder of the letter relates to the nomination for lieutenant-governor.

some swore, others grew faint and complained of the air of the room, others more collected called for adjournments and succeeded, all inquiring as they came down, "What shall we do?"

Another meeting was held, a new Committee softer and smoother were recommended for another attack on the present incumbent [William Phillips] of which your neighbor of the Senate was one. It was with difficulty they could see him, and very soon directed to inform the body that he would not be the candidate, and off they came with a flea in their ears as the saying is. In the meantime the Speaker grew sick, as you will see by the paper; a new meeting was summoned to decide on his fate, his friends flew to Medford and obtained a letter declining most fully and satisfactorily. The cry was again "What shall we do?" Some said "Let us consult out-doors among the common voters. Some of them may know something as well as the Court folks." Others said "It would please them and do no hurt — advised to delay 48 hours." In 24, they were assured Lieutenant Governor would stand; a new Committee appointed to wait on him with a vote that the Federal interest in this state imperiously demanded of him the sacrifice and nothing short of his compliance would satisfy the public sentiment and to request his permission to use his name. He replied that he had consulted conscience and duty and found himself bound to assent, and from that moment was as clay in the potter's hands.

"The caucus committee," which is mentioned in this letter, consisted of one member from each county in the state, and, as in this case, its recommendation was generally adopted by the whole body. Otis wrote William Sullivan in 1822, after intimating that he would accept the nomination for governor, "I venture only to suggest that a nomination of Governor ought not to be referred to a *Caucus Committee* — It is a most exceptionable mode." A letter from James Lloyd in 1808, addressed to "Honble. Mr. Otis, chairman of Federal meeting of the members of the Legislature,"[7] and accepting his nomination for Sen-

[7] *Proc. Mass. Hist. Soc.*, XLV, 374.

ator, indicates that the caucus then possessed a function that it has just lost—that of selecting United States Senators.

Either the legislative caucus, or the caucus committee, elected annually a smaller and permanent body, the Central Committee of the State. This body, consisting generally of seven Bostonians, not all of whom were necessarily members of the legislature, was the keystone and executive head of the Federalist machine in Massachusetts. It appointed the county committees, through which it controlled the town committees and all nominations to the General Court; it directed the campaigns, published an annual "address to the people," distributed literature, kept local leaders up to the mark, and saw to it that Federalist towns were fully represented; in short, it had every function of the modern state central committee, and possessed far more power. Its very existence, however, as well as that of the organization that flowed from it, was intended to be kept a profound secret; not only on account of its violation of New England traditions, but because, as a similar committee in Philadelphia observed in 1808, "Considerate people are convinced that measures must be digested by the few, nevertheless among the mass each is desirous that he should be one of the number." [8] The leaders must have been fairly confident that their secrecy could be maintained, for the *Centinel*, describing an exactly similar Democratic machine in 1808, had the effrontery to denounce its efforts as "wicked exertions of wicked men" and a "profanation of the temple of freedom." [9] The *Chronicle*, on the other hand, frequently

---

[8] *Am. Hist. Rev.*, xvii, 760.

[9] Article, "Freedom of Election," in *Centinel*, August 3, 1808. Cf. Luetscher, 105, 141–43. From what I have observed in the course of this study, I should say that the Democratic organization in Massachusetts was in all essentials the same as the Federalist, except for a substitution, from 1808 on, of the county

served up to its readers an exposé of the Federalist machine. Both parties, it seems, lived in glass houses, and threw stones freely.

Our principal source of information for the activities of the Central Committee consists in a few copies that have survived of printed circular letters, signed in manuscript, by which it communicated with the county and town committees.[10] The signatures indicate its personnel. Otis's name invariably stands first, suggesting that he was chairman— a supposition which several letters from local committee men among his papers, addressed to him in that capacity,[11] confirm. Associated with him are such men as Thomas Handasyd Perkins, William Sullivan, Daniel Sargent, John Welles, and John Phillips, all politicians, and members of leading Boston families; Israel Thorndike, one of the wealthiest merchants of Boston; Artemas Ward, son of the general of the same name, and Francis Dana Channing, a brother of William Ellery Channing. Although this list is notable for the absence of any member of the Essex Junto persuasion, yet we find that at this period the Essex Junto profoundly influenced Federalist policy, and that the committees which managed the presidential campaigns of 1808 and 1812 were chosen almost exclusively from its ranks. Probably the Junto considered the routine work of the central committee below its consideration.

convention for the county mass meeting, which gave the voter a slightly better chance of overruling the dictates of the men "higher up." See J. Q. Adams, *Memoirs*, I, 538–40; *Centinel*, March 30, 1811, April 3, 1819 (exposés of Democratic circular letters); Boston *Scourge*, September 17, 1811; *Centinel*, October 9, 1824; *Diary of William Bentley*, III, 303. The Democratic machine, it seems, was even then controlled by the federal office-holders in Boston — Aaron Hill, Henry Dearborn, Perez Morton, James Prince, etc.

[10] Besides the one here reproduced in facsimile, there is one dated February 9, 1810, in the Am. Antiq. Soc.; one of April 13, 1810, in the New York Hist. Soc. Another, dated April 19, 1811, is printed in the *Chronicle*, May 2, 1811.

[11] Cf. Josiah Dwight's letters, following this and the next chapter.

Circular letters were issued at least twice a year: before the governor's election, and between that date (the first Monday in April) and the election of state representatives. A page of stock remarks on French influence, Jacobin intolerance, etc., laying stress upon the particular need for exertion that year, was always followed by a confidential communication on methods and organization. The circular of February 9, 1810, for instance, states to the county committees:

You will impress the several town committees, with the necessity of dividing their towns into sections, of appointing committees for every district, of confirming the doubtful, and exciting those who are firm; and of sending the full number of representatives. The means of information must be placed in the hands of all who will make a right use of them.

You will recommend to the committees frequent meetings with the inhabitants, and the prompt distribution of any political papers they may receive, and communications of any intelligence they may obtain.

A correspondence should be maintained between the several county committees, and information given of the arts that may be resorted to by our opponents, in season to frustrate them.

The second page of the circular of February 19, 1811 (reproduced opposite in facsimile), shows the Central Committee ordering a change in the form of the county committees; and the circular of April 19, 1811, addressed to the town committees, gives such detailed instructions for getting out the vote, that it is difficult to see how a single Federalist voter escaped being dragged to the polls. Taken as a whole, these documents reveal a highly centralized party machine in a surprisingly advanced state of development: a hierarchy of committees, district, town, and county, all controlled and set in motion by a Central State Committee in Boston.

were of opinion that a great advantage might be derived from a different organization of our Committees. By the appointment of three in a principal Town of each County, it was expected an additional force and effect could be given to exertion, and a greater degree of responsibility might be had. You have been selected at a numerous and respectable meeting of Federalists, with a full confidence, that you will, in your County, give vigour and effect to all measures, that may promote the election of the Federal Candidates. You will correspond with the Town Committees, and stimulate their exertions in inducing the attendance of every qualified voter, and in every other correct and energetic measure, strive to realise the full benefit of this arrangement, in the high degree anticipated by the Federal meeting. Your friends have pledged themselves for your exertion ; and we have a full confidence their reliance is well placed. The Circular Letter which will be forwarded, you will distribute among the Towns in manner as you may judge proper.

We are respectfully,

Let us now turn to the practical workings of the machine. The county committees appointed and supervised the town committees, and summoned a county caucus some time in the month of March, to nominate a list of state senators.[12] This caucus was theoretically a mass-meeting open to every voter in the county, but, since only the inhabitants of the county town where it was held could well attend, the committee really made the nominations. In Boston, both a town and a county, the procedure was somewhat different. Here the machinery was controlled by the "Central Committee of Suffolk County," appointed by the Central Committee of the State; and by the ward committees. These last were elected by the ward caucuses, and were one of the few popular features of the Federalist organization. Twice a year (three times in even years), about two weeks before the elections for governor, for state representatives, and for Congress,[13] the Suffolk Central Committee called a Primary or Initial Caucus. This institution was composed of the Central Committee, the ward committees, and a carefully selected list of invited guests, which made it a very congenial little affair. It was held either at the Exchange Coffee-House, or at Jemmy Vila's "Concert Hall," and its privacy was respected by the Federalist press. At the March

[12] Senatorial districts coincided with county lines until the famous Gerrymander of 1811, which confused the Federalist machine considerably.

[13] The multiplicity of elections in Massachusetts before the Constitutional Amendment of 1831 is somewhat confusing. The election day for governor and state senators was the first Monday in April. State representatives could be chosen at any time "before ten days before the last Wednesday in May"; the first Monday in May was the usual date in Boston. The last Wednesday in May, when the governor was inaugurated and the legislative year began, was known as "General Election," or more popularly "Nigger 'lection," as it was the only day in the year on which negroes were allowed on the Common. Members of Congress and presidential electors were chosen, as now, early in November. The list of elections is further complicated by "Artillery Election," the first Monday in June, a great occasion upon which the Commander of the Ancient and Honorable Artillery Company was chosen on the Common.

meeting a list of state senators was agreed upon, and at
the October meeting, in even years, a member of Congress was nominated, without, it appears, taking the
slightest notice of the other towns that were in the same
district with Boston. Again, in May, the Initial Caucus
selected a list of representatives for the "Boston Seat" in
the General Court. Every town had a right to one member in the lower house for every 225 ratable polls, but
Boston never sent more than seven members until 1805.
Up to that year the courts insisted on a literal application of the constitutional provision that "every member
of the house of representatives shall be chosen by written
votes," which made the writing of ballots an onerous
task. After printed ballots were allowed, the Initial
Caucus availed itself of the town's full privilege, and
nominated annually between twenty-seven and forty-five
representatives, who were invariably elected, and constituted a welcome addition to the Federalist forces in the
General Court.

Nominations made by the Initial Caucus were announced in the newspapers as being "recommended"
from some mysterious source, and were formally adopted
by the General or Grand Federal Caucus at Faneuil Hall,
to which every Federalist in town was invited, on the
Sunday evening before election day. This was, however,
a mere matter of form; the Grand Caucus was practically
only a political rally. The April one was the great occasion
of the year, and invariably the scene of a brilliant forensic
display by Otis and the lesser Boston orators. John Quincy
Adams writes in his diary, under date of April 5, 1807:

Mr. Dexter called upon me this afternoon. I attended the
federal meeting at Faneuil Hall this evening. The hall was
nearly as full as it could hold. Mr. Quincy was speaking when
I went in. Mr. Otis and Mr. Gore succeeded him. But there

was no diversity of opinion. The vote was put for supporting Mr. Strong as Governor, at the election to morrow, and Mr. Robbins as Lieutenant Governor, with the last years list of Senators. They were all unanimously carried. Walking home with Mr. Dexter, I was remarking upon the questionable nature of this party organization, and its tendency under our Constitution. It is perhaps unavoidable, but it is not altogether reconcilable to the freedom of the elective principle.

Only two occasions are known of a revolt against the dictation of an Initial Caucus. The first was in 1814, when William H. Sumner was so nominated for Congress. A group of the younger Federalists, who were becoming tired of the old party methods, then waited upon Major Russell, in whose paper, the *Centinel*, the nomination had been announced, and asked him why they had not been consulted. He replied: "If the young men of Boston won't step into the traces, they must be whipped in!" This was enough for the young men. They called a separate caucus, nominated Andrew Ritchie, Jr., and presented his claims with such vigor at the Grand Caucus that the machine was forced to bring in a compromise candidate.[14] Again, in a congressional bye-election of 1817, the Initial Caucus was called to account by the Central Committee of the State for nominating Jonathan Mason, the purity of whose Federalism was then somewhat in doubt. The Central Committee called the Grand Caucus earlier than usual, and pushed through a new nomination; but the members of the Initial Caucus, tenacious of their privilege, insisted that this action was illegal, and ordered all true Federalists to vote for Mason.[15]

Election day in Boston was an exciting affair, under the old régime. The only polling place was Faneuil Hall. All

[14] William H. Sumner, *History of East Boston*, 743; Boston papers for November, 1814.
[15] *Centinel*, October 29–November 12, 1817; Niles, xxiii, 209.

day its steps were lined with young men of both parties,
offering to the voters as they arrived written or printed
ballots, and taking a last opportunity to strengthen the
wavering and alarm the timid. No secrecy was possible
under these circumstances; every man had to show his
colors or abstain from voting, and vigilant ward committees made life miserable for stay-at-homes. Otis was loath
to give up the old methods in 1822, when the city charter
was adopted, in favor of separate polling places in the
wards. Federalist supremacy, he wrote William Sullivan,

depends upon the influence and example of the most respectable persons in the various walks and professions who have
long been habituated to act together. — The force of these persons is increased by the sympathy and enthusiasm of numbers,
and by a feeling of shame or self reproach which attends the
consciousness of a *known* dereliction of duty — The class which
is *acted upon* by this example and influence realize a pride and
pleasure in shewing their colors upon a general review, which
they cannot feel when trained in a gun house. — The old leaders
have learned the art of giving a salutary impulse to the whole
body when collected together. — This impulse ought to be a
unit, to procure unity of action. — It is easier to manage the
town of B——by a *Lancastrian* system of political discipline
than to institute numerous schools.[16]

Judged by the results, this "Lancastrian system" had
been a complete success. While the Federal party existed,
Boston was its pocket borough. Between 1788 and 1828
it never failed to give a majority to the Federalist candidate for Congress. A Democratic candidate for governor
carried the town only twice (1800 and 1801) between 1797
and 1825; and the Democratic ticket for the Boston Seat
succeeded but once (1800) in the same period. No wonder,
then, that Federalists called stolid Boston "The Headquarters of Good Principles."

[16] January 19, 1822. MS. collection of N. Y. Public Library.

In spite of the scurrility and personal abuse with which newspapers of both parties were filled; in spite of the perfervid speeches of night-before caucuses, elections in New England during the Federalist epoch were never disgraced by disorder or violence. New England at that time had a rigid code of etiquette regarding political campaigns, which we would do well to return to nowadays. Stump-speaking, spellbinding, and whirlwind tours were unknown; political rallies, other than the grand caucuses, were rare; and best of all, candidates were absolutely forbidden by public opinion to canvass or electioneer in their own behalf. It was even considered improper for them to make a written denial of charges. Samuel Dexter, in 1814, apologized for publishing an explanation of his attitude, when unexpectedly nominated by the Democrats; and Otis's friends dissuaded him from publishing a denial of his opposition to war loans, when he was a candidate for governor in 1823.[17] But political conversation and newspaper campaigning never abated during the feverish period between 1807 and 1815. The State Street insurance offices became informal political clubs, at which leading Federalists would drop in during the morning to discuss the latest French outrage or Jacobin delusion. "The office of the Suffolk Insurance Company," writes Lucius Manlius Sargent,[18] "was more noted for its daily political harangues, than for its semi-annual dividends.... The voice of Mr. Parsons, then Chief Justice of the Commonwealth, was often heard in those conventicles; not in his official capacity, of course, but as the Magnus

---

[17] *Mr. Dexter's Address to the Electors of Massachusetts* (1814), 1, 9; Luetscher, 65; *Proc. Mass. Hist. Soc.*, 2d Ser., xiv, 74; Isaac Parker to Otis, January, 1823; "if intended for the public it [Otis's vindication] is introducing a mode of electioneering wholly new to our section of the Country & one which, as usual in the southern states, has been much condemned here."

[18] *Reminiscences of Samuel Dexter*, 84.

Apollo of the assembly." Formal dinners, especially the Federalist Fourth of July dinners, were occasions for the display of piquant political toasts, for which Otis was famous. Twenty formal toasts, accompanied by a band of music, and (if the dinner were out of doors) discharges of artillery, were not unusual on these occasions, and informal toasts followed until most of the diners were under the table or carried home. The following are a few of the formal ones at the Federalist dinner in Salem on July 4, 1812, just after war was declared:

*July 4th, 1812.* — We hail it as the commencement of a new Independence.[19]
  2 guns. "Yankee Doodle."

*Embargo.* — A base *retreat*, treacherously *beat*, while commercial prosperity was in full *march*.
  1 gun. "Austrian Retreat."

*Non-Importation.* — A vile measure calculated to introduce smuggling, deprave the public morals, and sap the foundation of *Northern* liberty.
  1 gun. "Jefferson's Delight."

*The Existing War.* — The Child of Prostitution, may no American acknowledge it legitimate.
  1 gun. "Wapping Landlady."

*Democratic Office Holders:* — They draw *double rations* and never go on *fatigue duty* except on days of election.
  1 gun. "Faith! The world's a good thing."

*Thos. Jefferson.* — May we never cease to continue to idolize the man who *copied off* the Declaration of Independence.
  1 gun. "Dicky Gossip is the man."

*Physical and Moral Strength.* — the STATE is favored of Heaven which sees itself STRONG in the field, STRONG, in the cabinet, and STRONG in the hearts of the people.
  3 guns. "Gov. Strongs March." [20]

----

[19] No doubt a hint that the author desired secession.
[20] Salem *Gazette*, July 7, 1812.

To return to the functions of the Central State Committee, we find one of its most important duties was that of "educating the voters." The "address to the people," which every year filled the front page of the *Centinel* in the latter part of March, was its production; and in many of them I have observed Otis's mannerisms of style. The members of the committee wrote political essays, and stimulated others to express their ideas. Newspapers were more extensively employed as a party weapon by the Federalists than by their opponents. Between 1801 and 1804, when the party organization was being established, many of the most famous party organs were founded, such as the Boston *New-England Palladium*, the Charleston *Courier*, and the New York *Evening Post*. As late as 1810 there were Federalist newspapers in every state, and in two of the territories; the total number was only two less than that of the Democratic journals.[21] Among Otis's manuscripts is a list of northern New England newspapers, containing many pithy comments,[22] which shows evidence of having been compiled in 1808 for the use of the committee that managed the presidential campaign of that year. When in 1812, a Boston Federalist paper, the *Weekly Messenger*, ventured to criticize the Federalist presidential nomination, Otis wrote William Sullivan, sputtering with rage against the "perfidy" of the editor "in thus perverting a paper set up with great pains trouble and expense by the Federal Party." The Central Committee, profiting by Josiah Dwight's sug-

[21] 157 Federalist (115 in New England and the Middle States), and 159 Democratic (87 in the same section). Isaiah Thomas, *History of Printing* (2d ed.), II, 517.

[22] For instance: "The *Watchman*, printed at Montpelier, Vt. by Samuel Goss. though federal — this watchman appears to sleep on his post — if roused to his duty and made acquainted with the importance of his trust, he may prove as serviceable to his country as the winged biped that saved Rome."

gestion[23] that pamphlets reached a class of readers who refused to read Federalist newspapers, circulated also that sort of literature in large quantities. Christopher Gore wrote in the spring of 1808 that five thousand copies of Timothy Pickering's pamphlet on the Embargo would be distributed, an estimate which was probably greatly exceeded before the campaign was over.

A standing grievance of both parties in Massachusetts was the failure of remote or indifferent towns to elect state representatives, in order to save the expense of salary and mileage. An interesting letter between two of Otis's fellow members of the Central Committee[24] shows that body making every effort to secure a full complement of Federalists. The results seem to indicate that they succeeded fairly well.[25] The Democratic legislature of 1811-12 passed an act providing for payment of members' salaries by the state; but this measure, which had the expected effect of securing more members from remote Democratic towns in Maine, raised the pay-roll of the General Court eighty-five per cent, and was repealed by the Federalists as soon as they returned to power.

The Federalist political organizations in New England and the Middle States possessed in the Washington Benevolent Societies a powerful auxiliary that corresponded to the modern national party clubs.[26] The first society of this name was founded in New York City in 1808, and probably acted as a central organization to all

---

[23] In his letter to Otis, following this chapter.

[24] T. H. Perkins's letter, following this chapter.

[25] The *Chronicle* of May 26, 1808, complains that Republican towns chose eighty-seven less than their full quota, but Federalist towns only twenty less.

[26] I am indebted for most of my data on this subject to Mr. Harland H. Ballard, of Pittsfield, and to his article, "A Forgotten Fraternity," in the Pittsfield *Berkshire Evening Eagle*, August 3, 1912. No other historian has so much as mentioned the Washington Benevolent Societies, which are quite as significant for the Federal party as the Democratic clubs of 1793 for its opponents.

the others; it was followed by the establishment of the Washington Benevolent Society of Berkshire, at Pittsfield, in 1811, and of the Washington Benevolent Society of Massachusetts, at Boston, in February, 1812. The movement so quickly spread that within two years almost every town of any size in New England, and points so remote as Canandaigua and Annapolis, had established branch societies. Each applicant for membership was obliged to take an oath to support the Constitution of the United States, to use his exertions to preserve it "against the inroads of despotism, monarchy, aristocracy, *and democracy*," and to be faithful to "those political principles which distinguished the Administration of Washington." He was then given a small pamphlet containing Washington's Farewell Address and the Constitution of the United States, with a certificate of membership on the flyleaf.

The objects of the Washington Benevolent Society were, according to the constitution of the Massachusetts society, "to support the constitution of the United States in its original purity," and "to supply the wants and alleviate the sufferings of unfortunate individuals within the sphere of our personal acquaintance."[27] Undoubtedly the real object was to strengthen and extend the Federal party, particularly among the lower classes, by a social bond. The society appealed to the poor, by dispensing charity,[28] and it greatly appealed to that most universal of human weaknesses, the desire to belong to something.

[27] MS. records in Mass. Hist. Society. William Sullivan, the only member of a Washington Benevolent Society to mention it in his writings, states in his *Familiar Letters* (1834), 325, that it was a movement for the defense of society and property, occasioned by the Baltimore riots of 1812, which, however, took place after the New York, Pittsfield, Boston, and many other branches were organized.

[28] William Cobbett compares the Washington Benevolent Society (in his *Weekly Register*, May 13, 1815) to the British Literary Fund, a scheme for attaching hack writers to the government under the garb of charity. A better comparison would be to the Primrose League of the modern Unionist Party.

Its annual dues were only a dollar; it had dinners, meetings, elaborate processions and badges, and in that period when the wealthy and powerful were far more respected and looked up to than now, it was a most desirable privilege to sit down at table with Harrison Gray Otis, Josiah Quincy, and Thomas Handasyd Perkins, and to be hailed by them as "brother." [29]  The Berkshire society had over twenty-three hundred members, and a directory of the Boston society, published in 1813, contains over fifteen hundred names, half the Federalist vote of the town, and including men in every walk of life. The officers were chosen for the most part among the younger generation of Federalists. [30]  Harrison Gray Otis, Jr., was secretary at one time, but his father was never an officer. An amusing (and very rare) satirical pamphlet of 1813, "The First Book of the 'Washington Benevolents,' otherwise called the Book of Knaves," [31] is dedicated, among others, "To the 'Beloved Harry,' otherwise 'the man of the People'"; and in "Chapter VI" assigns Harrison Gray Otis the following rôle in the organization of the Society:

Now it was far past the going down of the sun; and Harry who was surnamed the "beloved," proposed that the council

[29] Alexander Hamilton proposed in 1802 (*Works*, VI, 540–43) to strengthen the then declining Federal party by establishing a "Christian Constitutional Society," with a central organization and local branches, that should hold meetings, dispense charity, give instructions to mechanics, and combine at elections. Although the leaders to whom he communicated his plans gave them no encouragement, the New York founders of the Washington Benevolent Society were endeavoring apparently to carry out his ideas. It is interesting to note that President Taft, on November 6, 1912, expressed his hope to see organized a National Republican Club "which shall cherish the principles of the party, and be a source of political activity, not only during election years, but at all times." Boston *Herald*, November 7, 1912.

[30] The first board of officers of the Boston society consisted of Arnold and John Welles, William Sullivan, Josiah Quincy, Lemuel Blake, Andrew Ritchie, Jr., Daniel Messinger, Dr. John Collins Warren, and Benjamin Russell.

[31] The Berkshire Athenæum of Pittsfield, Mass., has the only copy of this pamphlet that I have been able to discover.

should make preparation for the great feast of the political passover.

2. Moreover he said, that albeit the name of *Tory* had become a bye-word, and a scoff among the people, he did propose that the tribe of the tories should forthwith be called *Washington Benevolents.*

3. And the council applauded Harry for his wisdom, and cried out with one voice, who is like unto the grand contriver?

4. He hath done wonderful things! yea he hath wrought miraculously, and we will praise him in the gates.

5. Verily he hath cast off the reproach of his ancestors, who did belong to the tribe of the republicans, and he is a man after our own hearts, who like the Boston Rebel [32] loveth *GROG* and feareth the King.

This pamphlet was published as a take-off on the pompous ceremonials in which every Washington Benevolent Society indulged on April 30, the anniversary of Washington's inauguration. On the whole, however, these organizations were taken quite seriously by the Democrats, since their growth in time of war could be viewed only as a menace. Charges of secret secessionist plots were frequently imputed to them, and in some places vigilance associations were formed to watch over the members. But there is no evidence that the society had any other objects than those I have stated. Most successful in these respects, it greatly increased the strength and solidarity of the Federal party during the War of 1812.

The most interesting development of the Massachusetts Federalist machine, on the whole, was its coöperation with the Federalist organizations in other states in calling secret meetings of delegates, in 1808 and 1812, in order to nominate candidates for the presidency and vice-presidency. These were the first national party conventions

[32] John Lowell.

ever held.[33] A peculiar problem of the Federal party, repeated in 1808 and in 1812, brought about this premature appearance of the capstone to modern party machinery. In each year an insurgent Democrat — in both cases a Clinton — entered the presidential race with more or less of the Federalist policies as his platform. The question before the Federalists then was whether to run their own candidates, or, with much greater chance of winning, to back the insurgent already in the field. Some method was necessary to reach a decision on this point that would be binding on the whole party. A congressional caucus was out of the question, because the growing unpopularity of this method of nomination, as practiced by the Republicans, was counted upon for political capital. A conference of leaders from all parts of the country was the natural alternative.

Harrison Gray Otis seems to have been the originator of this prototype of the national nominating convention. He probably broached the idea to New York and Philadelphia politicians during a visit to those cities in May, 1808. Shortly after his return came a letter from Charles Willing Hare,[34] of Philadelphia, alluding to conversations with Otis and suggesting that it was high time to do something about the presidential nomination. The hint was taken; the Grand Committee of the Federalist caucus in

[33] I have treated the 1808 convention at greater length in "*The First National Nominating Convention, 1808,*" *Amer. Hist. Rev.,* xvii, 744, an article in which references to statements made here on that subject will be found. The sources used for the 1812 convention are the Otis MSS., the memoirs of William Sullivan in his *Public Men of the Revolution* (1847), Rufus King's diary and correspondence in *King,* v, chap. xiv; letters of R. G. Harper in Steiner, *McHenry,* 583, ff. There is also a brief and inaccurate article on this subject in *Amer. Hist. Rev.,* i, 680.

[34] 1778-1827, a prominent lawyer and Federalist leader in Philadelphia; at this time a member of the state legislature and a candidate for Congress. He was a relative of Otis's old Philadelphia friends, the Willings and Harrisons, and was associated with him in the management of the Bingham estate.

the General Court appointed a special Committee of Correspondence to concert measures with the Federalists of other states for the approaching election. This committee had a distinguished membership: Otis, who was the chairman, the venerable George Cabot, Christopher Gore, Timothy Bigelow (Speaker of the House), and James Lloyd, who had just been elected to the United States Senate in place of John Quincy Adams. All except Otis were members of the Essex Junto, or its tools. At a meeting on June 10, this committee determined to call "a meeting of Federalists, from as many states as could be seasonably notified, at New York."

The easy and informal method by which the New York convention of 1808 was summoned was typically Federalist, and will no doubt be envied by party leaders of to-day. The Massachusetts Committee of Correspondence immediately notified Hare in Philadelphia, and Rufus King in New York, of their decision. Hare wrote Otis on June 19, as follows:

I received yours of the 11th on the 16. I immediately took measures for convening a few of our most active firm and discreet friends. A Meeting of about a dozen was held yesterday — at which your objects and reasoning were stated — and so far as regards the propriety of the proposed convention, immediately and without hesitation acquiesced in. A Committee consisting of Messrs Fitzsimons, R Waln, Latimer, Morgan and myself, were appointed to correspond with you — and in obedience to your suggestion to 'organise for the South.' We shall immediately write to some of our friends in Maryland and Delaware, and after having heard from them I shall again address you.

Judge Egbert Benson of New York, who happened to be in Boston shortly after the convention was decided upon, communicated with the leading Federalists in Connecticut and New Jersey on his way home, and suggested

"that they should instantly associate to themselves such
persons as they should think proper to form a Committee
of Correspondence,"[25] a method which they doubtless
followed. The Massachusetts Committee itself attended
to the rest of New England, sending Otis and Bigelow on
special missions to the different states, in order to insure
their coöperation. No attempt seems to have been made
to secure delegates from Virginia or North Carolina,
where Federalism was still strong, or from the West.

About thirty-five delegates from eight states,[26] chosen
by exclusive committees of the Philadelphia and Boston
types, met at New York in the third week in August. The
very existence of the convention was supposed to be a profound secret, and no hint of it was breathed by the Federalist journals; but the coming together of so many prominent Federalists did not escape the impudent Democratic
press. Among the delegates were Otis, Gore, and Lloyd
from Massachusetts, Hare and Thomas Fitzsimons from
Pennsylvania, Robert Goodloe Harper from Maryland,
and John Rutledge from South Carolina. No record as yet
has been found of the debates. We only know that the
proposed coalition with the Clintonians was rejected,
Charles Cotesworth Pinckney and Rufus King being
nominated for the presidency and vice-presidency. The
question between supporting Clinton and making separate
nominations was so thoroughly threshed out, however, in
Otis's correspondence, that we may fairly assume the line
of argument that prevailed. Otis believed that it was
hopeless to expect the success of a Federalist candidate,
and that to elect Clinton, whom he strongly favored,
would not only dethrone the Virginia dynasty, but secure
the repeal of the embargo and the abandonment of com-

[25] Benson to Otis, July 13, 1808.
[26] See the official notification, following this chapter.

mercial restriction. He was supported by the intellectual leader of the party, George Cabot, who saw that a page of democratic evolution had been turned; that the Federal party had better give up all hope of capturing the presidency, and ally itself with the best element among the Democrats. On the other side, it was argued in favor of separate candidates, first, that Clinton could not be trusted. The New York Federalists would have none of him. "We have condescended twice to tamper with Democratic Candidates," wrote Abraham Van Vechten to Otis, "and in both instances have been subjected to severe self-reproach. . . . Our experimental knowledge of the Clintonian. System is a powerful Antidote against affording it any facility here." Second, Clinton could not be elected unless he could carry one of the two factions representing Pennsylvania Democracy, both of which came out for Madison before the convention met. And, third, a coalition with Clinton would be a great dereliction of principle. As Judge Theodore Sedgwick wrote Otis (June 6):

It is of infinite importance that the leading federalists should conduct in such manner as to convince the publick that they are actuated by principle. This, I imagine, can hardly be the case unless they act by themselves, and keep themselves separate from the differant parties into which their adversaries are divided. . . . I cannot endure the humiliating idea that those who alone from education, fortune, character and principle are entitled to command should voluntarily arrange themselves under the banners of a party in all respects inferior, and in many odious, to them.

An amusing result of the secret methods of this convention was the fact that the Philadelphia committee, to which was confided the task of announcing the nominations, did not dare to make a statement. "We were led

to this conclusion," they wrote to the Massachusetts
committee, "from having observed something like a Jealousy, in our friends at having a Nomination so Important
decided on by so small a No. as we were, and without any
Special authority for the purpose, for altho there appears
to be no division of sentiment thr'out the state, as to the
Candidates, yet it was deemed most prudent that it should
appear rather the result of General sentiment than as
the Choice of a few to bind their party." The nominations were therefore given to the Boston papers, as being
the result of "information collected from every part of
the Union . . . without the aid of any Caucus, or other
preliminary." Many of the leading Federalist journals
never even published the nominations, but announced
that the Federalist electoral ticket was unpledged. This
was probably due to a desire in some quarters to swing
over to Clinton at the last moment. Otis, it seems,
favored this plan, and Theophilus Parsons attempted to
seduce the Connecticut legislature into the same course.
Evidently the first nominating convention did not succeed in impressing its members with loyalty to its
decision.

Again, in the presidential election of 1812, the Federal
party had to decide between making separate nominations and supporting a Clinton; De Witt Clinton having
come out for the presidency, as his uncle George had done
in 1808, as a Democratic insurgent. A Federalist national
convention at New York was decided upon in June, 1812,[37]
and organized, as in 1808, by irregularly chosen committees of correspondence in the several states.[38] Otis was

---

[37] Cf. William Sullivan, *Public Men*, 350, with *King*, v, 272.

[38] The Massachusetts Committee was presumably chosen by the Caucus
Committee, as in 1808. Otis, as chairman, received letters from a Philadelphia
"committee of correspondence and conference in regard to the Presidential
Election" (James Milnor, Robert Wharton, Horace Binney, and Andrew

chairman of a committee which elected the Massachusetts delegates, including himself, at a meeting consisting of only Cabot, Gore and Sullivan.

The convention met in New York on September 15, 16, and 17, 1812. About sixty-five delegates were present from eleven states, including three (Rhode Island, New Jersey, and Delaware) that were not represented in 1808. A brief diary that Rufus King kept of the convention, as well as the Otis correspondence, shows the arguments of 1808 being used over again. Otis was still strongly in favor of Clinton, and even refused to go to New York unless the entire Massachusetts delegation pledged itself in Clinton's favor. Besides the old arguments for Clinton, it was urged that there were no available Federalist candidates. John Jay and Chief Justice Marshall were mentioned, but as Samuel Dexter observed,[39] the former, superannuated and unpopular, "could no more play president than Seneca could Emperor," and the latter was needed in the Supreme Court. In addition, De Witt Clinton had promised to administer the government, if he were elected, in a manner satisfactory to the Federalists, and to sue for peace with Great Britain.[40] But Rufus King, unconvinced by these assurances, dilated upon Clinton's unscrupulousness and vacillation in recent years, and declared that his election would merely substitute Cæsar Borgia for James Madison. His speech produced, according to William Sullivan, a deadlock between Clin-

Bayard), appointed "at a meeting of Delegates from the several wards of this city"; from a similar New York committee consisting of Jacob Radcliff, Caleb S. Riggs, J. O. Hoffman, David B. Ogden, and John Welles; from Judge Griffith, of New Jersey, where a committee of correspondence was appointed by a Federalist state convention that met on July 4; and from Joseph Pearson, of North Carolina.

[39] To Otis, in letter following this chapter. C. C. Pinckney refused again to be the candidate.

[40] See Hoffman's letter to Otis, following this chapter, and *King*, v, 268-70.

ton's friends and enemies, which lasted until the convention was about to break up without result, when

> Mr. Otis arose, apparently much embarrassed, holding his
> hat in his hand, and seeming as if he were almost sorry he had
> arisen.  Soon he warmed with the subject, his hat fell from his
> hand, and he poured forth a strain of eloquence that chained
> all present to their seats; and when, at a late hour, the vote
> was taken, it was almost unanimously resolved to support
> Clinton.  This effort was unprepared, but only proves how
> entirely Mr. Otis deserves the reputation he enjoys of being a
> great orator.[41]

It is a pity to spoil this dramatic picture, but unfortunately more trustworthy sources than William Sullivan's
memory thirty-five years after the event show that Otis's
speech, powerful though it undoubtedly was, failed to
produce so definite a result as the nomination of De Witt
Clinton.  The convention adjourned after passing a set of
ambiguous resolutions that left the delegates in a state
of muddled incertitude.  It was voted, according to Rufus
King's diary, (1) that it was inexpedient to nominate
Federalist candidates; (2) that such candidates should be
supported "as would be likely to pursue a different course
of measures from that of the now President," and (3)
"that a committee of 5 persons (Pennsylvanians) be appointed to ascertain the results of the elections for Electors, and the Candidates whom they would be likely to
support, and to communicate the same as expeditiously as
practicable to the Electors of the several States."  No two
members seemed to be agreed as to the precise meaning
that these resolves were intended to convey.[42]  In most of

[41] *Public Men of the Revolution*, 351.
[42] Harper thought that they did not preclude the possibility of bringing in a
Federalist candidate (*McHenry*, 586); King, that they committed the party to
Clinton; George Tibbits, of New York, was so uncertain as to write Otis for his
opinion. If the third resolution were carried out literally, the Federalists and

the states, however, a "Clintonian" or "Peace" ticket of electors was supported by both Clintonian Democrats and Federalists.

These earliest of national conventions in 1808 and 1812 were typical of the Federal party. A few well-born and congenial gentlemen, who could afford the time and expense of travel, were chosen by their friends to settle, in a quiet and leisurely manner, the matter of nominations. From the body of voters neither authority nor advice was asked, and profound secrecy sheltered the convention's deliberations from vulgar scrutiny. Like the Federalist state machinery that we have examined, the two New York conventions were based on the right of the leaders to settle party matters without the slightest coöperation of the people. Of the voter, obedience only is required; he is to vote for candidates nominated he knows not how, because it is thought best by "those who alone from education, fortune, character, and principle are entitled to command."

Many will dispute the claim of these secret and exclusive meetings in New York to be classed with the modern national party conventions. There is not much outward resemblance, to be sure, but they are alike in the essentials: both were composed of delegates, chosen for the purpose of nominating presidential candidates, and both were national in their scope. Furthermore, the modern convention system, popular in theory, has proved quite as susceptible to boss rule as the old Federalist machine, which was frankly created for that purpose. I appeal for authority to an observation of our most acute political

Clintonians could not have combined on electoral tickets. As in 1808, the Federalists attempted to keep the convention secret, but the *National Intelligencer* published an account of it, stating the main facts correctly, and adding that a bargain had been made with Clinton during the sessions. Otis denied that in an indignant public letter. N. Y. *Evening Post*, October 20, 23, 1812.

seer, Mr. Dooley: "A naytional convintion, me boy, does nawthin' excipt whin it ain't in session. In manny a private room th' destinies iv this nation is bein' discussed be level-headed statesmen far frum th' tumult an' th' mob."

## LETTERS ON PARTY MATTERS, 1805–1812

### JOSIAH DWIGHT TO THE FEDERALIST CENTRAL COMMITTEE

Stockbridge, Nov 18 — 1805

Gentlemen

You have heretofore invited communication from your political brethren in the interior, whenever they should have any thing worthy of observation. The times with us are, at present, as they have been for sometime past, very little disturbed with the jargon of political Discord. Not that the spirit of Jacobinism is laid asleep. But, after being wearied with the tug of an electioneering campaign, both hostile parties seem glad of an opportunity to retire from the field, & enjoy the repose of a temporary truce. In the meantime each party maintains his own ground — no terms of mediation are proposed — nor are any offers, of permanent peace, made on either side. Each flatters himself that he is gaining new strength, which will enable him to attack his enemy with renewed vigor, and either, on one side, ensure a *more complete victory*, or, on the other, save him from a *more disgraceful defeat*. That we must again, in this section of the State, be defeated by numbers, cannot be a subject of doubt. But we are of opinion that the Jacobins cannot add an Unit to their former majority, and we are not without hopes of a very considerable reduction. To effect this desideratum, however, judicious means are to be used. The moderate Democrats are staggered with recent events in Pennsylvania & elsewhere, but they cannot at once be induced to detach their confidence from our *great political Demagogue,* in whom they have so long put their trust. Information must be disseminated among them. This cannot be done through the medium of Federal newspapers. This class of people have had their prejudices wrought up to such a degree as to believe that "their touch is poison." The measure adopted the last Spring of circulating Pamphlets, we think the only measure which can promise success. Men, who would not look into a Newspaper, will read a pamphlet with attention. Altho' for the want of time, we had very little chance to give them a general circulation, yet we are confident that they had a partial effect on the last Spring election. We therefore take the liberty to suggest the importance of immediately commencing a work of that kind, and issuing, at least, one number a month, from this time to April. We would not, however, be thought to assume a dictatorial authority over gentlemen far more competent than ourselves, and whose means of information, in the Metropolis, are much superior to ours, in a remote corner of the State. Altho' we have no doubt of the efficacy of the measures proposed, in this District, still if such effect, on the State at large, is dubious, we cannot expect it will be adopted. But if resort is at all to be had to such measure, you will pardon us for saying that, unless it be carried into operation at an earlier day than it was the last season, a very limited & partial effect, only, can be expected. Whereas if the means of communicating information to the deluded, are seasonably adopted, & pursued with unremitted exertion, during the time which intervenes the election, we flatter ourselves that much may be gained.

Your Committee, in this District, have holden a meeting & are organised agreeable to the recommendation in your letter of the 13th June. The undersigned has the honor of being appointed "to receive all communications" from the central Committee. The mode of communication may be, either by mail, via Springfield — or by private conveyance, either to this place, or to Northampton, to the care of Capt William Edwards, who will forward to this Town.

You may rely, Gentlemen, on our cordial cooperation in any measures you may in your wisdom devise, for the preservation of our Constitution & Government from the despoiling hands of Jacobins. I am, Gentlemen, In behalf of the Committee,

Very Respectfully Your Obedt Servt<br>JOSIAH DWIGHT

The Gentlemen of the
C Committee
[Address]: Hon Harrison G Otis Esqr

OFFICIAL NOTIFICATION OF THE RESULT OF THE FEDERALIST
NATIONAL CONVENTION OF 1808

*Manuscript copy sent Otis by the New York Committee of Correspondence,
October 9, 1808*

To the Federal Republican Committee [of]
Charleston, South Carolina
[New York, September, 1808]

Gentlemen,

We do ourselves the Honor of addressing you, in behalf of
the Federal corresponding Committee of this State, in respect
to the approaching Presidential Election. Several Conferences
on this subject have recently been held in this City, but from
Reasons of Expediency, it has hitherto been judged proper to
withold any Communications concerning the same. We feel
great Satisfaction in now being authorized to announce to you
the Result.

The States of Massachusetts, New Hampshire, Connecticut,
Vermont, New York, Pennsylvania and Maryland were sever-
ally represented at those Deliberations, as was likewise the
State of South Carolina by our respected Friend John Rutledge,
Esquire of your City.[43]

After several Meetings, and after the most mature and
dispassionate Consideration of the Subject, we formed a conclusive opinion, as to the Line of Conduct most proper for the
Federal Party to observe. It was decided to be our Correct and
dignified Policy to afford neither Aid nor Countenance, direct
or indirect, to any of our political opponents, but, holding
ourselves perfectly distinct, to nominate Federal Characters
for the offices of President and Vice President, and to support
them, with our uniform, zealous & vigorous Exertions. This
Determination, which we conceived best calculated to promote
the good of our Country — to concentrate the Activity and
Affections of our Party — to secure its Integrity, and to give
Energy to its Efforts, has likewise received the Approbation of
our Friends of New Jersey and Delaware.

[43] From Otis's correspondence it appears that Rhode Island was unable to
send a delegate, because no one could be spared from the state campaign that
was then going on, and that Delaware was unrepresented because James A.
Bayard disapproved of the meeting.

Having decided on the Measure, no difference of opinion could exist as to the Selection of Candidates, & Charles Cotesworth Pinckney for the Office of President, and Rufus King for the office of Vice President, became without the least Hesitation our Choice. In our Deliberations, we were governed by a calm and unbiassed View of the State, to which our Country is reduced, by the rash, though imbecile Measure of the Party now in Power. We perceived the energies of the Nation paralized; — Its Commerce suspended; — its Revenue nearly annihilated; — its most valuable Resources abandoned, and its Councils under the humiliating Influence of a foreign Power. Under such awful and hazardous Circumstances we felt a solemn Conviction that the Safety, Dignity, and Independence of our Union, demanded an immediate and radical Change in the Administration of its Government. . . .

With the States of Ohio, Kentucky and Tennessee we have no means of Communication. We have been informed, that a few Votes may be secured in those States by the Attention of Influential Characters in the State of South Carolina. This Suggestion is respectfully submitted to the Consideration of our Friends in Charleston — Urging and entreating them to lose no Time in adopting every proper and effectual Measure for communicating with those States, and to spare no Exertions to secure to our Candidates at least a Portion of the Votes of those States. We also rely with Confidence on your Attention to our Friends in North Carolina — their Distance prevents any safe and timely Correspondence with them on our Part. . . .

We shall be Happy, Gentlemen, to receive an Acknowledgement of the Receipt of this Letter, and such Information as you may think proper to communicate, which we trust will be as full & particular, as Circumstances will permit.

We are, Gentlemen, very respectfully

[JACOB RADCLIFF
JOS: OGDEN HOFFMAN
CADWALLADER D. COLDEN
S. JONES JUNR.][44]

[44] Signatures to the letter from the New York committee to Otis, in which this letter was enclosed.

### THOMAS HANDASYD PERKINS TO WILLIAM SULLIVAN

*From the Manuscript Collection of the New York Public Library.*

Tuesday Eve — [May 10, 1811][45]

My dear Sir,

I have just now learned from Bridgwater that the federalists are making overtures to send five Members to the Legislature — they sent from that town One Demo last year.[46]

Mr. Wm. Davis thinks we had best send our Ambassador — I have therefore engaged a Mr. Withington, a very ardent federalist & who formerly resided there, to get off to-morrow at 11 o'clock to visit the leaders there — and to whom we must address a letter, stating the importance it is to the issue that they should pursue the plan which we understand they have in agitation of sending five members — recommending unwearied exertions. Will you write and sign six letters to the Gentlemen whose names are below and send them to my store by 11 o'clock tomorrow.

You know how to address them to produce the best effect — I will get Sargent to sign and will do so myself. You have had much to do, but I trust you will be fully remunerated.

Yrs.

T H PERKINS

Honle Mr Baylis
Nahum Mitchell Esq
General Lazell
Nathan Lazell Esq
Honbl. Judge Howard
Dr. Orr.

### JOSIAH OGDEN HOFFMAN [47] TO OTIS

[New York], July 17, 1812.

My D Sir,

I have had a very full & satisfactory conversation with the Gentleman,[48] alluded to, in your Letter. He was not only

[45] Sullivan's endorsement.

[46] Marginal comment by Sullivan: "Difference six ! ! !"

[47] A Federalist leader in New York City, father of Ogden and of Charles Fenno Hoffman.

[48] De Witt Clinton.

explicit on all great points, but unsolicited by me, declared, there should be no distinction in selecting his Agents &c. Every thing is doing that he and his friends can do — and on Monday or Tuesday next, he will refer me to Names in your quarter. Hitherto our conferences have been entirely confined to ourselves — but in a few days, he will declare himself explicitly to at least three of our friends. This step, without the least hesitation, he acceded to, — indeed it was necessary for the union of our friends here. The Measure however is to have no publicity, but the Opinion of the Gentlemen selected is to be deemed authoritative and to have the force of ascertained facts. I cannot detail to you in a Letter all that passed. The Offers made to him to withdraw his pretensions, even within the last six days, have been of the most alluring kind. They were rejected with promptitude and disdain. His course of reasoning as to his future conduct exactly corresponds with that suggested in your Letter. On us & us only he in future could depend.

I have received Letters from Philadelphia. Our friends there and in Jersey will be prepared to act with us. It is not improbable, I shall go to Philadelphia for a day or so, in the course of two or three Weeks. South-Carolina & North-Carolina ought to be attended to. Our friends ought to be addressed in these States. You can do more in Boston there, than we can. In short we must be united.

I have some doubts at present of the expediency of a Convention. My fear is our Object might be misrepresented. We shall appoint a corresponding Committee next week, and our Letters will go to our friends through the U. States. You ought to do the same, and I am inclined to think, the Correspondence with us, had best commence on your part — and the sooner the better. I am obliged to write in great Haste. I am, D Sir

Respectfully Your friend

J. O. H.

OTIS TO WILLIAM SULLIVAN

*From the Manuscript Collection of the New York Public Library.*

Watertown, August 17—[1812]

My dear Sir,

The rain is so excessive that I cannot go to town. My presence at 12, on a certain subject is not necessary, as you are so well possessed of my opinions, that we have no other alternative but to support D W. C[linton].

As our friends propose a convention, it may be indispensable to accede to the suggestion — I earnestly pray I may not be a delegate, having many engagements at home. But in any event I should absolutely decline unless it is understood, *that we go to promote his election.* I should not choose to go to N York, and *there* find myself differing from my colleagues —

Permit me to suggest that I think Col. Thorndike would be a very proper person for this commission. Mr. Gore will I presume be also one — In fact, as they will have the privilege of paying their own expenses, there being no shot in the Locker, I can perceive no objection to a dozen. Perhaps it would be also advisable to let the Hampshire people know that they may send one or more but the affair should be *confidential.* I think Jackson and yourself would do for want of better fellows.

Yours very truly<br>H. G. O.

I shall be in tomorrow if I can hire a boat.

Pray send me news by bearer.

[*The following, written in pencil in Sullivan's hand on a blank page of the letter, is evidently a record of the committee meeting that elected the delegates to New York.*]

Aug. 18, 1812.

Voted — that D. W. C. be supported
- G. C[abot]
- C. G[ore]
- C. J[ackson]
- H. G. O[tis]
- W. P[rescott]
- W. S[ullivan]
- I. P.[49]

---

[49] Christopher Gore states in a letter of October 5, 1812, to Rufus King (*King*, v, 283), that only Cabot, Sullivan, and himself were present at this meeting. The others mentioned here must have voted by proxy.

That Hon C. Gore Esq.
   H. G. Otis
   I. Thorndike
   C. Jackson
   W. Sullivan
   S. Putnam
and somebody from Hampshire [County be] chosen.

SAMUEL DEXTER TO OTIS

Boston 12th Sept. 1812.

Dear Sir,

Some days ago Mr. Joy mentioned that you were so kind as to express a wish that I would join you in N. York. On examining the state of my engagements I find it would produce great derangement in my business; & as I have no belief that any important purpose could be attained by it I have declined the Journey, yet not without reluctance as I find Mr. Joy & Mr. Sullivan persevere in suggesting that it might be very useful. My opinions are of no great value, but I have no objection to stating them. The principal difficulty is said to be a disposition in some gentlemen to set up a federal candidate. When Piso conspired against Nero it was proposed to make Seneca Emperor; to this two objections of some weight appeared, 1st that it was not possible to make a sufficient party to put him in; & 2dly that if he were in he could not stay a moment in office, such was the state of public manners. Gov. Jay could no more play President than Seneca could Emperor. The great object is to prevent our annihilation as a commercial Nation. It is to me of little importance whether the rulers be of one party name or another. Every expedient will of necessity be temporary & only a choice of evils. Such indeed is Government itself. The great question is how can we escape with as little suffering as possible & for as long as possible. If these objects can best be obtained by a coalition with a portion of the opposite party why should pride or passion prevent it? An honorable peace is the present object; & I hope the Country can bear it & the prosperity that might attend it. Tho' sometimes I indulge gloom eno' to think that we are so corrupt as to need war. Everything that ought to be honorable in our Country seems to be at market as much as butcher's meat. To allude to the Roman history once more; when no formidable enemy remained corruption made them a fit prey for barbarians. While they were warlike they suffered, but they were magnanimous. The Greeks produced patriots, for posterity to admire, in the midst of War & Revolution. They have left a blaze of light behind them, but it was because their Country was on fire. I find I am only preaching. It is more easy to say what I do not want than what I do. I promised that I would write & I have performed my engagement.

Yours very truly
Sam. Dexter

# CHAPTER XVII

AFTER the *Chesapeake* incident, Jefferson lost the only
chance of declaring war against Great Britain, when such
a war would have secured unanimous support. Looking
back on 1807 from a period of Hague conferences and arbitration treaties, Jefferson's moderation and restraint at
that trying period seems most commendable. But the
sequel proved that none of his expedients could prevent
a war, which might far better have come in 1807, with the
entire nation up in arms over the insult to its flag, than in
1812, after one section of the Union had been led by four
years of commercial restriction into an attitude of violent
disaffection. Instead of commencing reprisals or encouraging the war spirit, Jefferson issued, on July 2, 1807, a proclamation closing American ports to British men-of-war,
and expressing his confidence that Great Britain would
apologize for the *Leopard's* action. The British government
did acknowledge its fault, though somewhat ungraciously,
and sent a special envoy to the United States to make
reparation for the damage done, but with such conditions
attached as to make it impossible for Jefferson to accept
the offer.

Before this envoy arrived, European affairs assumed
an aspect even more alarming for the United States than
before. It became evident that the British government and
Napoleon had determined that there should be no more
neutrals. In September, 1807, Copenhagen, the capital city
of a neutral nation, was bombarded by a British fleet, and

Denmark forced to surrender its fleet, simply in order to prevent its falling into the hands of France. The lesson was as applicable to the United States as had been the overthrow of Venice and Switzerland in the Federalist period. Already the Orders in Council of England and the Decrees of Napoleon had narrowed to a minimum the scope of trade permitted to neutrals.[1] In December, 1807, information arrived of a new and sweeping Order in Council, forbidding all direct trade between the United States and continental Europe, unless the cargo should first be landed in Great Britain and pay duty. Five days later came an official notice of the King's proclamation of October 17, requiring naval officers to exercise the right of impressment to its fullest extent. This was adding insult to the injury of the *Chesapeake* affair.

Jefferson felt that the moment had come for prompt and vigorous action, both to protect American shipping and sailors, and to coerce the two powerful belligerents into abandoning their anti-neutral systems. He had no desire for war. It was an opportunity to try an experiment he had dreamed of for years, — the appealing to Europe's self-interest by prohibiting commercial intercourse with it. At his dictation, the Republican majority in Congress passed the famous Embargo Act, which from December 22, 1807, until March 4, 1809, forbade the American merchant marine to engage in foreign commerce, and placed burdensome restrictions on coastwise traffic.

Jefferson intended the embargo to be the crowning measure of his administration; it remains as the typical example of his theoretical statesmanship. Theoretically, embargo was a perfect substitute for war, without the

---

[1] Napoleon's Berlin Decree of December 10, 1806, declaring the British Isles to be in a state of blockade, was applied to American vessels after August, 1807. The British Orders in Council of January 7, 1807, forbade to neutrals coastwise commerce between ports belonging to Napoleon or his allies.

attendant cost and loss of life; theoretically, it would at once protect vessels and produce from capture, and inflict such hardships on the two belligerents as to force them into compliance with our démands to observe the international law of neutrality. Practically, the embargo proved the greatest failure of any political experiment ever tried in the United States. It protected ships, but destroyed commerce; it produced no effect whatever on either belligerent, but threw the carrying trade into other hands; it was enforcible only by measures which violated popular ideas of liberty. Worst of all, it caused such economic distress in New England as to revive the decadent power of Federalism in that section, and to throw the Federal party into the arms of the Essex Junto.

The Federal party had experimented with a temporary embargo in Washington's second administration, and rejected it as a failure. When it was again proposed, in 1798, to offset the French spoliations, Otis declared:

A *general* Embargo would not protect either our commerce or navigation, but destroy both. . . . A *partial* Embargo upon our own vessels, while it puts an end to our navigation, would materially affect our commerce, and all that remains would be carried on by the belligerent nations or by neutrals, under great additional charges and expenses.[2]

These predictions were amply fulfilled in 1808, and especially in Massachusetts, where over one third of the tonnage of the United States was owned, and where the shipbuilding and cod-fishing industries almost wholly concentrated. Its lucrative carrying trade was entirely destroyed, except for those vessels which happened to be abroad at the time the embargo was laid; and the shipbuilding industry was completely tied up. It was useless to tell the shipowners that the embargo was for their own

[2] *Letter to the Hon. William Heath* (1798), 17.

protection, since the Orders in Council had left loopholes for lucrative trade under British protection, which they longed to enjoy. Nor did seamen and laborers in maritime industries see the advantage of embargo over war. Embargo forced them to depend on charity or to emigrate to Canada to keep from starving;[3] war would have continued or even increased the demand for their labor. Before the embargo had been in force many months, stagnation, bankruptcy, and distress were the rule along the New England coast. The farmers of the interior, now that exports had ceased, found their products a glut on the market, and prices of imported goods greatly enhanced. Except in regions that profited by the stimulus to domestic manufactures, there was throughout the Union the same state of exasperation and distress.[4]

To the Federalist leaders in Massachusetts, and especially to the Essex Junto, whose minds were working in the same old mercantile and pro-British groove, Jefferson's embargo seemed an insidious attempt to ruin New England's prosperity, and to provoke England to war. They could not attribute to Jefferson any genuine solicitude for

[3] Reports of John Howe, a British spy, in *Am. Hist. Rev.*, xvii, 89–90. Howe sarcastically called the embargo "An Act for the better encouragement of the British Colonies in America."

[4] Professor Channing, in his *Jeffersonian System*, 219, says that "The opposition to the embargo in New England was mainly political," and denies that it caused great or unusual distress. The Federal party naturally made political capital out of the embargo, and exaggerated its effects in newspapers and speeches. Much relief was also obtained through smuggling. But all economic data point to the correctness of the statements I have made above. Democratic leaders freely admitted as much in their private correspondence — see the Jefferson and Adams MSS. for the period — and foreign travelers and spies received the same impression. Many communities that remained faithful to the Democratic party all through the embargo period suffered most seriously from it; but they believed, like Jefferson, that the sacrifice was worth while in order to coerce England. And the embargo converted to Federalism many communities and sections that previously had been Democratic, viz., the coast districts of North Carolina. Cf. Mrs. St. J. Ravenel, *William Lowndes*, 75–78; C. H. Ambler, *Sectionalism in Virginia*, 87; S. Roads, *Marblehead*, 230–39.

commerce and shipping. From his "Notes on Virginia"
it was evident that he regarded commerce from the combined standpoint of a French physiocrat and a losing
farmer, and believed that the bulk of New England's
carrying trade was a positive detriment to the nation. If
he had since changed his opinion, why had he steadily
refused to provide a navy for the protection of commerce; why had he laid up the only effective vessels that
survived the French naval war, only two months before
the embargo was laid? If the embargo were for the protection of shipping, why was land traffic over the Canadian
border prohibited? Moreover, the Essex Junto had no
doubt that the embargo was laid at French dictation, in
order to aid Napoleon in his efforts to annihilate the British Empire, and was intended as a mere prelude to war
with England. If such were not the case, why was every
Democratic newspaper extolling Napoleon and decrying
England; denouncing the Orders in Council (which the Essex Junto considered legal methods of retaliation against
France), and apologizing for Napoleon's far more sweeping Berlin and Milan decrees? Napoleon, to these Federalists, was the living embodiment of the forces that
threatened the property and power of men of their class
all over the world. They were willing to grant England's
every claim in order to aid her in her battles; willing to
accept gratefully such crumbs of commerce as she might
graciously bestow. In spite of Jefferson's presumptuous
claims, argued Timothy Pickering, England had been for-
bearing and magnanimous to the United States. "Although Great Britain, with her thousand ships of war,
could have destroyed our commerce, she has really done
it no essential injury."[5]

[5] Pickering's *Letter to his Constituents* (1808). Cf. "Essex Resolutions" of
October 6, 1808, printed in Salem *Gazette*, October 14, 1808, and in pamphlet
form (Newburyport, 1808).

These arguments were tersely and effectively advanced·
by Senator Pickering, the leader of the Essex Junto, in a
letter dated February 16, 1808, to Governor Sullivan of
Massachusetts. Recognizing its force, Sullivan (a Republican) attempted to suppress it, but Pickering's friends
had it printed early in March. Within a few days the
Federalist party organizations throughout the state were
circulating thousands of copies of the "Letter from the
Hon. Timothy Pickering . . . exhibiting to his Constituents a View of the Imminent Danger of an Unnecessary
and Ruinous War," in newspapers, pamphlets, and broad-
sides.⁶ Although similar arguments had disgusted Massachusetts in 1804 and 1807, the economic effects of the
embargo had now prepared the people's minds for their
reception. "The Embargo will touch their bone and their
flesh, when they must curse its authors," wrote Pickering
in private;⁷ and election returns of April, 1808, proved
that for once he had gauged correctly the feelings of his
constituents. Jefferson lost his power over the General
Court of Massachusetts: the fruit of years of labor and
caution. The Federal party secured a majority in both
Senate and House, and returned Harrison Gray Otis and
Timothy Bigelow to the presiding chairs from which they
had been deposed two years before.⁸ This election marks
the beginning of a renaissance of Federalism, in which
that party, so crushingly defeated between 1800 and
1807, succeeded in establishing a powerful opposition,
under the shelter of state rights, to the Republican administrations.

⁶ See Dwight's letter following this chapter; cf. H. C. Lodge, *Cabot*, 379–82;
*Proc. Mass. Hist. Soc.*, XLV, 359; *King*, v, 88.

⁷ *N. E. Federalism*, 367. Cf. *Amer. Hist. Rev.*, XVII, 747.

⁸ The vote was 19–17, and 252–221; not a great majority. In the Senate then
elected Federalist measures were habitually carried by the Senators from Suffolk, Essex, Worcester, and Hampshire Counties, voting against those from
the rest of the state.

The victory would have been more complete had Otis, as was generally expected, been nominated for governor instead of Christopher Gore.[9] This nomination was distinctly the work of the Essex Junto, which had taken Gore into its full confidence, but distrusted Otis more than ever, since his memorable independence at the time of the *Chesapeake* affair. Gore was a gentleman of wealth and culture who lacked the popular talents that Otis possessed in so marked a degree. He was over-fond of displaying his great wealth, his oratory and manners were stiff and formal, and his father had been a refugee Tory. Further, he had resided many years in England, and his religious views were too liberal for the orthodox Connecticut Valley.[10] It is not surprising, therefore, that the Democratic candidate, ~~General~~ Sullivan, a popular old ~~hero~~ of the Revolution, was reëlected to the governorship.

The General Court of Massachusetts had been in session barely a week when its majority asserted itself by expelling John Quincy Adams from the Federal party.[11] Although elected to the United States Senate in 1803 as a Federalist, by a Federalist General Court, yet during the past six months Adams had gone completely over to Jefferson. He attended ~~and cast a vote~~ at the Democratic

[9] "Why was not Mr Otis, agreeably to the general expectation, selected as the federal candidate for the office of Governor, except that Mr. Gore's British attachments entitle him to a preference?" *Chronicle*, March 28, 1808. The *Democrat* (March 30) sneers at Otis as the dupe of the Essex Junto. "They will please his vanity, but never gratify his ambition." — "The British faction will never suffer one of the descendants of old whigs to hold any office of honor if they can help it."

[10] "Messrs Gore and Cobb, you see, are unanimously set up. The friends of Mr. Otis fell in, though sorry that the latter was not fixed upon last year. As you know, it is not the best nomination that could be made. General Cobb is too jolly. Mr. Otis is more regular at church than Mr. Gore." President Kirkland of Harvard to Josiah Quincy, *Proc. Mass. Hist. Soc.*, XVII, 113.

[11] Worthington C. Ford, "The Recall of John Quincy Adams," *Proc. Mass. Hist. Soc.*, XLV, 354.

congressional caucus that nominated Madison for the
presidency;[12] he voted for the embargo; he attacked his
colleague Pickering's arraignment of it in a published
"Letter to the Hon. Harrison Gray Otis on the Present
State of our National Affairs," which the Democratic
party circulated as a campaign document. If anything
under the sun could signify a change of party allegiance,
these three acts certainly did; but Adams always considered himself a martyr for his expulsion from the Federal
party, and affected to believe that it was a punishment for
his failure to defend the *Leopard's* attack on the *Chesapeake*.[13]

The Federal party of Massachusetts stripped John
Quincy Adams of his colors by prematurely choosing his
successor in the United States Senate on June 2, 1808.
He promptly took the hint, and resigned for the remainder
of his term. Otis was chairman of the legislative caucus
that nominated, as Adams's successor, James Lloyd, Jr.,
a Boston merchant and banker whom the Essex Junto
trusted; yet he does not seem to have sympathized with
that act. Otis and Adams both belonged to the liberal
wing of the Federal party, a fact which the latter recognized in addressing to Otis his attack on Pickering. Their
personal relations were cordial, though not intimate, and
there was a traditional bond of friendship between their
families. Adams wrote, in 1829, that his published *Letter*
was not entirely lost upon Otis. "He never answered it,
and, for some time, kept his opinions in reserve." He

[12] Adams wrote his mother on April 20, 1808, that in spite of this act it was
explicitly understood that he had no intention to join the party or become a
partisan of either candidate. It is difficult to understand what other object he
could have had in attending and voting.

[13] *N. E. Federalism*, 185. Adams had been an object of suspicion to the Essex
Junto for years, but not more so than Otis. Stephen Higginson, in 1804, sent
Pickering a private denunciation of Adams in almost the same words with which
he maligned Otis in 1797.

records a conversation with Samuel Allyne Otis, in which the latter said that his son "was mortified at the electing of another person in my place: that his son had done everything in his power to prevent it, but could not; that the tide ran too strong; that '*the Essex Junto were omnipotent.*'" [14]

If Otis felt this way, argued Adams, he too should have supported the embargo, especially since he had promised, in the town meeting of July 16, 1807, to support any measures judged necessary by the administration for the safety and honor of the country. No doubt a conflict was raging in Otis's mind as to the proper course for him to pursue. Probably the answer he would have given Adams would have been something like this: "My joint pledge with you in the town meeting related to the *Chesapeake* affair; and I fulfilled it by loyally supporting the administration while that question was pending. Great Britain has now disavowed the action of the *Leopard's* commander, and I consider that incident closed. I do not oppose the embargo by the same course of reasoning as Senator Pickering; I do not share his favorable views of British policy, and I trust that our administration is seeking neither to serve France nor to destroy the prosperity of New England. But the embargo falls with undue weight on the interests of our native state, without any corresponding benefit to the nation. You claim the embargo 'must in its nature be a temporary expedient,'[15] but we know that the president intends it to be a permanent policy; and a permanent embargo will sacrifice the very rights for which we are contending. You claim that national honor requires its united support, but I see neither honor nor dignity in this contemptible Chinese policy. Let Mr. Jefferson give us a pledge of his sincerity by restoring our

[14] *N. E. Federalism*, 202.          [15] *Letter to the Hon. H. G. Otis*, 11.

navy to the strength and prestige it had in your father's administration; let him then seek justice from England and France through diplomacy, and he will have my support, and, I believe, that of the greater portion of the Federal party. Meanwhile I shall remain a Federalist, and endeavor, without your aid, to counteract that British influence in the party which I deplore no less deeply than yourself."

Otis's influence is evident in the moderate course followed by his party until the winter. Governor Sullivan, in his opening speech of the spring session, asserted that Federalist opposition to the embargo could have but one end in view, the dissolution of the Union. The Senate and House in reply contented themselves, however, with repudiating the charge, and denouncing a permanent embargo as unconstitutional. In August came news of a change in the European situation, that made commercial restriction more irksome to New England than ever before. Spain had revolted against Napoleon and King Joseph; Great Britain had espoused her cause; and only the embargo prevented New England shippers from supplying the allied armies with provisions. In Boston, a special town meeting was called for August 9. Jonathan Mason opened it with a motion requesting the President to remove the embargo either wholly, or partially in regard to Spain and Portugal, under a recent power invested in him by Congress. Otis, Gore, and Daniel Sargent sustained the motion, which was carried by a strong majority, in spite of the opposition of prominent Democrats.[16] An exceedingly temperate set of resolutions was then adopted. The inhabitants express their willingness "to endure any privations which the public welfare may require," and apologize for not awaiting the meeting of Congress, on the

[16] *Centinel*, August 10, 1808.

ground of the change in European affairs, and their pressing desire for

relief from the pressure of this great calamity, which bears with
peculiar weight on the Eastern States. — Denied by nature
those valuable & luxuriant Staples which constitute the riches
of the south, they necessarily owe much of their prosperity
under the Blessing of Heaven to their own enterprise & Industry on the Ocean. . . They therefore pray that the Embargo in
whole or in part may be suspended.[17]

Evidently Boston Federalism was still independent
of the Essex Junto. In the debate, moreover, Otis and
Mason argued that war with England would be preferable
to embargo,[18] although Pickering's principal objection to
the embargo was the fact that it might lead to war. The
Boston resolutions, which were communicated to other
towns in the state, produced a crop of similar petitions to
the President.[19]

It soon became evident that Jefferson had no intention
of answering these prayers for relief. Jefferson refused
to modify the embargo in favor of the Spanish patriots,
whom Democratic journals denounced as "factious Reb-
els," both from fear of offending Napoleon, and from
a desire to share in the spoils of the Spanish empire.[20]
This attitude, serving further to spread the belief that
French influence was at the bottom of Jefferson's policy,
produced a vigorous demonstration of the Essex Junto in
favor of extreme measures, at an Essex County conven-

[17] *Boston Town Records 1796–1813,* 238.
[18] *Chronicle,* August 15, 1808.
[19] Down to September 28, 1808, at least seventy Massachusetts towns, seven
others in New England, and six in New York had memorialized the President
against the embargo. *Centinel,* September 28.
[20] H. Adams, *United States,* iv, 339–42, 385. Orchard Cook, a Democratic
member of Congress from Maine, wrote John Quincy Adams on January 1,
1809: "In short to be plain — Mr. Madison long since told me If we opened a
Trade with Spain & Portugal it would be War with France — & was so laid
down by Vattel." Adams, MSS. Cf. *King,* v, 110.

tion on October 6. But the Federal party as a whole was disposed to await the result of the presidential election before taking further steps to end the embargo.

During the summer and autumn the Federalist reaction continued in the Northern States. In May, the New York Federalists doubled their delegation in the state assembly which was to choose presidential electors, and placed themselves in a position to combine with the Clintonians, who had also adopted an anti-embargo policy. When state elections in the last days of August and early September swung back the rest of New England into the Federalist column, the prospect of electing Charles Cotesworth Pinckney, the nominee of the Federalist national convention,[21] appeared excellent to Otis's correspondents. "It seems by the accounts from all quarters," John Rutledge wrote him on September 10, "that a real & great change has taken place in the public sentiment & that we are about to return to the golden days when the government of the Country, placed in the ablest & best hands, will administer our affairs on manly & correct principles." Eighty-nine electoral votes were necessary for a choice. Otis's friends were certain of New England's forty-five, of at least ten from Delaware and the coast districts of Maryland and North Carolina, and confident of obtaining Pennsylvania's twenty and New Jersey's eight. The nomination of a "favorite son" of South Carolina led them to hope for success in that state, also, which would have given them a majority. But Pinckney secured only forty-seven electoral votes to Madison's one hundred and twenty-two. This was a notable increase over his fourteen votes of 1804; but it ended all chance of removing the embargo by a change of rulers. With the people of New England now facing another winter of privation and

[21] See chapter XVI.

distress, President Jefferson could hardly expect them henceforth to confine their opposition within prudent or constitutional bounds.

## LETTERS

### JOSIAH DWIGHT TO OTIS

Northampton March 16, 1808

Hon H G Otis Esqr

    Sir

In our former letter we communicated to you the anxious Sollicitude that pervaded all classes of people in this part of the Commonwealth, on the subject of our national affairs. Information received from all quarters, since the date of our last, was uniformly calculated to increase rather than diminish the general anxiety; and the receipt of Colo. Pickering's Letter has confirmed us in the opinion that the Executive Government of the United States are resolutely bent on the pursuance of measures which will bring ruin & destruction on the people. To avert the ruin which is now impending over us, we think the voice of the people ought immediately to be expressed, in that bold and dignified manner, which cannot be misunderstood by those who *mis-rule* the nation. Under this impression we have thought it wise & prudent to bring the subject before the Inhabitants of this place, assembled in Town meeting. After a lengthy, animated & candid Discussion, it was voted, almost unanimously, that the Selectmen should prepare to forward to Congress a Memorial,[22] & also an address to the several Towns within the County, requesting this concurrence in similar measures. The Court of sessions commenced their sitting in this place yesterday. A number of Gentlemen from different parts of the County are collected to attend this Court. These gentlemen attended a meeting which was holden last evening, and expressed their warm approbation of the proceedings of this Town, at the same time pledging themselves to use their exertions that similar measures should be adopted in the several Towns to

[22] Northampton evidently led the way in the policy of memorializing Congress on the embargo. Cf. *N. E. Federalism,* 369, and Steiner, *McHenry,* 546.

which they belong. Indeed each & every one of them declared his
sanguine belief that the minds of the people in his Town were
fully prepared to be active on this subject. We have also
taken measures to procure the printing & circulation of Colo.
Pickering's Letters, together with an address from the select
men.

We have thought proper thus far to inform you that, in this
hour of Peril & Distress, the people in this County are at their
Posts, & are prepared to cooperate with their political friends in
different parts of the Commonwealth, in any measures that
shall in wisdom be devised for the public good. We know little
of what is doing elsewhere, tho' we have been long anxiously
waiting for information from the "Headquarters of good principles." It gave us much pleasure, however, to see in the late
Boston Papers, the nomination of Messrs. Gore & Cobb for the
Offices of Govr. & Lt. Govr. — That the measures adopted by
us, & proposed for the adoption of others, if generally carried
into effect, — will have any influence, to check the mad career
of the man, who now rules with absolute sway, the councils of
the nation, may perhaps be somewhat problematical. But even
should the Idol chief of the dominant Party turn a deaf ear to
our remonstrances, & refuse us relief from our anxiety & distress,
we have another object in view, in the attainment of which
we think these measures will have a very happy influence. Colo.
Pickering's letter, tho' it contains little information entirely
new, yet coming in such a form & from such high authority, it is
calculated to excite the attention of the people, & rouse many
from that Lethargy which had almost fatally seized them.
The unwarranted suppression of that letter also, by the chief
Magistrate of the Commonwealth, when it was expressly intended to be communicated to the Legislature, is a violation of
official duty which ought to be seized on with avidity, & made
the theme of popular clamor, to blast the reputation of the
man who would thus dare to conceal from his constituents, a
document so highly interesting. We do believe, Sir, that if we
meet our political enemies manfully, with the weapons which
are thus providentially put into our hands, it will insure us success at the approaching election. We can assure you of the utmost exertions of all good people in this large County, & we
think that existing circumstances justify us in the belief, that a

greater number of Federalists may be brought to the Polls than in any former year. . . .

By order of the corresponding Committee, I am sir

Very respectfully your Obedt Servt

JOSIAH DWIGHT

### GEORGE CABOT TO OTIS

Boston Augt 14, 1808

My Dear Sir —

\*   \*   \*   \*   \*   \*   \*   \*   \*   \*   \*  [23]

I recollect it was said last winter that the restraints contemplated on the coasting trade wou'd never be enacted because it must be foreseen that our people wou'd not tolerate them — "they wou'd seize upon the Castle" if it shou'd be used to enforce such grievous measures; yet we find that the passage of a single canoe is not allowed but by special license & no violence or opposition is heard of.—the reason is plain & Mr. J acts upon the knowledge of it. Mr. Jefferson is the man of the *populace* & both are gratified too well in seeing those they hate humbled — the *populace* consider Mr. J *their* head, & this silences their complaints. on the whole I am persuaded if it were not for the sufferings brought on us by the Embargo Mr. J & Mr. M wou'd be immoveable — yet they have managed ill for 7 years; how then can gentlemen insist that 4 years more wou'd produce a contrary effect? it wou'd not, experience as well as reason teaches clearly that the people will adhere to those who are the instruments of their passions & will shun those who wou'd controul them — if Mr. J *cou'd* at this moment remove the embargo without a quarrel with France I think he cou'd quarrel with England in spite of her equity & moderation.

yours truly

G C

[23] The first part of this letter relates to the Federalist presidential nominations, and is printed in *Amer. Hist. Rev.*, XVII, 755.

END OF VOLUME I